contents

publisher
RICHARD POULTER

editor
JEREMY SHAW

art editor
STEVE SMALL

production manager
STEVEN PALMER

managing editor
PETER LOVERING

business development manager
SIMON MAURICE

sales promotion
CLARE KRISTENSEN

chief photographer
MICHAEL C. BROWN

US advertising representative
Barry Pigot
2421 N. Center Street
Suite 128
Hickory, North Carolina 28601
Telephone and fax: (704) 322 1645

INDY CAR 1996-97
is published by
Hazleton Publishing Ltd.,
3 Richmond Hill,
Richmond, Surrey
TW10 6RE, England.

Color reproduction by
Barrett Berkeley Ltd., London, England.

Printed in England by
Butler and Tanner Ltd.,
Frome.

FOREWORD *by Jimmy Vasser*	5
EDITOR'S INTRODUCTION	8
A LONG AND WINDING ROAD *A profile of PPG Cup winning team owner Chip Ganassi by David Phillips*	14
TOP TEN DRIVERS	23
HALL OF FAME *Jeremy Shaw looks back at the career of retiring team owner Jim Hall*	36
PLAYING BY THE RULES *David Phillips considers the rule changes introduced by IndyCar for 1996*	42
PPG's CONTRIBUTION TO INDY CAR RACING	46
TEAM-BY-TEAM REVIEW *by Jeremy Shaw*	49
TRIBUTES TO SCOTT BRAYTON, JEFF KROSNOFF AND GARY AVRIN *by Jeremy Shaw*	86
FACTS & FIGURES	87
PPG INDY CAR WORLD SERIES	89
PPG-FIRESTONE INDY LIGHTS CHAMPIONSHIP REVIEW	186
SCCA PLAYER'S/TOYOTA ATLANTIC CHAMPIONSHIP REVIEW	190
RACING ROUND-UP	192

acknowledgments

The Editor and publishers wish to thank the following for their assistance in compiling the *Autocourse Indy Car Yearbook 1996-97*: Andrew Craig, Randy Dzierzawski, Cathie Lyon, T.E. McHale; CeCe Pappas, Adam Saal, Steve Shunck, Mike Zizzo; Marc Abel, Tom Blattler, Susan Bradshaw, Kim Carmine, Francois Cartier, Steve Chassey, Mark Christian, Mark Coughlin, Amy Dangler, Kevin Diamond, Deanna Griffith, Bronko Gruichich, Jade Gurss, Heather Handley, Robbin Herring, Christine Horne, Trevor Hoskins, Deke Houlgate, Hank Ives, Dan Luginbuhl, Brett Kear, Kevin Kennedy, Michael Knight, Kathi Lauterbach, Mai Lindstrom, Scott McKee, Chris Mears, David Phillips, Shannon Poskon, Steve Potter, John Procida, Patty Reid, Scott Reisz, Mike Sack, Rick Shaffer, Barry Smith, Marc Spiegel, Mike Stoller, Carole Swartz, Scott Tingwald, Tony Troiano, Brian Wagner, Kathy Weida, Carol Wilkins; and Tamy Valkosky.

This book is dedicated to the entire Indy Car community and especially the families and friends of Gary Avrin, Scott Brayton and Jeff Krosnoff.

DISTRIBUTORS

UNITED KINGDOM
Bookpoint Ltd.
39 Milton Park
Abingdon
Oxfordshire OX14 4TD
Telephone: 01235 400400
Fax: 01235 861038

NORTH AMERICA
Motorbooks International
PO Box 1
729 Prospect Ave., Osceola
Wisconsin 54020, USA
Telephone: (1) 715 294 3345
Fax: (1) 715 294 4448

AUSTRALIA
Technical Book and Magazine
Co. Pty.
295 Swanston Street
Melbourne, Victoria 3000
Telephone: (03) 9663 3951
Fax: (03) 9663 2094

NEW ZEALAND
David Bateman Ltd.
P.O. Box 100-242
North Shore Mail Centre
Auckland 1330
Telephone: (9) 415 7664
Fax: (9) 415 8892

SOUTH AFRICA
Motorbooks
341 Jan Smuts Avenue
Craighall Park
Johannesburg
Telephone: (011) 325 4458/60
Fax: (011) 325 4146

Back when racing began, our decals were a lot easier to read.

When J. Frank Duryea's race car streamed across the finish line at a breathtaking 5 mph, Mobil helped get it there. Of course, Mobil Motor Oil has protected somewhat more sophisticated engines since then. In fact, Mobil 1 is the official oil of Team Penske, the most successful team in Indy history. So whether you work in racing or race to work, call 1-800-ASK-MOBIL and find out more about any of our advanced oils. After all, we've found there's really only one place to promote our name. Under the hood.

Mobil. Changing oil for over 125 years.

foreword

by Jimmy Vasser • 1996 PPG Cup champion

I am told it is traditional for the PPG Indy Car World Series champion to write the introduction for the *Autocourse Indy Car Yearbook*. If that's true, I hope I will get to fill this space for many years to come!

As I write this, it is just a few weeks since the final race of the season at Laguna Seca, where I clinched the championship. All of the special things that happened during this most special season are just now beginning to come into focus for me. I'm sure they all will be faithfully recounted here in the pages of the *Autocourse Indy Car Yearbook*.

As you review the Indy Car season through the photos and stories between these covers, I would like you to remember the PPG Cup championship resulted from a total team effort by Target/Chip Ganassi Racing. No driver achieves his success alone. I am extremely proud of the fact we finished each of the 16 races. It's the first time the PPG Cup title-winner has done so. That's a tremendous achievement and a great tribute to the performance and reliability of our Reynard chassis, Honda engines and Firestone tires.

Equally, it says so much for the talents and professionalism of the guys on my Target team. I want to take this opportunity to thank managing director Tom Anderson – who calls the shots for me on the radio – team manager Mike Hull, my engineer Julian Robertson, chief mechanic Grant Weaver and the rest of the crew. Great job guys!

Of course, I have to pay tribute to Chip Ganassi for putting the entire package together. Chip made some bold moves before the start of the season and they all paid off. Chip's been working since 1990 with our primary sponsor, Target Stores, to put all the elements of a championship team in place. I'm glad to be the driver who brought Chip the title.

I also want to compliment my teammate, Alex Zanardi, who is not only a great driver but also a very nice person. I think Alex and I worked very well together and that was important in obtaining the results we achieved. Formula 1's loss was definitely Target/Ganassi's gain!

I hope you'll be cheering for us as we try to do it again in 1997.

Sincerely

Jimmy Vasser

Michael C. Brown

the carrousel SPINS

The entire spectrum of human emotion was exposed at one time or another during the 1996 PPG Indy Car World Series. There was joy at some notable firsts – maiden wins for Jimmy Vasser, Alex Zanardi and Adrian Fernandez; a first pole for (again) Zanardi and Vasser, and also Scott Pruett. There was bitter disappointment for Al Unser Jr. and Marlboro Team Penske, robbed of almost certain victory by an engine failure within a mile of the finish line at Road America. There was palpable relief when rookie Mark Blundell emerged with relatively minor injuries after experiencing a devastating impact in Rio de Janeiro; and similarly when it became apparent veteran Emerson Fittipaldi would not be permanently disabled after he, too, hit the wall at M.I.S. There was the emptiness of defeat and elation of victory experienced almost simultaneously by, respectively, Bryan Herta and Zanardi following the Italian's stunning last-lap pass at Laguna Seca. And then there was utter despair when first Scott Brayton died during practice for the IRL's Indianapolis 500 and then Jeff Krosnoff and a course worker, Gary Avrin, lost their lives in Toronto.

The accidents served as vivid reminders of the inherent dangers involved in auto racing. The competitors, of course, willingly accept the risks. In the 1960s and '70s, auto racing was never far removed from tragedy, but since then enormous advances have been made in the name of safety. Technological breakthroughs have meant the propensity for serious injury has been significantly reduced. The Championship Auto Racing Teams/IndyCar organization, however, has maintained an unerring focus upon safety-related issues.

Over the winter of 1995/96, IndyCar enacted some new regulations (outlined elsewhere in these pages) aimed at curbing the escalation in speeds and minimizing the likelihood of driver injury in the event of an accident. For 1997, more changes will be introduced with the same goals in mind. And judging by initial tests at Mid-Ohio shortly after the season was concluded, the modifications represent another step in the right direction.

'The rules make quite a big difference because they take away quite a lot of downforce as well as horsepower,' declared Newman/Haas race engineer Brian Lisles after completing two days of testing with Christian Fittipaldi in an updated Lola-Ford/Cosworth. 'That was the plan, of course.'

The alterations are subtle rather than drastic. They perpetuate the overriding philosophy of the team owners which is to maintain a stable rules structure and, as far as possible, ensure a level playing field for the participants. The success of that aim becomes apparent when one considers that seven different race teams and as many drivers have emerged to win the PPG Cup championship during the past eight years.

In 1996, furthermore, three drivers representing three engine manufacturers, three chassis suppliers and two tire companies retained a chance to win the championship prior to the season finale. No wonder Chip Ganassi, the champion team owner, was moved to exclaim: 'Is this a great series, or what?!'

The overall standard of the competition has continued its upward trend, and this in spite of the potential fragmentation caused by the rift between IndyCar and its upstart rival, the Indy Racing League. The IRL chose to rely upon 1995 equipment for its inaugural season, which at least ensured a ready supply of cars and engines. However, in contrast to the aims of CART, speeds in the IRL series continued to rise commensurate with the ongoing improvements made by Ford/Cosworth, which furnished the majority of engines, and the tire companies, Goodyear and Firestone.

It was not until the month of May

TO THE ORDER OF **JIMMY VASSER** 5/26/96
ONE MILLION AND 00/100 $1,000,000.00

Michael C. Brown

ON

The PPG Indy Car World Series once again provided thrilling racing on a big stage. However, it was also a season of contrasting emotions: elation for Jimmy Vasser and Chip Ganassi *(bottom left)* following their win in the U.S. 500, but despair at Toronto, where Jeff Krosnoff *(right)* was to pay racing's ultimate price.

Prepared for the worst

IndyCar's commitment to safety was clearly illustrated with the unveiling of a brand-new, $1 million, fully equipped, state-of-the-art IndyCar Mobile Medical Facility during the first race of the 1996 season at the equally new and impressive Metro-Dade Homestead Motorsports Complex.

The unit features X-ray machines, a heart monitor and defibrillator, a high-frequency ventilator and its own pharmacy as well as the capability to conduct physical therapy and minor surgical procedures.

'About 99 percent of the injuries we treat are minor, such as cuts, bruises or even stomach flu,' said Dr. Steve Olvey, IndyCar's director of medical affairs, 'but we are prepared for that other one percent if necessary.'

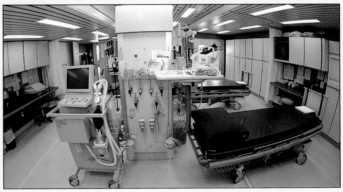

---

that the true disparity between the two series became apparent. In 1995, the last time all the Indy Car teams raced together at Indianapolis, the entire 33-car starting field was blanketed by 6.579 mph. This year, while Arie Luyendyk annihilated the outright track record by posting a four-lap qualifying average of 236.986 mph, the slowest IRL qualifier was a full 14.801 mph adrift.

In reality, and contrary to some expectations, the split did not appear to cause any serious problems for the PPG Cup series. Grid sizes remained virtually constant (27.06 cars per race compared to 27.25 in 1995) and the number of drivers contesting more than one event fell by just two, from 38 to 36.

The biggest test for the CART organization came in its bold – and controversial – decision to host its own 500-mile race, the U.S. 500, on Memorial Day weekend at Michigan International Speedway. Some naysayers predicted an embarrassing failure. It proved to be nothing of the sort. The start itself *was* a shambles, delayed by more than an hour following a cataclysmic accident even before the green flag; but frankly, that could have happened anywhere. It was no more than 'a racing accident.'

What followed was a spectacular auto race, featuring wide-open, wheel-to-wheel combat for the entire 500 miles. It was witnessed by a full-house crowd in excess of 110,000. In addition, the ESPN television broadcast garnered a 2.8 rating, which, while hardly extravagant, was in fact the station's largest audience ever for an IndyCar-sanctioned event. The Indy 500, meanwhile, drew a comparatively slim 6.8 rating on the ABC Sports network – its lowest rating in more than 10 years.

The arguments about which side 'won' and which 'lost' will go on, of course, but U.S. 500 winner Jimmy Vasser was justifiably ecstatic after earning prizes totaling over $1.15 million, as well as the glorious Vanderbilt Cup which was awarded for the first time since 1937.

'The U.S. 500 was our biggest race of the year,' said Vasser, who by the end of the season had added the PPG Cup championship, worth another $1 million. 'The drivers didn't have any control over the decision to race in the U.S. 500 and not in the Indianapolis 500. The way I look at it, to win a 500-mile race on Memorial Day for $1 million against the best drivers and teams in Indy Car racing is very special.'

The victory was Vasser's fourth of the season. It was also the fifth win from six races for Firestone, which began the season on a tear. The rival tire engineers at Goodyear, meanwhile, were hard at work. Goodyear duly rebounded to win the next two races as the two giant corporations sustained a close, clean battle throughout the 16-race season. In the end, Firestone could boast the upper hand after winning 10 times to Goodyear's six; but perhaps a more accurate barometer can be gleaned by the statistics relating to laps led during the season. In this they proved rather more closely matched, with Firestone leading 1077 laps (53.72 percent) and Goodyear 928 laps (46.28 percent).

The series truly lived up to expectations during 1996, and the intensity among competitors never wavered. In all, 17 drivers representing 12 different teams claimed

Emerson Fittipaldi, whose successes have done so much to popularize Indy Car racing in South America, is thought to be considering retirement after he was injured in a violent accident on the first lap of the Marlboro 500 in July.

Bottom: Competition was fierce throughout the field: Mauricio Gugelmin, Greg Moore, Mark Blundell and Scott Pruett fight it out for the minor placings at Laguna Seca.

at least one podium finish. The difference between winning and losing boiled down to the individual teams being able to optimize the equipment at their disposal. In ultimate terms, a Reynard chassis, Honda engine and Firestone tires, as used by the Target/Chip Ganassi team, represented the most successful combination. Nevertheless, an amazing 11 different permutations of chassis, engine and tires proved good enough to lead a race at one point or another.

Vasser's championship, his first and also the first for Target/Chip Ganassi Racing, served once again to exemplify the constantly changing face of auto racing. Out with the old, in with the new, so to speak.

In 1996, the arrival of a fourth engine supplier, Toyota, to challenge the established might of Ford/Cosworth, Mercedes-Benz and Honda, added yet more luster to the global appeal of the burgeoning sport. The PPG Cup series also visited two new venues in Homestead, Fla., and Rio de Janeiro, Brazil. Both drew large crowds and provided excellent races.

A few months later, Indy Car racing bade farewell to one of its most innovative and imaginative team owners, Jim Hall, who announced in July his impending retirement at the end of the season. The following day, one of Indy Car racing's most popular, accomplished and enduring drivers, Emerson Fittipaldi, was injured in a wreck on the first lap of the Marlboro 500. The veteran Brazilian, after undergoing surgery to repair the damage, was expected to make a full recovery, and while he had made no firm announcement, he clearly hinted that his spectacular career may be reaching toward its conclusion.

The never-ending carrousel continues. A fresh crop of rookie drivers will join the fray in 1997, along with at least two new regular teams. Gerald Davis, formerly team manager for Hall Racing, seems poised to take over the remnants of Jim Hall's operation as he joins forces with Gualter Salles. The young Brazilian is yet another graduate from the thriving PPG-Firestone Indy Lights Championship, which in recent years has produced such bright young talents as Adrian Fernandez, Bryan Herta, Andre Ribeiro and Greg Moore. Della Penna Motorsports, which dipped a toe in the water during the 1996 season by contesting three races with former Player's Toyota Atlantic champion Richie Hearn, also is slated to undertake a full campaign.

The signs are entirely positive as the growth of the PPG Cup series continues unabated. As we look forward, though, so we must also take the opportunity to pause every once in a while and reflect upon the past. The glorious past. And the not so glorious past. Auto racing can be such a cruel sport. But the memories of those who are gone will remain with us always.

Jeremy Shaw
Dublin, Ohio
September 1996

Everyone

who lives dies,

but not everyone

who dies,

has lived.

Jeff Krosnoff
September 24, 1964 - July 14, 1996

C3

16 mg "tar," 1.1 mg nicotine av. per cigarette by FTC method.

SURGEON GENERAL'S WARNING: Smoking By Pregnant Women May Result in Fetal Injury, Premature Birth, And Low Birth Weight.

A long and winding road

by David Phillips

On the face of it, Chip Ganassi paved the way to Jimmy Vasser's 1996 PPG Indy Car World Series championship with a series of critical decisions following the 1995 season. He switched allegiance from Ford to Honda in October, then announced his Target-backed team was changing from Goodyear to Firestone tires, and added the finishing touch by selecting the little-known (at least in the United States) Alessandro Zanardi to be Vasser's teammate.

The off-season moves returned handsome dividends. The Honda demonstrated itself to be not only the most powerful but also the most reliable engine, while Firestone was the tire to have and Zanardi's technical savvy proved the perfect compliment to Vasser's Indy Car experience. The

result was one of the most successful seasons in PPG Cup history.

The decisions, however, represented the culmination of an eight-year journey which began in 1988, when Ganassi joined forces with long-time Indy Car team owner Pat Patrick. The association scooped the 1989 PPG Cup, but the subsequent defection of Emerson Fittipaldi and Marlboro to Penske Racing effectively spawned two new teams – Patrick Racing International and Ganassi Racing. In addition to Patrick Racing's physical assets, Ganassi retained the services of several key members of the 1989 championship-winning team, including Tom Anderson.

'First and foremost, Tom [pictured below] is as steady as they come,'

says Ganassi of the only team manager he has ever had – until promoting Anderson to managing director this year. 'Plus he's been everywhere and done everything there is to do in Indy Car racing. He started off as a mechanic and worked his way up to chief mechanic on a championship-winning team. He's been in business for himself; he's run an Indy Lights team. There aren't many guys these days who can rebuild a gearbox and run a spreadsheet on Windows '95, but Tom can.'

No less important was the fact that Ganassi soon attracted the support of Target Stores, one of the country's leading discount department store chains. Although that first season Ganassi's plain white cars were adorned simply with Target's bull's

Photos: Michael C. Brown

eye trademark, it wasn't long before the team's cars were festooned with a multitude of associate sponsors participating in cooperative merchandizing programs with the retailing giant. But the relationship between team and sponsor is deeper than a few layers of paint on the race cars.

'They've been a huge help not just in the sponsorship but in lending their management expertise and advice to the decisions we make,' says Ganassi, 'from choosing Alex Zanardi to producing employee handbooks. We can tap into resources at Target that are not normally available to a small business like a race team.'

The partnership between team and sponsor would ultimately be reflected in the team's name change to Target/Chip Ganassi Racing in 1995. But there were a multitude of steps – not all of which bore fruit – before that came to pass. Formula 1 refugee Eddie Cheever was recruited to drive in 1990 and, after two seasons of indifferent results, Ganassi made the first of what would become

a pattern of dynamic moves by joining with Newman/Haas Racing in casting his lot with the new Ford/Cosworth XB engine.

Although the Target Lola-Ford was fast, results fell short of expectations. Cheever was replaced by Arie Luyendyk, who brought the team a taste of success in 1993 by taking the pole at Indianapolis and finishing a close second on race day. But Ganassi realized additional moves would be required if his team was to play anything more than a supporting role in the Indy Car drama. Thus midway through 1993 he joined forces with Reynard to bring the ultra-successful race car manufacturer into Indy Car racing.

'Reynard was another important part of the foundation,' he says, 'because it gave us more control over our own destiny.'

Not content with re-inventing the Indy Car chassis game, Ganassi hired the best driver available – Michael Andretti. Andretti, of course, had won the 1991 PPG Cup and some 18 Indy Car races in the 1990s with Newman/Haas, but was coming off a horrific season in Formula 1.

'It's so important in this business to have the complete package,' says Ganassi. 'Without the proper engine, the chassis means nothing; without the proper driver, your engine–chassis package means nothing. With Michael we completed the loop.'

Ganassi's personnel moves were not limited to a headline driver. They also included assembling the best possible supporting cast. Thus he brought promising young race engineer Julian Robertson into the fold together with the vastly experienced Morris Nunn. Grant Weaver joined veteran Mike Hull as chief mechanic when the team added a second entry for ex-Formula 1 campaigner Mauricio Gugelmin.

The season got off to a storied start with a win in the first race at Surfers Paradise that not only brought Andretti a measure of redemption after his Formula 1 travails but kept Reynard's streak of winning debuts in new formulae alive and well. The remainder of the year was less successful, though, as Andretti won just once more in the face of a Penske juggernaut that saw Al Unser Jr., Paul Tracy and Fittipaldi win 12 races.

What's more, Ganassi found himself looking for new drivers at year's end when Andretti returned to Newman/Haas and Gugelmin defected to the PacWest team. Ganassi took a new path, hiring two young talents in Vasser and Bryan Herta in an effort to bring some stability to the cockpits of the Target/Ganassi cars.

'It was the next logical step,' says Ganassi. 'With Michael we'd proved to ourselves that, given the right driver, we had a team that could win races. We didn't make any major changes after Michael left, so it was a case of finding a couple of guys who we thought could really blossom into something.'

If the driver line-up was ever-changing, the rest of the team was finally achieving some continuity. In fact, the most significant personnel change was an addition, rather than a replacement. And what an addition.

Two-time NFL MVP Joe Montana who, ironically, hails from the same Western Pennsylvania town where Ganassi was born and raised, joined the team. Like the Target sponsorship, Montana's contribution is more than skin deep.

'No question Joe brings marquee value to the team,' says Ganassi. 'Invaluable as that may be, what I really look to Joe for is his application of leadership. Winning is contagious.'

The winning habit did not become full-blown in 1995, but there were promising symptoms. Herta earned his first pole at Phoenix and Vasser 'won' a disputed victory at Portland after Al Unser Jr. was disqualified on a technicality. The decision was later overturned, but it didn't tarnish a breakthrough season that saw Vasser earn 'Most Improved Driver' honors. Ganassi and Herta parted company at year's end, however, with Bryan heading to Team Rahal and Ganassi

Michael C. Brown

A triumphant Chip Ganassi celebrates his team's third win in the season's first four races on the podium at Long Beach with team co-owner Joe Montana and victorious driver Jimmy Vasser.

Bottom: In the second half of the season new recruit Alex Zanardi *(left)* moved into the foreground while Vasser concentrated on securing the coveted PPG Cup championship.

tabbing Zanardi – at the urging of Reynard – as his successor.

Aside from driver and equipment changes, the team stayed largely intact. Again. For the first time in his career, Vasser enjoyed the luxury of a second season with the same core group of engineers and mechanics, including Robertson and Weaver, while Zanardi joined a largely intact unit featuring Nunn and chief mechanic Robin Hill, lately of Rahal/Hogan. Meanwhile, Anderson was promoted to managing director as Hull assumed the team manager role.

'We changed some things, but we also had some good continuity on the engineering and mechanical side,' says Ganassi. 'That's where our strength comes from. When you change an outside supplier like an engine or tire manufacturer it's not as big a move as when you make a management change or an engineering change where you have to absorb whole new ideologies.'

While Vasser's four wins in the first six races got the team off to a rocket start, and Zanardi's three wins in the last 10 kept it going, the key to the championship was the fact that Vasser finished each of the 16 races, all but one in the points.

'Jimmy began building towards this year in 1995 when he led some races. It was a confidence thing,' says Ganassi. 'I also think he matured over the winter and developed his ability to focus on his career and what was attainable. He took a big step as a driver and as a person.

'I don't think the victories in the early part of the season should rest solely on Jimmy's shoulders, but by the same token, I don't think our so-called "mid-season slump" rested squarely on his shoulders either. There were a couple of races where we didn't help him much, and don't underestimate the fact that a lot of

other people – tire manufacturers, engine manufacturers and the teams themselves – raised their game.

'In the beginning of the season, Jimmy won some races with his own style, no question. There's also no question at some parts of the season he was driving for points. But championships are what this business is all about. There were some people who criticized Jimmy for driving just for the championship, but I never heard anybody who's won a championship criticize him.'

Zanardi added his share to the success story as well.

'I said at the beginning of the season that Alex was going to help Jimmy win the championship, and he did,' says Ganassi proudly. 'With five of the first seven races on ovals it was quite a learning curve, but he came through with flying colors and then just got stronger and stronger at mid-season. I'm sure he'll be even stronger next year. I couldn't be hap-

pier with my relationship with Alex or the job he's done.'

But the goal posts are always moving in racing. This time last year, Ganassi's goal was to win the PPG Cup. Now the goal is to repeat. He knows it won't be easy.

'Each year the championship gets more and more competitive,' he says, 'and I'm sure the 1997 PPG Indy Car World Series will be the most competitive yet. What were the chances that three drivers on three teams with three different engine and chassis manufacturers and two different brands of tires would go to Laguna Seca with a chance to win the championship?

'Just think of the thousands of people who had a vested interest in any one of those three cars and drivers winning the championship. I don't think they're going to be any less determined to win the championship in 1997. I know the Target/Ganassi team won't.'

Michael C. Brown

DREAM SEASON

While the U.S.A.'s Dream Team II fashioned its roundball domination at the Olympics, Firestone was fast-breaking to a dream season in Indycar racing. In its second year of competition following a 21-year absence, the tire supplier provided support to 10 of the 16 winners in the PPG Indycar World Series and all the frontrunners in the Indy Racing League's first campaign.

Firestone's tires won every superspeedway race, including its 49th Indy 500® crown and the inaugural U.S. 500 checkered flag, 16 pole positions, Target/Chip Ganassi Racing Jimmy Vasser's 1996 PPG Cup Points Championship and his teammate Alex Zanardi's Rookie-of the-Year award and Bradley Motorsports' Buzz Calkins' IRL co-championship.

"Sometimes I have to pinch myself to make sure it's all real," said Bridgestone/Firestone motorsports manager Al Speyer. "You can take the blueprint and tear it up as we are far ahead of our original schedule. It was a fabulous run and we're determined for it to continue."

What sparked Firestone's drive to success so quickly? If you dissect its program you'll conclude: hard work, talented people, talented teams, a wealth of technology and excellent planning.

"Firestone had a grand plan and executed it perfectly. I've spent a lot of time with their race tire engineers and you won't find more focused people committed to achieving their goals. Firestone's success came from its hard work," said Patrick Racing and Firestone test driver Scott Pruett.

Firestone has drawn on its global resources for racing. The Firehawk™ Indy® tire makes its home in two locations — the Bridgestone/Firestone Akron, Ohio technical center and the Bridgestone Corporation technical center in Tokyo. Of the 15 races Firestone has won since the start of 1995 — tires built in Akron were on eight of the winning cars and

tires built in Tokyo were on seven.

"We are fortunate to have two very fine technical centers," said Speyer. "We've benefited from a development and production standpoint and it's also been a source of pride and motivation for our people. The technical and moral support each center has given the other has been outstanding."

The Firestone family featured a host of speed merchants. In Indycar, Vasser led the way with Zanardi, Tasman Motorsports' Andre Ribeiro and Adrian Fernandez, Forsythe Racing's Greg Moore and Patrick's Pruett. Seldom did an IRL run go by without Bradley Motorsports' Buzz Calkins, Treadway Racing's Arie Luyendyk, Team Menard's Tony Stewart or Hemelgarn Racing's Buddy Lazier setting a speed record or grabbing a checkered flag.

"It was great to have Firestone tires; they were definitely the dominant tire in '96," said Vasser. "The tires were consistent and always there. What more can you say – we won races and won a championship on Firestone, that says a lot."

"Firestone has done a very good job for us," said Tasman Motorsports owner Steve Horne. "We've been associated with them for a long time, having graduated from Indy Lights. They're dedicated and if there's a problem, they respond."

The beat goes on. Racing is how Firestone goes to market. The main reason for Firestone's return was to energize the brand – increase its tire sales. It's worked, as sales of Firestone passenger tires have increased significantly each year over the last several years. Speyer notes, from racing to marketing Firestone is barreling down the straightaway to success.

"The famous slogan goes, 'Win on Sunday, sell on Monday'. We like to think we're doing a pretty good job and want to do better."

Perhaps Lazier's comment following his Indy 500® victory, Firestone's 49th at the Brickyard, puts this story to bed best. "The Firestone tires were awesome."

For Firestone, it's all sweet dreams.

Firestone®
America's Tire Since 1900

Firestone Wins Indy 500® Again!

Comeback Marks Record 49th Indy® Win

On Firestone tires, Buddy Lazier wins the Indy 500®.

Firestone® tires made history once again on May 26, 1996, at the 80th Indy 500® In a Firestone-equipped Ford-Reynard, Buddy Lazier raced to victory in Indianapolis. Firestone also established new Indy records for the fastest race lap, fastest qualifying lap, and fastest qualifying speed ever.

Lazier's win is the 49th Indy 500 victory for Firestone, capping a record unmatched by all other tire companies combined. It's a winning tradition that began in 1911, when Ray Harroun

"The Firestone Tires Were Awesome."
—Buddy Lazier

won the very first Indy 500 on Firestone tires.

Firestone congratulates Lazier on his remarkable performance, and his refusal to accept anything less than a first-place finish. It's a quality all of us at Firestone know something about. Because—more than two decades since we left Indy competition and 25 years after our last Indy 500 victory—Firestone has not only returned, we have returned triumphant.

Firestone. The Legend.™

Race-Winning Firestone Firehawk Indy Racing Slick & Firestone Firehawk SS10™ Street Tire

Firestone
America's Tire Since 1900

Firestone Firehawk Indy Racing Rain Tire & Firestone Firehawk SZ50™ Ultra-High Performance Tire (Available Soon)

Our 33,450 American employees are proud of Firestone's Indy 500® Performance!

Indy® Indy 500® and Indianapolis 500® are registered trademarks of the Indianapolis Motor Speedway.

Firestone Wins U.S. 500™

On Firestone tires, Jimmy Vasser wins the U.S. 500.™

Firestone® established a new tradition on May 26, 1996, with Jimmy Vasser's win at the inaugural U.S. 500.™ This historic victory marks the fourth time this season that Vasser has finished first in his Honda-Reynard on Firestone Firehawk tires.

Firestone-equipped cars dominated the event with ease, leading 241 out of 250 laps and establishing records

"The Firestone Tires Were Fantastic—Just Super."
—*Jimmy Vasser*

for the five fastest U.S. 500 race laps.

Firestone congratulates Jimmy Vasser on his latest victory, and salutes all the drivers and teams that choose to compete on Firestone Firehawk tires. And to all those who choose Firestone tires every day on the streets of this country— thanks for being part of our winning tradition.

Firestone. The Legend.™

Race-Winning Firestone Firehawk Indy Racing Slick & Firestone Firehawk SS10™ Street Tire

Firestone®
America's Tire Since 1900

Firestone Firehawk Indy Racing Rain Tire & Firestone Firehawk SZ50™Ultra-High Performance Tire (Available Soon)

Our 33,450 American employees are proud of Firestone's U.S. 500™ Performance!

FIREHAWK

AFTER PERFORMING AT 172 MPH IN THE RAIN, 55 MPH IS A PIECE OF CAKE.

INDY PERFORMANCE. FOR THE RAIN. FOR THE ROAD. Introducing the new Firehawk SZ50 ultra-high performance tire. With a tire tread patterned after our original Firehawk Indy* racing rain tire, the Firehawk SZ50 is well equipped to handle a wide range of conditions from heat-baked highways to rain-drenched curves.

 FOR THE RAIN. The Firehawk SZ50 derives its **Power-V**™ tread from **POWER-V** our original Firehawk Indy* racing rain tire. This unique tread pattern channels water out of the tire's path. It's so effective, it gives Indy* drivers the confidence they need to scream into wet turns. It's a difference you can actually feel in your own driving.

FOR THE ROAD. The Firehawk SZ50 delivers all the performance characteristics you'd expect from an ultra-high performance tire. The feel of the road. The tight handling. The precise cornering. And one more. It's exceptionally quiet.

COOL PERFORMANCE. You might not know it, but temperature has a lot to do with a tire's performance. Most traditional high-performance tires perform better in high temperature ranges. But the Firehawk SZ50, thanks to our high-tech compound called **Broad Grip Silica,**™ maintains **BG SILICA** exceptional performance when it's hot and when it's cool.

*Indy® is a registered trademark of the Indianapolis Motor Speedway.

From hot to cool, the Firehawk SZ50 has a relentless grip on the road.

THE FIRST FIRESTONE TIRE TO BENEFIT FROM UNI-T.™ Two years ago, we set out to develop the most for-ward-thinking tire tech-nologies on the planet. Everything that could be improved was improved. The result is **UNI-T**, the ultimate tire technology. The **UNI-T** technologies incorporated into the Firehawk SZ50 are:

Ultimate Tire Technology

CO•CS. It stands for Computer Optimized Component System. **CO-CS** Stated simply, computers calculate the ideal combination of tread design, material composition and tire shape to achieve mind-blowing levels of handling, grip, noise reduction and maneuverability.

L.L.CARBON. L.L.Carbon is a long-link carbon molecule that **L.L. Carbon** reinforces and stabilizes the tread rubber to provide long tread life without sacrificing grip.

O-BEAD. You probably never thought about how well your tire **O-Bead** fits your wheel. We did. Our O-Bead changes the way the tire holds the rim and creates a "tire-wheel unit" that is more pre-cisely round. This rounder shape minimizes steering shake. The result: precise, responsive steering for consistent control.

HIGH-PERFORMANCE CARS DESERVE HIGH-PERFORMANCE TIRES. Get the performance you paid for when you bought your high-performance car. Performance technology that comes from the tires of the highest-performing cars in America. The Indy* cars. And the ultra-high performance that the Firehawk SZ50 can deliver. So, ask your Firestone retailer about the Firehawk SZ50. And find out what Indy* proven technology can do for your high-performance car.

INTRODUCING
FIREHAWK SZ50

For the Rain. For the Road.

Firehawk Indy* Racing Rain Tire   Firehawk SZ50

Firestone ®
America's Tire Since 1900

WE MOVE IN THE BEST OF CIRCLES.

(AS WELL AS ROAD COURSES AND CITY STREETS)

THE OFFICIAL SPONSORS OF INDYCAR

Championship Auto Racing Teams, Inc. • 755 W. Big Beaver Road, Suite 800, Troy, MI 48084 • Tel: 810-362-8800 • Fax: 810-362-8810
http://www.indycar.com

Our fastest moving parts.

The piston in the Ford Zetec-R Formula One engine accelerates from 0-100 miles per hour in just one thousandth of a second.

Moving quickly on, the turbo in the Ford Cosworth engine which won the 1995 Indy 500 and PPG Indy Car Championship spins at 80,000rpm.

And yet, from 1996, Cosworth's fastest moving parts will be castings. Up to one million castings per year will be produced using the patented Cosworth process at a new, highly automated UK foundry in which £25 million has been invested.

Phase A alone has already produced full order books to supply high quality, precision engine castings to companies such as General Motors, Jaguar, Ford and many other manufacturers around the world.

This is all part of our fast moving success in the field of automotive technology.

COSWORTH

CASTINGS • ENGINEERING • MANUFACTURING • RACING

Vickers

A division of Vickers PLC

St James Mill Rd   Northampton NN5 5JJ   United Kingdom   Tel: + 44 1604 732100   Fax: + 44 1604 732113

Cosworth is a registered trade mark belonging to Vickers PLC.

1992

TOP TEN DRIVERS

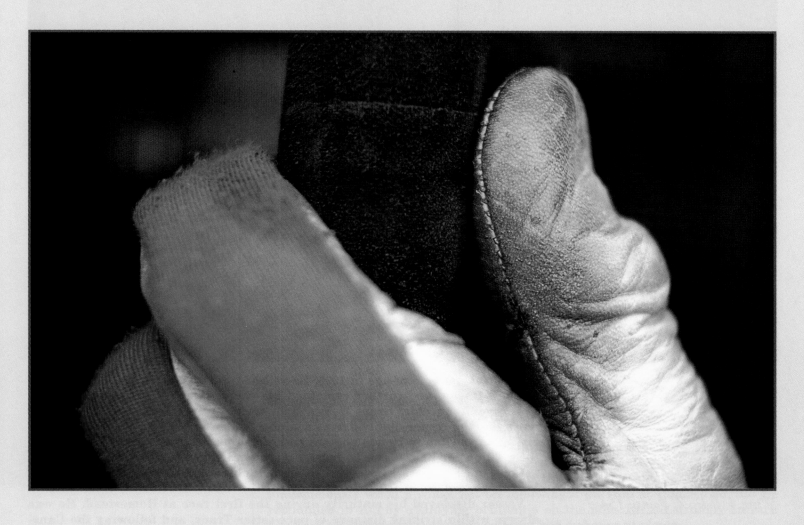

The 1996 season has been perhaps the most competitive in the history of the PPG Indy Car World Series. The overall quality of the drivers has been extremely high. In the following pages, Editor Jeremy Shaw offers his personal ranking of the best of the best, taking into account their individual performances, their level of experience and the equipment at their disposal

Photographs by Michael C. Brown

michael andretti

3

Michael Andretti

Date of birth: October 5, 1962

Residence: Nazareth, Pa.

Indy Car starts in 1996: 16

PPG Cup ranking: 2nd

Wins: 5; Poles: 0; Points: 132

One could make a case for placing any of the top three drivers at the head of the ranking – and perhaps even one or two more. The difference, however, came down to Vasser's consistency and coolness under pressure; Zanardi's stunning performances as a rookie; and the fact Andretti, even with all his experience, allowed aggression and eagerness to overcome common sense in some early races. The blemishes earned him a probation following Long Beach. Thereafter he put barely a wheel wrong.

Andretti left not a crumb on the table in 1996. He extracted every last ounce of potential from his Lola/Ford/Goodyear combination. Five wins represented a remarkable achievement, and there is no doubt that if his car had been more reliable, he might have won the PPG Cup title.

The Milwaukee victory was vintage Andretti. He would have been content to finish second to Unser, who had chosen the harder Goodyear tire and was firmly in control as the race drew toward its conclusion. But a late caution put Andretti back in the frame. He promptly took advantage of his softer tires by pouncing past Unser on a restart. His win at Detroit was equally opportunistic.

For me, two other drives were even more outstanding. At Portland he pitted with an electrical problem almost immediately after the green flag and lost almost two laps. He drove his heart out to finish 11th. At Cleveland, meanwhile, excellent strategy enabled Andretti to take the lead soon after halfway. His Ford engine was no match for the rival Hondas, yet a string of fast laps – on a circuit where consistency is hard to achieve – kept him in contention until his transmission failed. Brilliant.

al unser jr.

Al Unser Jr.
Date of birth: April 19, 1962
Residence: Albuquerque, N.M.
Indy Car starts in 1996: 16
PPG Cup ranking: 4th
Wins: 0; Poles: 0; Points: 125

Who would have guessed that Unser (and Team Penske) would fail to win a race in 1996, especially after making a solid start to the season? Nevertheless, he remained in title contention until the final race, despite the fact his car frequently seemed no match for the other front-runners. But the crux of the matter is, *why* was his car not more competitive? His Mercedes-Benz engines might have lacked a little on some courses in comparison to the Hondas, but they were at least as good as the Fords. Teammate Paul Tracy, meanwhile, often was appreciably faster in qualifying, evidenced by the Canadian's tally of three poles and an average grid position of 7.6 compared to Unser's 10.6. In spite of all his experience, testing and resources, both human and financial, Unser rarely secured a comfortable handle on the car.

Of course, he usually made up the deficit on race day with his all-business, heads-up style. Team owner Roger Penske also sometimes came to the rescue with typically astute strategy, yet all too often Unser left himself with too much work to do, too many cars to pass – especially given how competitive the series had become.

Unser made a rare mistake in Australia where he spun after making contact with de Ferran. At Detroit he slid into the tires after Tracy, crassly, refused to allow him room despite the fact Unser was clearly much faster. A seldom seen frustration also surfaced on occasion, notably at Mid-Ohio where Unser attempted a desperate maneuver to pass Parker Johnstone – for 11th place – on the last lap. On balance, this was a far cry from Unser's best campaign, but equally he showed he's not ready to be counted out just yet!

gil de ferran

9

Gil de Ferran
Date of birth: November 11, 1967
Residence: Indianapolis, Ind.
Indy Car starts in 1996: 16
PPG Cup ranking: 6th
Wins: 1; Poles: 1; Points: 104

Gil de Ferran was much in demand during the month of July. His victory at Cleveland moved him firmly into contention for the PPG Cup title and he was engaged in talks with several team owners about a drive in 1997. His name also had been linked to at least a couple of Formula 1 opportunities. De Ferran ultimately signed for Derrick Walker following Jim Hall's decision to retire, although the fact he slipped to sixth in the point standings represented a major disappointment.

It was truly a topsy-turvy year for the Brazilian, who began as one of the favorites for honors following his superb victory at the end of the 1995 season and Hall's subsequent decision to switch to Honda engines. A second-place finish at Homestead represented a promising start. De Ferran ran equally well in front of his home fans in Rio, only to be delayed by a fuel system problem. But that setback paled into insignificance at Long Beach, where he controlled the event until a hose-clamp failure robbed his engine of boost with just five laps remaining. Fifth place represented scant reward.

His drive to victory in Cleveland was exemplary, but in the latter part of the year he became involved in a series of first-lap mishaps. Matters came to a head when he accused Zanardi of pushing him off the road at Road America; but de Ferran had been under strict instructions from his team not to try any bold moves on the first lap . . .

De Ferran was curiously inconsistent during his sophomore season. He will need to improve upon that anomaly, and curb his enthusiasm in the early laps, if he is to fully realize his obvious potential.

scott pruett

10

Scott Pruett
Date of birth: March 24, 1960
Residence: Crystal Bay, Nev.
Indy Car starts in 1996: 16
PPG Cup ranking: 10th
Wins: 0; Poles: 1; Points: 82

Fourth place at Homestead followed by a well-earned third in Rio saw Scott Pruett leading the PPG Cup standings after two races. A runner-up finish in Australia, where he also started second, wasn't enough to stave off the advances of Vasser, who took over the points lead – ultimately, as it turned out, for good – but Pruett nevertheless had gotten off to a good start for Patrick Racing.

The Californian continued to run well, only to be hamstrung by a series of niggly problems. He was restricted to 11th place at Long Beach by a broken coil and retired early in the U.S. 500 with a blown engine. He, like most Firestone runners, struggled on the short ovals yet he battled hard to claim valuable points. Next, as further evidence of a dramatic improvement in his qualifying performances, came a magnificent maiden Indy Car pole at Detroit. Race day, though, dawned wet, and the Firestone wet weather tires were a disaster.

His season continued in similar vein, moments of elation tempered by cruel disappointment. In the Marlboro 500, after being content to run a steady pace in the early stages, he stepped up his challenge and had just passed Ribeiro for the lead when his engine blew less than 20 miles from the finish. His frustration grew even more intense following more XD failures at Mid-Ohio and Vancouver.

Pruett, nevertheless, can be proud of his accomplishments. He accumulated the third-best qualifying record of the season, his average grid position of 7.44 bettered only by the Ganassi pair. He showed he can mix it with the best. Given proper reliability in 1997, Pruett could become a serious championship challenger.

On the left, the McLaren F1 road car. 6.1 litre normally aspirated V12 engine. 0-60mph in 3.2 seconds. 103bhp per litre.

On the right, the new BMW M3 Evolution.

3.2 litre normally aspirated straight six engine. 0-60mph in 5.3 seconds. 100.3 bhp per litre.

It is no coincidence that these two extraordinary engines both offer the elusive 100bhp

per litre. For they both also carry the name BMW M Power.

Since its inception in 1972, the BMW motorsport division has rewritten many engineering

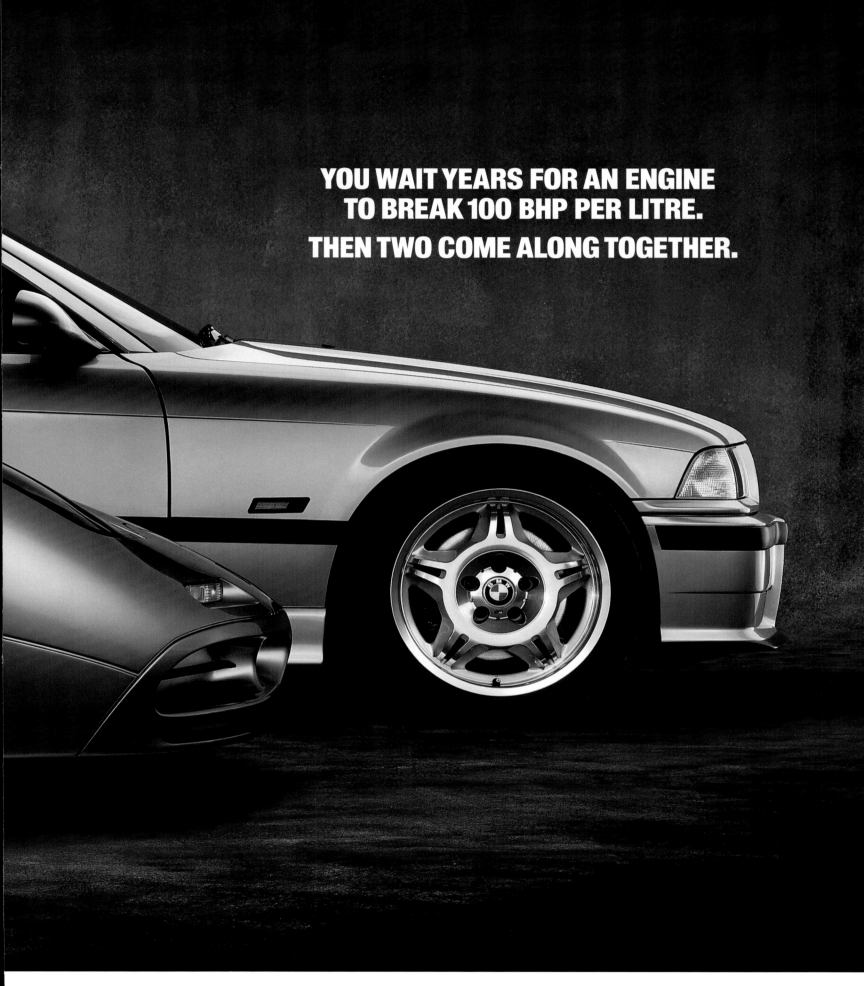

YOU WAIT YEARS FOR AN ENGINE TO BREAK 100 BHP PER LITRE.

THEN TWO COME ALONG TOGETHER.

rules. Not to mention record books. And in so doing has helped create some of the world's most revered cars. (In the 1995 Le Mans 24 hour race, the F1 won and took 4 of the top 5 places.)

Small wonder then that the M3 Evolution has the critics swooning.

Autocar magazine summed up the feelings of its press colleagues when it used the phrase "...a mind-blowing supercar..."[†]

Very kind, but we can't help thinking we've heard that before somewhere.

THE ULTIMATE DRIVING MACHINE

The universally admired enthusiast/driver/engineer-turned-team owner Jim Hall announced during the Marlboro 500 weekend that he would retire from the sport at the end of the 1996 season. His driver for the past two years, Gil de Ferran, was firmly in the hunt for the PPG Cup title when Hall made his intentions public, and while he was ultimately unsuccessful in his quest for one final championship, the tall Texan still departed the scene with a host of credits to his name.

Hall, born in Abilene, Texas, on July 23, 1935, saw his boyhood interest in automobiles blossom when he attended college at the California Institute of Technology. He initially studied geology, intent upon developing his family's extensive oil interests in his home state, but soon started to race his older brother

Richard's Austin-Healey sports car and after two years switched to a major in mechanical engineering. It was to stand him in good stead.

Hall raced a variety of Maserati sports cars upon graduating from college, and for a while he and his brother were involved in a sports car business in Dallas with another soon-to-be-legendary name in American motorsport, Carroll Shelby. Hall and Shelby traveled to England in 1958 and together they met with Brian Lister, who at the time was producing a successful Jaguar-powered sports car. The Americans persuaded Lister to install a Chevrolet engine in one of his bulbous designs, which Hall raced with modest success at home until replacing it with the more sophisticated 'Birdcage' Maserati.

It wasn't long before Hall figured

he could build at least as good a car himself, and so the Chaparral marque – named after the Southwestern road runner bird – was born. The first car, a traditional front-engine design, was built under contract in California, although in 1962 Hall and his like-minded neighbor and friend, Hap Sharp, decided to set up shop together in their home town of Midland, Texas.

During the rear-engined, Chevy-powered Chaparral 2's gestation, Hall grasped the opportunity to race for one complete season in Europe, driving a Lotus-BRM 24 for Reg Parnell in the 1963 World Drivers Championship. His best finish was a fifth at the Nurburgring. His heart, however, remained in the United States, and while he made some spectacular and successful forays to Europe with later Chaparral creations, Hall decided to

concentrate his efforts on racing in North America.

Hall himself won the burgeoning United States Road Racing Championship in 1964, and as the USRRC developed into the Can-Am, Hall and the Chaparrals led the way with a series of innovations including the use of airplane-type wings, semi-automatic transmissions, ground effects and plastic composite materials, all of which are widely used in the sport today.

Hall retired from driving following a bad crash at Stardust Raceway, Las Vegas in 1968, in which both legs were badly broken, but his pioneering nature remained intact. The Chaparral 2J, which appeared in 1970, represented perhaps his most outrageous design, featuring 'skirts' reaching from the bottom of the car to the ground and a powerful electric

by Jeremy Shaw

HALL
of fame

What They Said:

James C. Pate, chief executive officer of Pennzoil Company: 'No one person has had as profound an effect on motor racing as Jim Hall. Many of his innovations on the race track have found their way into the automotive product that is currently driven by the general public.'

Carl Haas, a former partner of Hall and now co-owner of Newman/Haas Racing: 'I have always had the highest regard for Jim's technical expertise and racing knowledge. Above all he is an honorable gentleman who I am very sorry to see leaving the sport.'

Andrew Craig, president and chief executive officer of IndyCar/Championship Auto Racing Teams: 'I have only had the pleasure of knowing Jim Hall for a few years but apart from being a legendary figure in the sport, he has always been a voice of wisdom and reason and a significant contributor to the IndyCar board meetings. He will always be a welcome face in IndyCar.'

Roger Penske, who drove for Hall when the Texan was sidelined by a broken arm in 1964 and now heads Marlboro Team Penske: 'Jim Hall, as well as possessing the highest moral standards, has been one of the greatest innovators in the history of motor sports.'

Les Richter, former vice president of NASCAR and now executive vice president of The California Speedway: 'Like the creatures escaping from Pandora's Box, his ideas could not be confined once they have been let loose. Jim Hall's influence on modern motor racing has been very significant.'

the sport in the 1980s, but in 1991 he returned once more to the Indy Car scene, again with sponsorship from Pennzoil. The new Hall-VDS team, originally comprised of Hall and his son, Jim II, and VDS Engines' Franz Weis, scored a fairy-tale debut victory at Surfers Paradise, Australia with John Andretti at the helm of its Lola-Chevrolet.

The team, still based in Midland, underwent several changes, with Hall regaining sole ownership, but it wasn't until the arrival of European-based Brazilian Gil de Ferran in 1995 that the yellow cars returned to full front-runner status. De Ferran scored a superb victory at Laguna Seca to secure Rookie of the Year honors, and in 1996 continued to be a major contender after switching to Honda power. After adding one more victory, in Cleveland, however, Hall decided enough was enough.

'I've had a great time in this sport and I'm definitely gonna miss it,' said an emotional Hall in confirming his impending retirement immediately following qualifying at Michigan International Speedway. 'It's been my life. It's been a lot of fun. This is certainly one of the toughest decisions I've ever had to make.

'There's never a perfect time [to make this announcement]. I guess if you wrote the script, you'd grab the trophy girl and run off in the pace car – but I've already got the girl,' he added with a grin, nodding in the direction of his wife, Sandy. 'But now is the right time to do it because it will give my guys an opportunity to get good jobs for next year.'

Hall said that his decision to withdraw from the sport was not predicated upon sponsorship, despite the rumor mill suggesting that primary sponsor Pennzoil was not planning on renewing its support in 1997. In fact, Hall said he had 'plenty of proposals' and that he considered the PPG Cup series 'to be in the best shape it's ever been in.'

'I consider it the most competitive open-wheel series in the world today,' he said. 'That's why I'm in it, because I've always wanted to beat the best there is.'

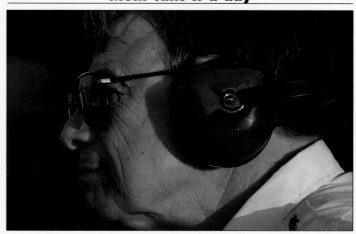

Mehl calls it a day

Photos: Michael C. Brown

Leo Mehl, Goodyear's director of worldwide racing for the past 22 years, officially retired on March 1, one month before his 60th birthday. Mehl, universally admired within the auto racing community both for his legendary integrity and his ready wit, joined Goodyear as a trainee in 1959, after graduating from West Virginia University and spending three years in the Air Force. He moved into race tire development in 1963 and has overseen countless victories in every imaginable aspect of the sport.

There is no question that Leo will be missed by Goodyear and by racing,' said Goodyear Chairman Stan Gault. 'Along with establishing the success of our overall racing program, he has built countless friendships and relationships around the world. We aggressively will continue the winning tradition that Leo has been instrumental in developing.'

fan which evacuated the air and created additional downforce – hence its nickname, the 'vacuum cleaner.' The car was immediately successful in Jackie Stewart's hands, but like Hall's previous 'flipper' wing which flattened out on the straightaways and then tilted dramatically under braking to provide downforce through the corners, it was also controversial and before the end of the season was ruled as ineligible for competition by the FIA. Hall quit the scene in disgust.

'Basically, almost everything I had done with sports cars and the Can-Am was outlawed,' said Hall. 'I just sat on the sidelines for a while.'

But Hall couldn't escape the lure of auto racing. He returned in 1973 to Formula 5000 competition in partnership with another sports car convert, Carl Haas. The Haas/Hall combination won three consecutive championships with British driver Brian Redman before Hall moved on alone into Indy Car racing in 1978. Once again he was immediately successful, teaming with Lola Cars and Al Unser to win the coveted Triple Crown by claiming victory in all three 500-mile races at Indianapolis, Pocono (Pa.) and Ontario (Calif.).

Hall was among the founding fathers of the Championship Auto Racing Teams organization toward the end of that season. Nevertheless, his penchant for engineering excellence continued with the stunning 'yellow submarine' Pennzoil Chaparral 2K, which introduced the concept of 'ground-effects' technology to Indy Car racing in 1979. The following year, Johnny Rutherford swept to victory at Indianapolis en route to capturing the PPG Indy Car World Series crown.

Hall took another sabbatical from

Goodyear's commitment to auto racing

is unequaled by any other tire company in the world. On any given weekend, at any number of places around the world, Goodyear Eagle racing tires are competing – from Formula One, stock cars, Indy cars and drag racing to trucks, sports cars, sprints and off-road racing. No other tire company in the world competes in as many different types of racing and racing series as Goodyear – or wins as many championships.

At world headquarters in Akron, Ohio, Goodyear associates thrive on competition. Racing energizes the entire company and provides an arena to develop new technology and transfer much of what they learn to street tire advancements.

'Our years of involvement in all aspects of racing give us the unique advantage of being able to transfer applicable technology, not only from one racing series to another, but from the track to the street as well,' said Stu Grant, general manager of racing worldwide. 'When we receive a challenge from a tire company, which often chooses just one high-profile series to concentrate on, we do whatever it takes to provide our drivers and teams with the best, most technologically advanced product possible. And, it's done without compromising our commitment to those involved in other racing series.'

GOODYEAR
#1 in Racing. #1 in Tires.

Nowhere was Goodyear's race tire development more intense in 1996 than in the IndyCar series. Facing the second year of competition from Bridgestone/Firestone, Inc., Goodyear made big strides in compounds, molds and construction, not only for short tracks and superspeedways, but for the varied road courses and street courses as well.

'Competition pushed us to put in more time and effort this year with IndyCar than we have at any other time in recent history,' Grant said. 'We've been able to make a lot of improvements in the tire over a very short period of time.'

Goodyear accelerated its approach to testing and building race tires. Engineers brought out new tires virtually every race weekend, developing a different product for each track in the Indy Car series.

Stu Grant, Goodyear's general manager of racing, worldwide

'In the beginning of 1996, we felt we were behind, but by the end of the season the tide turned back to where our tires were once again the baseline of performance,' said Grant.

The company's Eagle racing radials won six IndyCar events, sweeping the top three podium positions in three races and taking the top five positions in one race and four of the top five positions in four events.

Goodyear's rain tire proved spectacular in its first outing at the Detroit Grand Prix. Eagle-shod cars overpowered the Firestone teams in every corner and every straight to take the podium and lead all but one lap.

'The dual-channel, asymmetric, directional tread Eagles had a three-second advantage,' said Steve Myers, director of racing tire sales and marketing. 'We were proud that our tires were the common denominator in bringing top finishes to all the engine suppliers.'

Indeed, competition is everything according to Goodyear's Don Vera, manager of race tire product development.

'We may not be driving the cars, but we feel like we're sitting there beside the driver as he goes around, because he's using our product,' said Vera. 'And it's so critical to the performance. We do everything we can to give our Goodyear teams the best tire possible for every track.

'Competition is what keeps us coming back year after year. The race itself is like icing on the cake, especially if you win. It shows that you have been able to improve the product. But during a competitive situation like we have now, the real development work is done during testing, not during the race.

'We've tested at more tracks with more teams and with more different drivers this year than ever before. You are going to see that carry over into '97, improving our performance even more.'

The new racing season promises to be as exciting and challenging as it was in 1996.

Another challenge for the 1997 racing season is the addition of new race tracks in Las Vegas, Dallas, California and Colorado Springs.

A new track presents myriad variables for tire engineers to consider – what the speeds are going to be, the banking, what lines the cars will run, how much grip the surface has, how much heat the tires will generate ... the list goes on. Engineers first gather as much data on the track

as possible, sometimes relying on satellite photography for overviews. Then, after exhaustive testing sessions, by computer and on the track, specific tire recommendations are made for each track.

'For every track, not just the new ones, you start with a known tire and always look to improve it,' Vera said. 'Every test you go to, you're trying to make it better than what you had before. That's what it's all about, not only for race tires, but for our entire line of products. We want to be the baseline of performance.'

That baseline of performance extends from Indy racing to virtually every form of motor sport. Goodyear continually advances race tire technology in all areas of racing, all over the globe.

In Formula One, a new three-aqua channel rain tire proved its mettle, while a deep-water Monsoon tire stood by to tackle the extremes.

Goodyear was co-champion in the Indy Racing League's first season. With alterations in chassis and engine combinations being introduced for the second season, Goodyear engineers are approaching it as a brand-new series . . . baselining with current technology and tire construction.

With speeds in the pro classes of drag racing showing consistent, over 300 mph runs, a new, stronger rear Eagle has become a key component in these record-setting events.

New sports car tires won the overall victory at the 24 Hours of Le Mans.

New, successful stock car tire ideas continue to evolve in NASCAR Winston Cup, Busch Grand National and Craftsman Truck series.

Expansion continues in the short track arena, with sales doubled since last year. In 1997, the asphalt area will see significant growth, but an even larger focus will be on the high-sales volume dirt-track segment.

'We've got the commitment from the entire company and the backing and resources to do what it takes to win not only in Indy racing, but across the board,' said Grant. 'This company remains committed to serving the entire sport with the best possible technology and highest quality product. No other tire company in the world represents what Goodyear does in racing. We win an average of 83 per cent in all major series in which we participate. We're number one in racing and we intend to stay there.'

Left: Goodyear's spectacularly successful Eagle racing rain tire introduced in the 1996 season.

Below: Goodyear equals success at Nazareth, with the first three finishers all on Eagle race tires.

PLAYING BY T

Few things are as vital to open, fair and safe competition in auto racing as a logical set of rules governing the design, construction and performance of chassis, engines and tires. There are as many ways of making rules in the sport as there are sanctioning bodies, with no one method necessarily the best.

IndyCar's approach to rules-making, however, where a technical committee made up of representatives from all facets of the sport makes recommendations to the board of directors, has proven to be remarkably effective in balancing the often conflicting concerns of cost, safety and open competition. The fact that three drivers using three different makes of chassis, three different engine manufacturers and two different brands of tires took the green flag at the Toyota Grand Prix of Monterey with a chance of winning the 1996 PPG Indy Car World Series is testament to that fact.

Chaired by Penske Racing's Teddy Mayer, the technical committee also includes team owners Derrick Walker, Dale Coyne and Jim Hall, driver/team owner Bobby Rahal, Target/Chip Ganassi team manager Tom Anderson, Newman/Haas race engineer Peter Gibbons and Kirk Russell, IndyCar's vice president of competition and technical director.

'The committee only has three objectives,' says Russell. 'Driver safety, cost containment and providing a rules base which ensures close competition among a major part of the field.

'It's an ongoing process which includes the people who are closest to the product. Manufacturers, their engineering staffs, our drivers, anyone that has any interest definitely has the ability to give an opinion or direction on where we're going with these rules. We spend a considerable amount of time with these groups discussing the direction we're going to go and how we make the changes so we can get a consensus to put a rules package together.'

Early in 1995, the board of directors approved the technical committee's recommendations designed to curtail the escalation in speeds on the mile ovals and superspeedways of the PPG Indy Car World Series for the 1996 season. The new rules also mandated specific steps in the construction of the chassis to better protect drivers during impacts.

The 1996 rules package featured significant restrictions in the effectiveness of the chassis aerodynamic packages, including a reduction in the size of the underbody tunnels; raised and repositioned sidepods; limitations on the speedway wings'

Michael C. Brown

angle of attack; and restrictions on the placement of the bodywork and underbody relative to the rear wheels. In total, the new rules were designed to reduce downforce by as much as 30 percent and, simultaneously, place a renewed emphasis on the mechanical grip generated by the suspension geometry, springs and dampers.

'The concern was performance,' says Russell. 'The mechanical efficiency of the cars and the improved performance of the tires and engines have just increased the capability of these cars to go ever faster. I don't think there's necessarily a performance concern at most road circuits, but when we start looking at ovals and the speeds on ovals – when on one mile ovals speeds approach 200 mph – and especially the speeds we're seeing at Michigan – we need to keep looking at this.'

The committee was not only concerned about reigning in the escalation in performance, it also wanted to ensure that in its efforts to mandate slower cars it did not unwittingly mandate uncontrollable cars.

'The way you look at it is where you are as a baseline, what kind of developments you think are going to be part of the performance enhancement for the upcoming season and what you can do to alter that package,' says Russell. 'Not to the point that you change the car totally, but that you can produce a rules package that contains perfor-

mance but at the same time produces a predictable vehicle.

'It would not be very astute for us to produce a package that gave us proportionally more incidents at a little bit lower speed, and that balance is always considered. Essentially we know as we started to take downforce away from the cars the stability changes, but we have to differentiate between stability and predictability.

'Predictability is the key there. We don't want cars that put drivers in uncomfortable positions because the car "gave up" where a couple of laps before, in the same set of circumstances that the driver recognizes, the car was in a comfortable position.'

Additional measures were adopted for 1996 which were intended to directly enhance driver safety. These included higher cockpit surrounds to protect the driver's head during a side impact, as well as a 30 percent increase in the 'skin' thickness of the chassis in the cockpit area. In addition, the repositioned sidepods afforded increased protection against wheels intruding into the cockpit in the event of an impact.

Much to everyone's surprise, the 1996 rule changes did not result in slower speeds and lap times. Thanks to continual gains by the engine makers and tire companies, together with ongoing aerodynamic and mechanical development of the chassis, new lap records were set at more than half of the circuits this season. Were it not for the new rules, however, speeds undoubtedly would have escalated to an even greater degree.

The year was also marred by fatalities and serious injuries, underlining the omnipresent need for continual improvements in safety. Thus new rules for 1997 address the most critical safety aspects brought to light this past season, primarily with regard to a series of back and neck injuries suffered by drivers. As a result, all Indy cars in 1997 will be required to have energy absorbing seats.

'Evolution is an important part of what we do from a safety standpoint, both in car design and in circuit design,' says Russell. 'And there's another component to that, which is there are many people who are knowledgeable about the things that produce good, safe race cars. Everything from the design concept up through the actual driver's particular position in the car: how he sits in the car, where his seat-belts are; the objects inside the car that in the event of an impact could affect him and the placement of those things.'

Nor is the technical committee

HE RULES

by David Phillips

Opposite: Safety measures introduced as part of IndyCar's 1996 rules package included raised cockpit sides and padded headrests *(top)* to provide additional protection for drivers' heads in the event of an accident. Underbody tunnels *(bottom)* were reduced in size in order to restrict cornering speeds.

Below: A comparison between the 1995 Lola, the T95/00, and the four designs produced to the 1996 rules makes clear the changes to the height and position of the cars' sidepods.

Lola T95/00

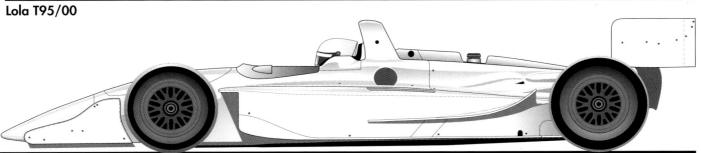

Lola T96/00

Reynard 96I

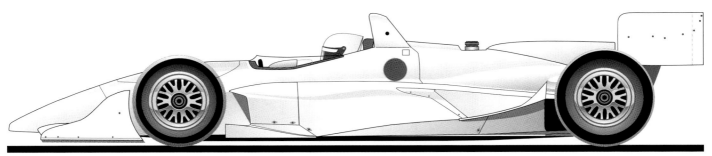

Penske PC25

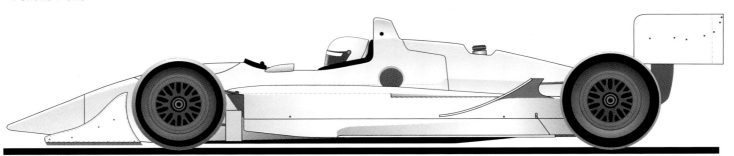

Eagle Mk.V

The new rules allowed designers considerable scope to apply their creativity, with suspension layout assuming particular importance. In these plan views, the differences between the four 1996 designs are particularly noticeable.

Despite the adoption of regulations intended to limit performance, development continued unabated during the season. Reynard, for example, introduced the modified front wing design carried by Alex Zanardi's #4 Target/Chip Ganassi car *(below).*

Michael C. Brown

An inexact science

Despite IndyCar's new rules mandating reductions in aerodynamic downforce, new lap records were established at eight of the 13 venues common to the 1995 and '96 seasons, with Jimmy Vasser setting a new closed course record with a qualifying lap of 234.665 mph at Michigan International Speedway in July. There were a variety of reasons for the continuing escalation in speeds, not the least of which was the spirited battle between Honda, Mercedes-Benz, Ford/Cosworth and Toyota, the tire 'war' between Goodyear and Firestone, and in the cases of Milwaukee and Laguna Seca, grippy new pavement.

Chassis designers and race engineers also contributed to the increasing speeds through their efforts to improve the cars' mechanical grip, or the traction generated by the non-aerodynamic components of the chassis such as the suspension, springs and shock absorbers.

'The rules meant that we basically lost 30 percent of the downforce,' said Bruce Ashmore, technical director for Reynard North America. 'So the big challenge was to gain some of that back. To achieve that we realized we had to improve the car mechanically, which meant placing a large emphasis on the suspension geometry.'

Chassis-makers weren't the only ones taking a renewed interest in suspension geometry. Most of the top teams using customer cars – including Target/Chip Ganassi, Newman/Haas and Patrick Racing – went one step farther by developing their own suspension pieces and geometries.

'In the past if the car wasn't working properly, especially under braking, the easiest thing to do was to just crank on some more

downforce,' said Tom Brown, Hogan Penske race engineer. 'But you can't do that anymore – we had to work much more with the suspension to make gains.'

Nor was the quest for mechanical grip limited to A-arms, trailing links and sway bars. Optimized shock absorber setups, already a vital component of chassis configuration, became even more critical.

'We used Koni, Penske and Ohlins shocks during the season,' said Morris Nunn, Target/Chip Ganassi race engineer for Alex Zanardi, 'and we won races with all of 'em.'

Meanwhile, progress continued on the aerodynamic front. In contrast to the standard issue Lola T96/00s, the Newman/Haas entries featured subtly reprofiled bodywork at the rear of their sidepods, while Team Rahal introduced winglets immediately in front of the rear wheels (said to improve downforce and top speed) at Portland. These later became standard issue on all Reynards, with Penske employing similar changes at Vancouver and Laguna Seca.

However much the rules were changed though, the game remained the same.

'You look at the elements to the setup individually, like the suspension geometry, the shock valving, the spring rate and the aerodynamics and try to optimize each one,' said Don Halliday, Tasman Motorsports race engineer for Andre Ribeiro. 'But the real trick is to feel where each is at its best in harmony with the others.

'It's fun . . . but it's not exact.'

David Phillips

---

standing still in its efforts to curtail the escalation in speeds and costs. Next year will see the manifold boost pressure reduced from 45 inches to 40 inches at all IndyCar races (this limitation has been in effect at M.I.S. the past two years), while fuel cells will be reduced from 40 gallons to 35 gallons and a greater emphasis will be placed on fuel economy, with Valvoline methanol distributed to each team on the basis of a maximum consumption of 2.0 miles per gallon rather than the previous 1.8 mpg. In addition, new rules will limit speedway rear wings to two elements in an effort to both limit speeds and reduce costs by controlling the number of wing elements teams need to bring to the track.

There will also be a reduction in on-board instrumentation permitted during race weekends as well as the beginnings of an effort to increase the lifespan of ancillary parts and equipment.

'There will be a trend towards – not standardized components but the ability for components to be used from one design to the next,' says Russell. 'For example, wheels, brake calipers, those sort of things eventually will function on one car for a long period of time, so that design changes that are incorporated in the updates will have to allow for the fact that these components will be able to be brought forward; and the teams won't have to retire spares because they aren't usable anymore.'

Other cost saving regulations will include a mandate to 'freeze' the development of each engine design's primary exhaust headers early in the season, as well as requiring that wing supports be constructed of aluminum alloy plate instead of composites.

None of the changes, of themselves, is particularly dramatic. In total, however, they represent a cohesive package aimed at providing stability for the individual designers while continuing to upgrade the overriding issue of providing as much protection for the drivers as is practically possible.

As IndyCar President Andrew Craig has said so often: 'Safety is job one for us. It always will be.'

What They Said:

Michael Andretti (#6 Kmart/Texaco Havoline Lola-Ford/Cosworth: '[The new rules] definitely slow the car through the corners, and the car feels a lot lighter. That's what they were supposed to do. The car is very drivable and not at all pitch-sensitive. They really did their homework.'

Tom Anderson, managing director, Target/Chip Ganassi Racing: 'The tires and engines were only going to get better. We needed to do something in order to slow the cars down before we had a serious problem.'

Raul Boesel (#1 Brahma Sports Team Reynard-Ford/Cosworth): 'You have the sensation of the car floating under you. The car does not have a bad balance, front to rear, but you really notice it in the braking areas: The car just doesn't stop. You feel the loss of downforce for sure. You have to brake much earlier.'

Mauricio Gugelmin (#17 Hollywood Reynard-Ford/Cosworth): 'The first time I drove [the '96 Reynard], it felt like driving on ice.'

Bryan Herta (#28 Shell Reynard-Mercedes): 'The new cars are very nice to drive. It seems like the rules have been well thought out because they've accomplished their goals in terms of slowing the car down, but it doesn't seem to have made the car twitchy because of the loss of downforce.'

Tom Brown, race engineer, Hogan Penske Racing: 'Before, aerodynamics was the most important factor in determining a car's competitiveness. Now mechanical balance has taken over.

'Also, the driver has to be much more precise under braking, because he doesn't have the downforce any more; and he has to be much more sensitive on the throttle.'

Derrick Walker, team owner, Walker Racing: 'Each year the engineers and the rules committee work on improving the car and, as always, they come up with things that make each car better and safer. We have struggled for years and years in the rules committee to make a big enough step to really make an impact and slow the cars down, but we always try to pick something that is going to maintain stability, and that is always tough to do.'

Mark Blundell (#21 VISA/PacWest Reynard-Ford/Cosworth): 'Obviously I don't have any real experience of what the cars were like before this season, but I have to say, after my crash in Rio, I'm seriously impressed with how strong the cars really are. I gave it a pretty good test.'

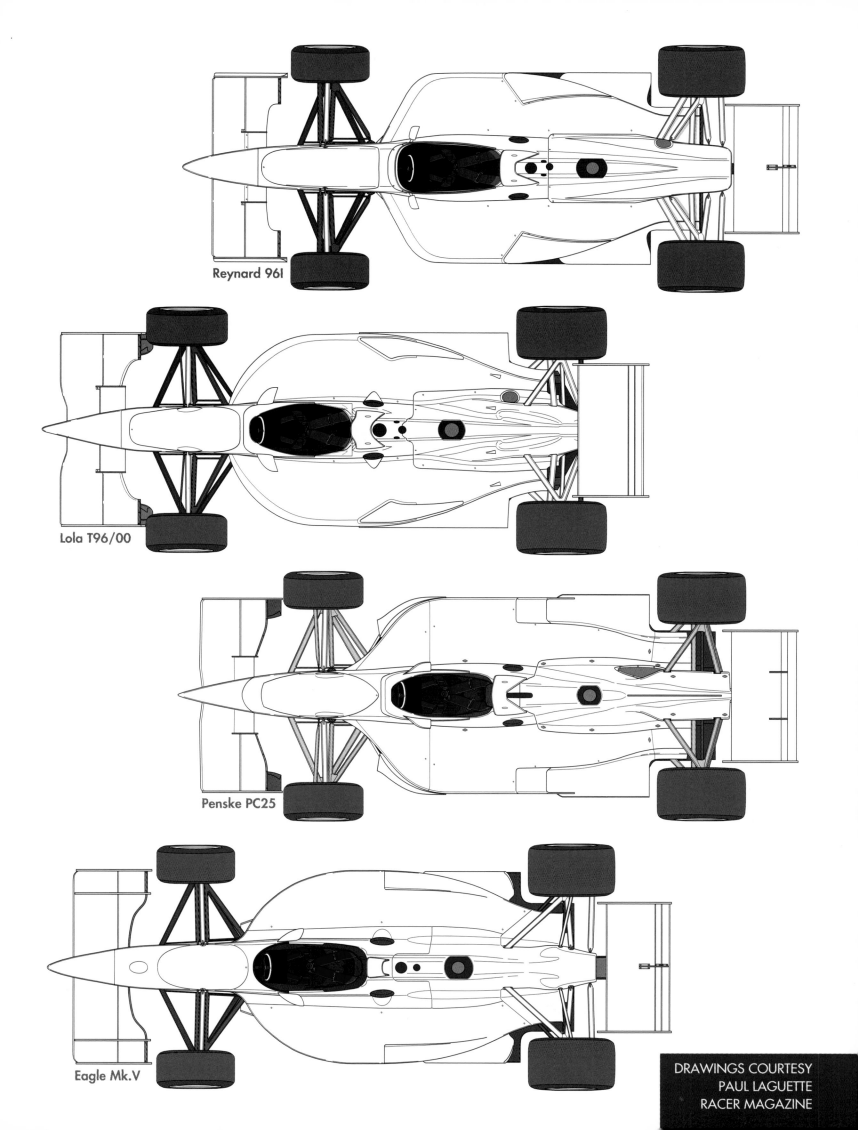

Reynard 96I

Lola T96/00

Penske PC25

Eagle Mk.V

PRIMARY COLORS

The PPG Indy Car World Series represents a unique challenge to drivers, teams and manufacturers. Teams and drivers must constantly adapt to a variety of circuits, conditions and technical challenges against a deep and powerful field of outstanding competitors.

This season Target/Chip Ganassi Racing and Jimmy Vasser became the eighth different team and driver to claim the PPG Cup title in the last 10 seasons. That is a mark of competition unmatched in major motorsports worldwide.

And the continued growth of the series not only brings new fans and venues to the series, but new manufacturers, sponsors and racing talent. This past season, for example, the PPG Cup series visited the brand-new Metro-Dade Homestead Motorsports Complex in south Florida and made its first ever foray to Brazil for the Rio 400. Both represented exciting additions.

The challenges which teams, drivers and manufacturers face in their quest for the PPG Cup are not unlike those PPG as a worldwide supplier to industry, particularly the automobile industry, faces every day.

'Our customers around the world challenge us daily to meet new requirements, create new products and processes and develop strategic advantages, all in the face of strong competition,' says PPG Vice President–Automotive Rich Zahren.

'Competition challenges people and companies to test themselves, to stay focused, adapt to rapid change, and work constantly to create new opportunities, advantages and breakthroughs.'

During the past year, PPG turned the same institutional and creative processes which it uses every day in its many businesses to the company's involvement in Indy Car racing. PPG asked a lot of questions, did a lot of homework, adopted some new approaches and came to a series of very positive conclusions.

'Indy Car racing is growing in terms of audience, television, manufacturer involvement and the depth and quality of competition,' says Zahren. 'We at PPG continue to benefit from our relationships within the series.

'Our PPG Pace Car Team is the centerpiece of our program and one which we expect to build upon in the years ahead. We not only set the standard by which other pace car programs are based, we created the standard. And we are proud to continue to raise the standard through rigorous specifications, maintenance and training which our PPG Pace Car Team requires.'

The PPG Colorful Characters program continues to single out people whose style, personality and efforts bring fun and excitement to the racing community and race fans. During the past season, PPG recognized Mario Andretti, Shav Glick, Jim McGee, Kirk Russell, Mike Nealy, Al Speyer, Ned Wicker, Ned and Ann Miller, Michelle Trueman-Gajoch, Jim Melvin, Jim Hall, Dan Gurney and Pat Patrick as Colorful Characters and already has a long list of nominees for 1997 honors.

Photos: Michael C. Brown

maximum IMPACT
For television

Branding is nothing without impact.
Sponsorship at *all* levels should receive maximum impact.
Hutchinson Motorsport Design is recognised as the leading livery design company in making sponsorship and logo awareness <u>work</u> - especially for television, where the race car must become a moving billboard, selling an instant message to the consumer. By using logo and color enhancement techniques developed by Hutchinson, teams and sponsors will gain from <u>greater television exposure</u>.

HUTCHINSON

For further information and a copy of
Hutchinson - Principles of Livery Design Brochure, please contact:
Nicola Fox, Hutchinson Motorsport Design
14-16 Star Hill, Rochester, Kent, England ME1 1XB
Telephone: +44 1634 409773
Facsimile: +44 1634 409774

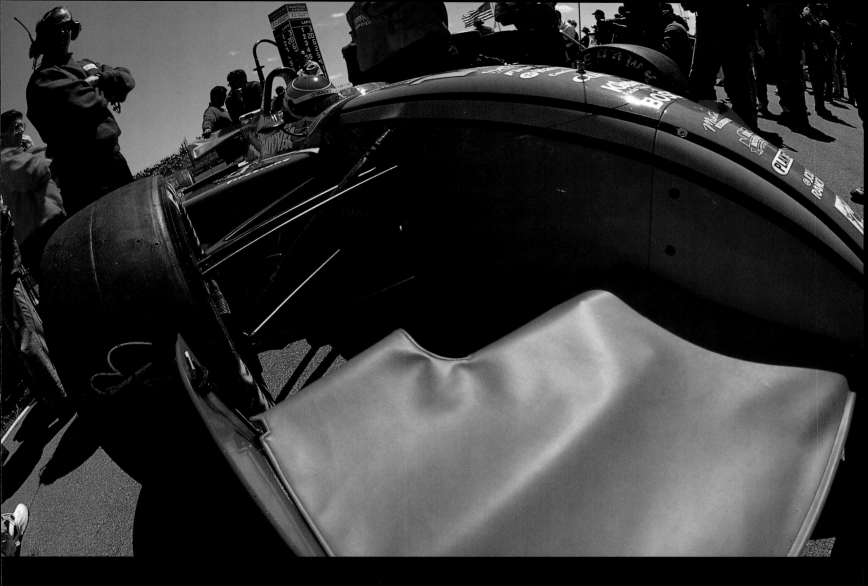

review

by Jeremy Shaw

*A total of 40 drivers made an appearance during
the 1996 PPG Indy Car World Series, of whom
32, representing 20 different teams, earned points
from the 16 races.
In the following pages, Editor Jeremy Shaw
assesses some of the strengths and weaknesses
of each team.*

A blend of raw speed and impressive consistency enabled Jimmy Vasser *(left)* to claim the PPG Cup championship for team owner Chip Ganassi *(below)*.

Far left: Vasser received vital support from managing director Tom Anderson, who looked after his race strategy, and engineer Julian Robertson *(below)*.

As the season developed, it was the second Target Reynard-Honda of Alex Zanardi *(below center)* that set the pace. Benefiting hugely from the experience of veteran race engineer Morris Nunn (seen bottom center on the left, chatting with Reynard's Bruce Ashmore), the talented Italian *(bottom right)* took the Rookie of the Year crown in style.

Target/Chip Ganassi Racing
Base: Indianapolis, Ind.
Drivers: Jimmy Vasser, Alex Zanardi (R)
Sponsor: Target Stores
Chassis: Reynard 96I
Engines: Honda Indy V8
Tires: Firestone
Wins: 7 (Vasser 4, Zanardi 3); Poles: 10 (Zanardi 6, Vasser 4)
PPG Cup points: 286
Vasser 154 (1st), Zanardi 132 (3rd)

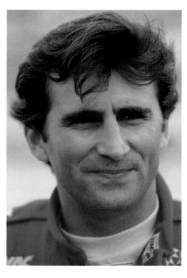

Everyone on the well-drilled Ganassi team played a role. The respective crew chiefs, Grant Weaver (Vasser) and Rob Hill (Zanardi), performed almost flawlessly, and both crews were superbly marshaled by Mike Hull. Tom Anderson, who gained new responsibility at the beginning of the season as managing director, did a fine job. He also took charge of calling the strategy on Vasser's car during the races.

The team was extremely well prepared prior to the first event at Homestead, and therein lay the key to its success. The only problems seemed to occur on the short ovals, where race engineers Morris Nunn (Zanardi) and Julian Robertson (Vasser) never did secure a consistent balance for their drivers. They were perhaps fortunate that due to the IRL conflict, only Milwaukee and Nazareth remained on the schedule. Nevertheless, on every other type of circuit, the Target cars were always a force to be reckoned with. The drivers took full advantage.

The switch last winter from Ford/Cosworth and Goodyear to Honda and Firestone proved to be an astute move by Chip Ganassi. The engines and tires, both of Japanese/American lineage, were consistently competitive and seemed to be especially potent when mated to the Reynard chassis. The decision to hire Alex Zanardi, previously unheralded in North America, also was an inspired choice.

In reality, the statistics tell the story. Ten poles and seven wins would represent an impressive tally in any championship, let alone one as competitive as the 1996 PPG Indy Car World Series. Jimmy Vasser, while never a totally dominant force, rattled off four wins in the first six races. He also demonstrated his raw speed by winning four poles during his championship year. Zanardi, meanwhile, was on the pace pretty much right away, although he did suffer a variety of misfortunes in the early part of the season.

Between them Zanardi and Vasser led a total of 772 laps – or 38.5 percent – during the 16-race season. Vasser, furthermore, was a paragon of consistency. His #12 Target Reynard-Honda finished every single race, comfortably leading the categories for most laps and miles completed.

Congratulations to the best Sunday drivers in the world.

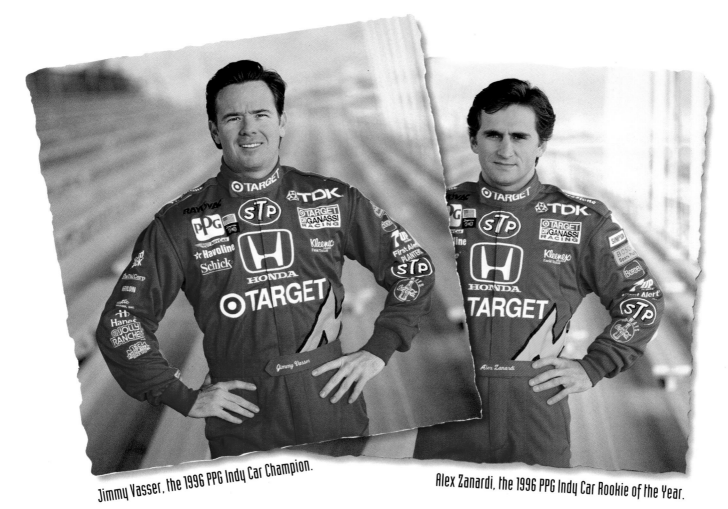

Jimmy Vasser, the 1996 PPG Indy Car Champion.

Alex Zanardi, the 1996 PPG Indy Car Rookie of the Year.

10 poles. 7 wins. First and third in the 1996 PPG Indy Car Points Championship. They all add up to the best team in Indy Car Racing. Congratulations, Target/Chip Ganassi Racing, on a spectacular season.

Michael Andretti *(right)* scored more wins than any of his rivals but reliability problems weakened his championship challenge. Team co-owner Paul Newman *(far right)* enjoyed his driver's success.

Carl Haas *(below right)* has decided to end his partnership with Lola and forge a new link with Swift for 1997.

Below: Andretti's aggressive style proved particularly effective on the street circuits.

The fruitful relationship between the team's drivers and race engineers Brian Lisles and Peter Gibbons *(bottom left)* helped newcomer Christian Fittipaldi *(bottom right)* demonstrate his potential.

Newman/Haas Racing
Base: Lincolnshire, Ill.
Drivers: Michael Andretti, Christian Fittipaldi
Sponsors: Kmart, Texaco Havoline, Budweiser
Chassis: Lola T96/00
Engines: Ford/Cosworth XD
Tires: Goodyear
Wins: 5 (Andretti); Poles: 0
PPG Cup points: 242
Andretti 132 (2nd), Fittipaldi 110 (5th)

For the second straight campaign, Newman/Haas Racing succeeded in placing both its drivers among the top six in the final PPG Cup standings. The transition from Paul Tracy to Christian Fittipaldi in the Kmart/Budweiser car went remarkably smoothly as the young Brazil-ian quickly established a good rapport both with the crew and his new teammate, Andretti. Between them they scored four points more than the team managed in 1995.

At Long Beach in April, team co-owner Carl Haas confirmed the impending termination of a long-standing partnership with Lola Cars. The decision brought to an end a relationship which had begun in the late 1960s, since when Haas had imported literally thousands of the British-built cars into North America.

For 1997, indeed, Newman/Haas will rely upon a brand-new design from Swift Engineering.

It would perhaps have been understandable if the switch had taken its toll on the team as it sought to prepare for the future. But nothing could be further from the truth. Andretti and Fittipaldi worked steadily on improving their steeds and did so in the face of a string of problems with the latest Ford/Cosworth XD engines. Both men, in fact, endured heavy acci-dents during testing at Michigan due to engine failures, and by the end of the year, the respective crews, headed by Tim Bumps (Andretti) and Billy Simmonds (Fittipaldi), were well practiced in the art of changing motors!

Andretti, working well, as ever, with race engineer Peter Gibbons, continued to adopt a policy of concen-trating on preparation for the races rather than qualifying. The strategy seemed to work, although from time to time Andretti did rue the fact he was starting farther down the grid than he would have liked. The part-nership between Fittipaldi and Brian Lisles was equally fruitful.

As usual, the team was expertly managed by Lee White. It was a credit to the entire organization that both drivers scored points every time they reached the finish line.

When your goal is to advance

TECHNOLOGY

it is nice to be

DRIVEN

by the best.

THE SCIENCE BEHIND OUR SUCCESS

Havoline Formula $\frac{3}{8}$ - - - - - - - - - - - - - - - - - -  - - - - - - - - - CleanSystem $\frac{3}{8}$ Gasoline

Think fast. At Texaco, these are words to live by-not just on the track, but in the lab. Fact is, some days it's easier to keep pace with our drivers than it is to keep up with our scientists. Backing their research with results, the Texaco crew leads the pack with products like Havoline Formula $\frac{3}{8}$, an advanced motor oil perfected under racing conditions but available on retail shelves. Havoline's proven formulation controls volatility, fights vaporization and provides complete engine protection. Further innovations include our CleanSystem $\frac{3}{8}$ Power Plus and Power Premium gasolines, each specifically designed for smooth starts and sure acceleration. And then there's Havoline® Extended Life Anti-Freeze/Coolant, DEX-COOL,™* yet another success story in our drive for better technology-a drive that glorifies engineers as much as it does engines. The proof is in the performance. On the track and off, the most celebrated team in racing really only has one star: Texaco.

ADD MORE LIFE TO YOUR CAR. TAKE IT TO THE STAR®

TEXACO

*DEX-COOL™ is a trademark of General Motors Corp.   Internet address: HTTP://WWW.TEXACO.COM/tlc

BOSS

HUGO BOSS

Photograph by Richard Avedon

The talent gathered at Marlboro Team Penske is formidable, but in 1996 the team's handling problems proved insurmountable. Teddy Mayer, Rick Mears, Nigel Beresford, Chuck Sprague and Jon Bouslog confer.

Below, left to right: With the Penske Indy Car team failing to win a race for the first time since 1976, Al Unser Jr., team owner Roger Penske and Paul Tracy endured a frustrating season.

The recalcitrant PC25 *(below left)* was by no means the best car designer Nigel Bennett *(middle right)* has produced, but that did not prevent Unser *(bottom right)* from mounting a spirited bid for the PPG Cup championship.

Marlboro Team Penske
Base: Reading, Pa.
Drivers: Al Unser Jr., Paul Tracy, Jan Magnussen (R)
Sponsor: Marlboro
Chassis: Penske PC25
Engines: Mercedes-Benz IC108C
Tires: Goodyear
Wins: 0; Poles: 3 (Tracy)
PPG Cup points: 185
Unser 125 (4th), Tracy 60 (13th)

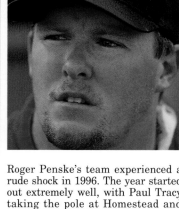

Roger Penske's team experienced a rude shock in 1996. The year started out extremely well, with Paul Tracy taking the pole at Homestead and leading the race in convincing fashion until felled by a transmission failure. Teammate Al Unser Jr. never matched the Canadian's pace in the season opener yet he drove with characteristic guile to finish second in Rio. The omens appeared to be good, especially when both drivers were competitive at Surfers Paradise and Long Beach. Next, on the one-mile ovals at Nazareth and Milwaukee, they were virtually dominant.

On both occasions, however, due to differing circumstances, they were eclipsed in the final stages by a fired-up Andretti. For some reason, the team was never to display such force again. Nigel Bennett's Penske PC25 chassis was obviously a marvel on the ovals, yet it resisted all attempts at achieving a consistent balance on road courses. According to its drivers the car was overly pitch-sensitive, extremely difficult to drive on bumpy circuits and easily upset by elevation changes. It was especially evil at Mid-Ohio and Laguna Seca.

Penske, of course, had its usual phalanx of top-quality engineers, yet even their combined efforts failed to uncover a true fix for the car. The arrival of John Travis, latterly of Lola Cars, didn't seem to help much either. Travis will assist Bennett in the design of the team's 1997 challenger, although the team also purchased a couple of Reynards with which to conduct back-to-back testing once the 1996 season had been completed.

Tracy, as ever, attempted to extract every last ounce of the car's potential, especially in qualifying. Once again, though, he was involved in rather too many incidents. Some, assuredly, were not his fault, notably in Australia, where he was collected by Andretti, but he threw away points at Long Beach, Nazareth, Detroit and Portland. He also crashed heavily during practice at Michigan, injuring his neck and back which caused him to miss the next two races. As a result of all the dramas he finished a disappointing 13th in the point standings – by far his worst season since joining the PPG Cup circuit on a regular basis in 1992.

A few racy lines explain Sunseeker's performance.

The essence of a Sunseeker lies in its beautiful, fluid lines. That sleek shape is what makes us so different from other marques. And not just to look at, either. Evolved from racing hulls, our designs deliver exceptional levels of performance and manoeuvrability in the most demanding conditions.

Sunseeker

Choose from seventeen models in four ranges: Performance Motoryachts, Flybridge Motoryachts, Performance Powerboats and Offshore Cruisers. No two models are exactly alike and the final specification is down to you. But all are built along the same race-proven lines.

What do you expect from a country known for no speed limits?

Mercedes-Benz is the "Official Car of IndyCar."

Brazil's Andre Ribeiro *(left)* confirmed the promise he had shown in 1995, taking two wins with his LCI Lola-Honda *(below left)*.

Below: Steve Horne's team continued to make impressive progress in its second season in Indy Car racing.

Bottom: Slick work by Ribeiro's pit crew led by Steve Ragan *(left)*, who won the coveted Snap-on/CAM 'Top Wrench' award from the Championship Association of Mechanics.

Tasman Motorsports Group

Base: Hilliard, Ohio
Drivers: Andre Ribeiro, Adrian Fernandez
Sponsors: LCI International, Marlboro, Tecate Beer, Quaker State Oil
Chassis: Lola T96/00
Engines: Honda Indy V8
Tires: Firestone
Wins: 3 (Ribeiro 2, Fernandez 1); **Poles:** 1 (Ribeiro)
PPG Cup points: 147
Ribeiro 76 (11th), Fernandez 71 (12th)

Three wins in its sophomore season represented a magnificent achievement by Steve Horne's Tasman team. Andre Ribeiro drove to a brilliant and wildly emotional victory in Rio de Janeiro, then added a similarly mature performance to scoop the Marlboro 500 spoils. Adrian Fernandez also made great strides under Horne's guidance. His victory in Toronto was thoroughly well-deserved.

A lack of consistency was the team's bug-bear. And these days, perhaps more than ever, it takes consistency to win championships at this level – which explains why neither Ribeiro nor Fernandez appears in our Top Ten ranking of individual drivers. Both men made too many mistakes to be considered as true championship challengers.

Ribeiro's relationship with engineer Don Halliday paid off in spades on the longer ovals, while on the mile tracks their efforts often were stymied by a lack of grip from the Firestone tires. The Brazilian also tended to struggle on the road courses. For example, he crashed at Long Beach, was involved in two incidents at Road America, made a mistake in Vancouver, and failed to capitalize on a fine strategy at Laguna Seca.

Right: Adrian Fernandez produced some strong mid-season performances at the wheel of the Tecate Lola-Honda *(below left)*, recording the first Indy Car win of his career at Toronto.

Below right: While experienced engineer Don Halliday *(left)* continued his effective relationship with Andre Ribeiro, it took a few races for Fernandez to establish a rapport with Diane Holl.

Bottom: The Tecate car was immaculately presented, the Tasman team handling the expansion necessary to field a second entry without apparent difficulty.

Fernandez, meanwhile, took some time to develop a rapport with his race engineer, Diane Holl. The Mexican also tended to drive on his instincts rather than his feel. Nevertheless, the quality of his feedback improved dramatically during the season. His confidence was boosted enormously by the Toronto win, and Fernandez was looking good at the Marlboro 500 until forced out by a clutch failure. However, like his teammate, he was brought down to earth by a few mistakes in the later races.

Both drivers proved they have an immense amount of natural ability. The team, too, is still improving. Certainly, in 1996, Tasman was not overly endowed in financial terms, so the drivers were not able to conduct much testing, which severely curtailed their opportunity to fully optimize the Lola chassis. Next year, with the benefit of a larger budget, more testing, renewed focus and the additional experience, Ribeiro and Fernandez can be expected to make an even firmer mark on the series.

Labatt USA wants to stop and say "thanks" to Adrian Fernandez.

Just one problem.

Adrian doesn't like to stop.

Labatt USA, proud sponsor of the Tecate car, salutes Adrian Fernandez,

The Tecate/Quaker State Team and The Tasman Motor Sports Group.

Hey, when you race, it's nice to have people behind you.

TECATE
QUAKER STATE
INDY CAR RACING TEAM
©1996 Labatt U.S.A., Darien, CT.

TASMAN
MOTORSPORTS GROUP

Labatt

Darien, CT. 203-656-1876

CERVEZA
TECATE
IMPORTED BEER
PRODUCT OF MEXICO

Talented Brazilian Gil de Ferran *(right)* has yet to fulfill his undoubted potential. His second season in Indy Car racing was spoiled by a number of unnecessary first-lap accidents.

Below right: With team owner Jim Hall *(left)* announcing his retirement from racing, de Ferran is switching to Derrick Walker's team in 1997.

Bottom: The Pennzoil Reynard-Honda was expected to be a regular race winner but a disappointing season yielded only a single win at Cleveland.

Hall Racing
Base: Midland, Texas
Driver: Gil de Ferran
Sponsor: Pennzoil
Chassis: Reynard 96I
Engines: Honda Indy V8
Tires: Goodyear
Wins: 1; Poles: 1
PPG Cup points: 104 (6th)

Hall Racing held a great deal of promise in 1996. Gil de Ferran's confidence had been boosted by a superb victory in the previous year's finale at Laguna Seca and the Gerald Davis-managed team was properly prepared after a concerted test program following its switch to Honda engines. A second-place finish at Homestead was surely a portent of things to come.

For a variety of reasons, however, the season did not go at all according to plan. Quite why is harder to assess.

The team was hobbled by all manner of glitches in the early part of the year, and the excruciating loss in Long Beach, where de Ferran led handily until felled by a broken hose clamp, of all things, was especially hard to take. The Brazilian worked well with his two engineers, Bill Pappas and Chuck Matthews, and Alex Hering's crew always presented him with two of the most immaculate cars to be found anywhere along pit lane.

The victory in Cleveland was a true team effort. A decision was made early on to employ a two-stop strategy, which turned out to be a smart move. Excellent pit stops and a disciplined drive by de Ferran brought a welcome reward.

Surprisingly, apart from his pole in Long Beach and a second on the grid at Road America, de Ferran rarely qualified well. Perhaps that fact contributed to his involvement in a series of first-lap incidents, which effectively killed his chances of winning the championship after working his way into contention three-quarters of the way through the season.

Bruce McCaw *(right)* put his faith in a pair of well-seasoned drivers, experienced Brazilian Mauricio Gugelmin *(center)* lining up alongside popular Englishman Mark Blundell.

Blundell *(below right)* was lucky to survive his horrifying crash in Rio, but put in some sterling drives on his return to the cockpit.

Bottom right: Gugelmin's determined drive to fourth place at Surfers Paradise helped set the team on the right path.

Without a regular ride after losing his place in the Forsythe team to Greg Moore, Teo Fabi *(bottom left)* stood in for Blundell in a couple of races.

PacWest Racing Group
Base: Indianapolis, Ind.
Drivers: Mauricio Gugelmin, Mark Blundell (R), Teo Fabi
Sponsors: Hollywood, VISA
Chassis: Reynard 96I
Engines: Ford/Cosworth XB SII
Tires: Goodyear
Wins: 0; Poles: 0
PPG Cup points: 94
Gugelmin 53 (14th), Blundell 41 (16th)

Bruce McCaw's team endured an absolutely appalling start to the season. Mauricio Gugelmin, after qualifying a promising eighth at Homestead, was effectively taken out of contention by a first-lap incident with Andretti, while newly recruited teammate Mark Blundell endured all manner of difficulties before finishing a dismal 17th. Afterward the Briton was moved to comment: 'Things can only get better.'

Well, in fact, they got worse first. In Rio, a brake component failure pitched his Hollywood/VISA Reynard into one of the most terrifying accidents of all time. Blundell was extremely fortunate to escape serious injury. Even so, he was forced to sit out the next three races due to a broken foot and severe internal bruising.

Gugelmin retired from the race due to a similar problem, albeit, thankfully, without such dramatic consequences. With his confidence in tatters, the Brazilian deserved enormous credit for a gritty drive to fourth place at Surfers Paradise despite continuing brake difficulties. Gugelmin's performance proved to be the turning point.

The team soon decided to place more emphasis on in-house engineers

Andy Brown and Tim Neff, rather than rely on its British-based Galmer design studio. Several other changes among the John Anderson-managed team also served to restore morale, which was bolstered still further when both Gugelmin and Blundell ran strongly in the U.S. 500.

The pair made full use of the proven reliability of their older Ford/Cosworth XB engines, while their combined talents brought a significant up-turn in performance toward the end of the season. A switch to Mercedes engines and Firestone tires for 1997 could elevate them to consistent front-runner status.

Jerry Forsythe *(right)* **promoted brilliant young Canadian Greg Moore** *(far right)* **from his Indy Lights team to the PPG Indy Car World Series and was repaid with a series of thrilling displays at the wheel of the beautifully presented Player's Reynard-Mercedes** *(bottom).*

Player's/Forsythe Racing

Base: Indianapolis, Ind.
Driver: Greg Moore (R)
Sponsors: Player's Ltd./Indeck
Chassis: Reynard 96I
Engines: Mercedes-Benz IC108C
Tires: Firestone
Wins: 0; Poles: 0
PPG Cup points: 84 (9th)

The combination of a rookie driver, Greg Moore, and a rookie race engineer, Steve Challis, allied to a switch in equipment from Ford and Goodyear to Mercedes and Firestone, would have given Gerald Forsythe's Tony Brunetti-managed team ample excuse for a lack of performance. None was required.

The organization, overseen for Forsythe by the experienced Neil Micklewright, was well-structured. Crew chief Phil LePan always ensured there were two perfectly prepared Player's Reynards in ready-to-run condition, whereupon Moore and Challis went to work.

Their partnership, established through a graduation from Formula Ford to Formula Ford 2000, followed by three years of Indy Lights, has reached an elevated state. The two understand each other perfectly, and Challis always seems able to provide a car with which Moore can excel.

A concerted winter test program ensured they were ready to go when the season began at Homestead in March. Nevertheless, Moore's form in the early races was a revelation. He could have won both of the first two events. Only plain bad luck, and perhaps a share of rookie impetuosity, kept Moore out of victory circle.

Although driver Scott Pruett *(right)*, general manager Jim McGee *(below right)*, race engineer Steve Newey *(below far right)* and other key personnel remained on board, the team was unable to build on the foundations that were laid in 1995.

Veteran team owner Pat Patrick *(below center)* is planning to field a second car in 1997 for Raul Boesel.

The disappointing reliability of the Ford XD engine prevented Pruett from achieving the results he had hoped for with the Firestone Lola *(bottom)*.

Patrick Racing

Base: Indianapolis, Ind.
Driver: Scott Pruett
Sponsors: Firestone, Pennzoil
Chassis: Lola T96/00
Engines: Ford/Cosworth XD
Tires: Firestone
Wins: 0; Poles: 1
PPG Cup points: 82 (10th)

Pat Patrick's team remained virtually unchanged from the 1995 season, and many pundits expected the stability to pay dividends. Scott Pruett reinforced that viewpoint after finishing fourth, third and second in the first three races. Curiously, that was as good as it got. The team had to wait until the final race of the season before recording another strong finish.

The Ford/Cosworth XD engine appeared to be markedly inferior to the Honda and Mercedes-Benz opposition, both in terms of outright horsepower and (especially) reliability, but general manager Jim McGee's team still was able to extract consistently good performance, especially in qualifying as Pruett amassed a record beaten only by the Ganassi pair. Race engineer Steve Newey and Pruett continued to work well together and it seemed only a matter of time before they would return to Victory Lane.

Instead, a variety of ailments hindered their efforts, and through the latter half of the season, especially following another engine failure which cost the chance of a repeat victory in the Marlboro 500, the frustration began to show.

Photos: Michael C. Brown

Right: Hopes that a switch to contemporary equipment would give a substantial boost to the competitiveness of Tony Bettenhausen's small team proved ill-founded.

Stefan Johansson *(far right)* will not be driving for the team in 1997 after a largely frustrating campaign.

Johansson frequently showed well on race day, notably at Road America where he took the Alumax Reynard to fourth place, but a lack of pace in qualifying blighted the amiable Swede's season.

Bettenhausen Motorsports

Base: Indianapolis, Ind.
Drivers: Stefan Johansson, Gary Bettenhausen
Sponsor: Alumax Aluminum
Chassis: Reynard 96I
Tires: Goodyear
Engines: Mercedes-Benz IC108C
Wins: 0; Poles: 0
PPG Cup points: 43 Johansson (15th)

Qualifying remained the biggest problem for Tony Bettenhausen's team, which entered the season full of optimism after purchasing a pair of new Reynards for Stefan Johansson. The Swede enjoyed his relationship with race engineer Bernie Marcus, but an inability to coax ultimate speed from the Alumax cars during qualifying proved a difficult hurdle to overcome.

A lack of testing and several mechanical problems combined to hinder progress. At Road America in the fall, for example, he experienced engine failures during both qualifying sessions. Nevertheless, Johansson generally ran far more strongly once the green flag was flown on race day. Road America was a case in point. He started way back in 21st position but soon began to work his way forward. A fourth-place finish represented his best result of the season and by far his most competitive outing.

At Laguna Seca, after again running well (on his 40th birthday) until crashing heavily when the car's rear wing fell loose, Johansson announced he would not be returning for a sixth year with the team. Bettenhausen, though, will be back, once again with high expectations after luring away talented race/design engineer Tom Brown from Team Penske.

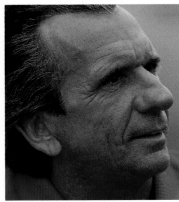

Having parted company with Bobby Rahal, Carl Hogan *(far left)* formed a new association with Roger Penske. Emerson Fittipaldi *(left)* handled the driving duties.

Below left: Fittipaldi rarely produced his best form, although his polished style paid dividends on the short ovals. Jan Magnussen *(bottom left)* showed great promise in his three races for the team.

After a season punctuated by accidents and engine problems, Robby Gordon *(right)* has decided to switch to NASCAR racing in 1997.

Below (clockwise from top left): Derrick Walker's second car was driven by Scott Goodyear, Fredrik Ekblom and Mike Groff.

Hogan Penske Racing
Base: Reading, Pa.
Drivers: Emerson Fittipaldi, Jan Magnussen (R)
Sponsor: Marlboro Latin America
Chassis: Penske PC25
Engines: Mercedes-Benz IC108C
Tires: Goodyear
Wins: 0; Poles: 0
PPG Cup points: 34
Fittipaldi 29 (19th), Magnussen 5 (24th)

Walker Racing
Base: Indianapolis, Ind.
Drivers: Robby Gordon, Scott Goodyear,
Fredrik Ekblom (R), Mike Groff
Sponsors: Valvoline, Cummins, Craftsman
Chassis: Reynard 96I
Engines: Ford/Cosworth XD
Tires: Goodyear
Wins: 0; Poles: 0
PPG Cup points: 34 – Gordon 29 (18th), Goodyear 5 (25th)

There was precious little for team owner Derrick Walker to cheer about in 1996. The season began well enough, with Robby Gordon driving aggressively to finish third at Homestead, despite an incident with Ribeiro. That was to prove a lone highlight.

Gordon crashed at Rio, Long Beach, Nazareth and Detroit, mainly through over-exuberance, and was further frustrated by engine problems which ended promising runs at Mid-Ohio and Road America. By then the Californian had decided his future lay in NASCAR racing. Nevertheless, the manner in which he lambasted Ford with regard to its reliability problems left a sour taste.

Scott Goodyear began the year with the intention of running the majority of the races in a second car, albeit motivated by the older XB engine rather than the XD. Sadly, he suffered a severe injury to his back when he crashed at Rio in March. The Canadian was not fit enough to resume driving until June, and by then his source of funding had almost dried up. He contested just three more races, and only heavy attrition at Vancouver enabled him to record a season-best ninth.

Fredrik Ekblom, invited to sit in for Goodyear at the U.S. 500, once again acquitted himself well before being ousted by engine failure. The Swede would be a potent force in a properly funded car. Mike Groff also guested for the team once at Nazareth, where he moved up strongly from 20th on the grid to 14th.

A pair of fourth-place finishes on the one-mile ovals remained the highlight for Carl Hogan, who entered a new partnership with longtime friend and rival Roger Penske following the culmination of his relationship with Bobby Rahal.

Veteran Emerson Fittipaldi, 49, rarely seemed at ease on the road or street circuits, although he did appear to rekindle his old enthusiasm at Portland, where he charged into contention following a brief shower of rain in the early stages. Sadly, a broken transmission ended his hopes that day in June.

Fittipaldi's smooth style, allied to the Penske chassis' excellent performance on the short ovals, allowed him to shine at Nazareth and Milwaukee. Ultimately, however, on each occasion he was shuffled out of podium contention in the closing stages by more youthful rivals.

The Brazilian seemed set for a strong showing, too, in the Marlboro 500, only to crash massively on the opening lap. Fittipaldi sustained a serious neck injury in the mishap, which seemed likely to bring his illustrious career to a close.

Jan Magnussen, drafted in to replace the injured Tracy at Mid-Ohio, shuffled across to fill Fittipaldi's place for the final three races. The young Dane showed great promise by setting fastest time in the warmup at Road America, only to be involved in an incident on the opening lap, while at Laguna Seca he drove steadily to finish eighth.

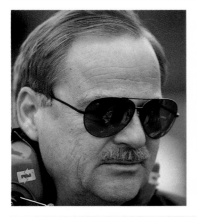

The commercial activities of businessman Harry Brix *(far left)* enabled Parker Johnstone *(left)* to tackle the full PPG Cup schedule in 1996. With sponsor Motorola pledging its support to the small California-based team for a further three seasons, Comptech owners Doug Peterson and Don Erb *(below left)* should be able to maintain their steady progress. The Motorola Reynard-Honda *(bottom left)* was at its best on the street courses.

Underrated Brazilian Roberto Moreno *(right)* caught the eye with some doughty early-season performances in the Data Control Lola *(below)*, to the delight of team owner Dale Coyne *(middle)*. A second '96 Lola was entrusted to Hiro Matsushita *(bottom right)*.

Brix Comptech Racing
Base: El Dorado Hills, Calif.
Driver: Parker Johnstone
Sponsor: Motorola
Chassis: Reynard 96I
Engines: Honda Indy V8
Tires: Firestone
Wins: 0; Poles: 0
PPG Cup points: 33 (13th)

Payton/Coyne Racing
Base: Plainfield, Ill.
Drivers: Roberto Moreno, Hiro Matsushita
Sponsors: Data Control, Mi-Jack, Panasonic, Duskin
Chassis: Lola T96/00
Engines: Ford/Cosworth XB
Tires: Firestone
Wins: 0; Poles: 0
PPG Cup points: 28 – Moreno 25 (21st), Matsushita 3 (28th)

Sponsorship from Motorola, procured by businessman/racing aficionado Harry Brix, enabled long-time Comptech proprietors Doug Peterson and Don Erb to extend their relationship with Parker Johnstone and, together, embark upon their first full season of PPG Cup competition. Given the obvious limitations of a new team and a budget which allowed precious little testing – and was stretched to its limits by several expensive accidents – both team and driver should be proud of their accomplishments.

The undoubted highlight came at Long Beach, where Johnstone's fascination for auto racing was cemented by a visit to watch the Formula 1 cars compete in the late 1970s. The immensely enthusiastic Johnstone was delighted to qualify sixth fastest, and was almost overcome with emotion when he held off a challenge from Unser to finish a sensational second. It was no more than he – and the team – deserved.

Johnstone also qualified strongly in Brazil (fifth) and Australia (seventh), and after struggling on the short ovals at Nazareth and Milwaukee, he bounced back by securing fourth on the grid in Detroit and sixth in Toronto. Clearly, Johnstone and vastly experienced race engineer Ed Nathman had concocted an excellent setup for the street courses. The small team, led by veterans Jonesy Morris and Barry Brooke and talented young crew chief Shad Huntley, couldn't match that form on the permanent road courses, although Johnstone did work his way through from 15th to fifth at Portland. Undoubtedly there will be even better days ahead.

The procurement of two new Lola chassis and a top-line driver in Roberto Moreno enabled Walter Payton and Dale Coyne to continue their slow but steady rise in stature. As ever, the budget was tight and allowed virtually no testing, but Moreno, after embarrassing himself by spinning out of the first race even before the green flag, proceeded to score points in four of his next five starts. Included among that string was a spectacular run to third place in the prestigious U.S. 500, comfortably eclipsing Coyne's previous best result, a sixth-place finish by Robbie Buhl at Long Beach in 1993.

Moreno, indeed, ran some laps at better than 232 mph in the dramatic closing stages as he tucked into the draft of race winner Jimmy Vasser and overtook Andre Ribeiro on the final lap to ensure his position on the podium. Great effort.

Predictably, Moreno struggled in the later stages of the season as other teams were able to gain a better understanding of their cars. He also was hobbled by a series of niggling mechanical problems. Nevertheless, Moreno provided another excellent display in the series finale at Laguna Seca when he hustled hard throughout the race and rewarded his sponsors, Data Control, with another hard-earned PPG Cup point.

Hiro Matsushita, in his seventh year of Indy Car racing, once again failed to make much of an impression. He managed one point-scoring finish, a 10th in Surfers Paradise.

Photos: Michael C. Brown

It was another wretched season for team owner Rick Galles *(right)*. Former motorcycle world champion Eddie Lawson *(bottom left)* performed respectably, given his lack of experience, notching up four points-scoring finishes with the Delco Electronics Lola *(below)*, but left the team at mid-season, to be replaced by Davy Jones *(bottom right)*.

Raul Boesel *(center)* was hired by Barry Green *(far right)* to fill the void left by the departed Jacques Villeneuve, the 1995 PPG Cup champion, but the pair suffered an endless series of disappointments, the Brahma/Klein Tools-backed Reynard-Ford *(middle right)* falling prey to a catalog of engine and electrical gremlins.

Galles Racing International

Base:	Albuquerque, N.M.
Drivers:	Eddie Lawson (R), Davy Jones
Sponsor:	Delco Electronics
Chassis:	Lola T96/00
Engines:	Mercedes-Benz IC108C
Tires:	Goodyear
Wins: 0; **Poles:** 0	
PPG Cup points: 27 – Lawson 26 (20th), Jones 1 (32nd)	

Brahma Sports Team

Base:	Indianapolis, Ind.
Driver:	Raul Boesel
Sponsors:	Brahma Brewery/Klein Tools/Raybestos
Chassis:	Reynard 96I
Engines:	Ford/Cosworth XD
Tires:	Goodyear
Wins: 0; **Poles:** 0	
PPG Cup points: 12 (22nd)	

Rick Galles was cautiously optimistic at the start of the year. He said he realized his new recruit, four-time 500cc motorcycle world champion Eddie Lawson, would have some difficulty in adapting to the Indy cars, especially after sitting out a year following a promising season with Tasman's Indy Lights team in 1994; but both men agreed they were prepared to be patient.

Not patient enough, unfortunately.

Lawson certainly struggled to match the pace in qualifying, and he became increasingly frustrated at the lack of a full-time race engineer after Lola's Mike Wright had failed to get along with veteran crew chief Owen Snyder during the early races. Still, Lawson posted several excellent drives. Granted, his seventh in Australia was achieved more through attrition than speed, but he ran well to ninth at Long Beach and added a solid seventh in the U.S. 500. A sixth in difficult conditions at Detroit also served to show he was moving in the right direction.

Sadly, Lawson's promise remains unfulfilled following a parting of the ways prior to the Marlboro 500.

Davy Jones, who scored a marvelous victory for the Joest Porsche team at Le Mans and finished second for Galles at Indianapolis, took over the ride but never looked like matching Lawson's achievements.

How is the mighty fallen! Team owner Barry Green, after winning the 1995 PPG Cup championship in magnificent style, hustled like mad to fill the void left by Jacques Villeneuve, who departed the Indy Car scene in favor of a fresh challenge in Formula 1, and Player's, who instead joined Greg Moore and the Forsythe team.

Green duly signed a fresh agreement with Brahma, the largest beer producer in South America, and after failing to lure Andre Ribeiro away from the Tasman team, he was more than satisfied to procure the services of veteran Raul Boesel. The deal was put together relatively late, which didn't allow much time for testing, but even so he had no reason to believe the season would turn out so disastrously.

Boesel, after turning down the opportunity to remain with Team Rahal, developed a good friendship with race engineer Tino Belli, who worked well with Teo Fabi in '95. Professionally, however, the pair never really gelled. The team remained unable to dial in the car to Boesel's satisfaction.

Even when there were signs of improvement, like when the Brazilian qualified 10th for the U.S. 500

and eighth for the following race on the Milwaukee Mile, other factors intervened. At M.I.S. he was stricken early by an engine problem, while in Milwaukee he collided with a slower car. Then came an unbelievable string of Ford/Cosworth engine/electrical failures which ensured retirement in seven of the last eight races.

Klein Tools... for Professionals... since 1857™

A generation before an automobile ever took to the road and more than half a century before the first Indy 500, tools manufactured by the earlier generations of the Klein family were the choice of master tradesmen. Like their counterparts of yesteryear, today's professionals, whose reputation and livelihood depend on the tools they use, still demand the quality found only in Klein tools.

Klein, the mark of quality since 1857, is still the most sought after and recognized name among professional tool users. Today, the professional, who takes pride in and realizes the importance of quality tools, can now select from more than 4,000 job-matched Klein tools.

As an IndyCar sponsor, Klein Tools is proud to support Barry Green and the professionals that make up Team Green in their pursuit of excellence in the IndyCar World Championship Series.

96299

Chicago, Illinois USA

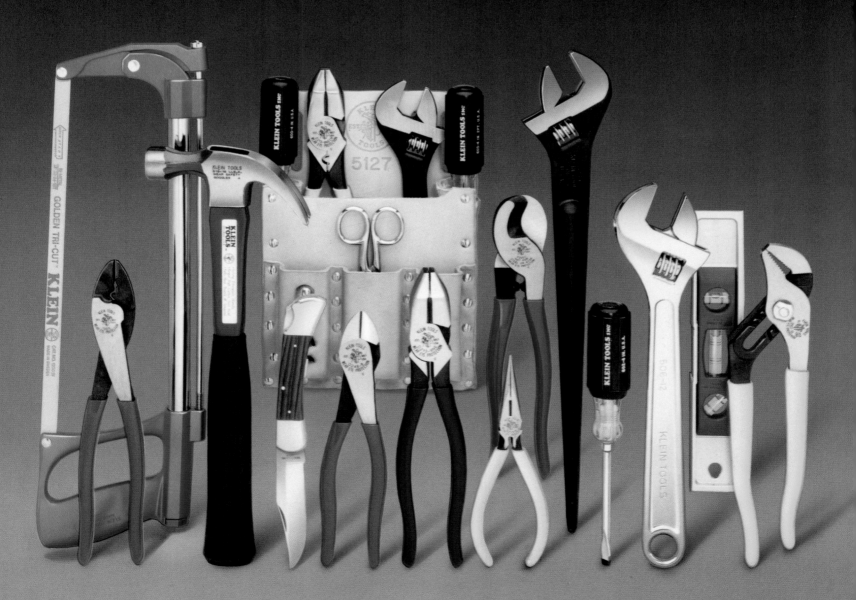

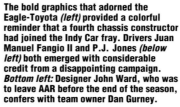

The bold graphics that adorned the Eagle-Toyota (left) provided a colorful reminder that a fourth chassis constructor had joined the Indy Car fray. Drivers Juan Manuel Fangio II and P.J. Jones (below left) both emerged with considerable credit from a disappointing campaign. Bottom left: Designer John Ward, who was to leave AAR before the end of the season, confers with team owner Dan Gurney.

Team co-owners Frank Arciero (below left) and Cal Wells III (below right) suffered a devastating blow with the loss of Jeff Krosnoff, tragically killed at Toronto. Max Papis showed well in his three end-of-season outings with the MCI Reynard-Toyota (bottom), securing a place in the team for 1997.

Near right: Richie Hearn shone on his occasional appearances with John Della Penna's '95 Reynard.

Far right: Marco Greco and Eliseo Salazar scraped a meager few points for Andy Evans' Team Scandia.

Opposite middle: Mexican teenager Michel Jourdain Jr. (above) enjoyed rather better fortune than fellow countryman Carlos Guerrero (below), who was dropped from the team after a string of accidents in the Herdez Lola (bottom right).

Opposite bottom left: Dennis Vitolo made a single appearance at Long Beach and hopes to return in 1997, once again with backing from SmithKline Beecham.

All American Racers
Base: Santa Ana, Calif.
Drivers: Juan Fangio II, P.J. Jones (R)
Sponsor: Castrol
Chassis: Eagle Mk.V
Engines: Toyota RV8A
Tires: Goodyear
Wins: 0; Poles: 0
PPG Cup points: 9
Fangio 5 (23rd), Jones 4 (26th)

Arciero-Wells Racing
Base: Rancho Santa Margarita, Calif.
Drivers: Jeff Krosnoff (R), Max Papis (R)
Sponsors: MCI, Toyota
Chassis: Reynard 96I
Engines: Toyota RV8A
Tires: Firestone
Wins: 0; Poles: 0
PPG Cup points: 4
Papis (27th)

Dan Boyd

Dan Gurney knew going into the season it would be a character-builder. It was. The California-based team had been preparing for two years for its return to the Indy Car wars following a 10-year hiatus, but that in itself didn't make the task any less arduous. Furthermore, the first definitive Toyota engines were not ready until relatively late, which precluded much in the way of serious testing.

Juan Fangio II, who set out with a lone Eagle Mk.V, was already at a disadvantage, yet he kept his nose to the grindstone and never allowed himself to become discouraged. The first of two visits to Michigan International Speedway served to show just how much both Toyota and the team had to learn.

P.J. Jones joined the fray at Milwaukee, and a week later posted one of the best individual drives of the season when he took advantage of wet weather conditions to move from 25th to ninth. In the fall, Fangio also had his moment in the sun, so to speak, when high attrition at Road America allowed him to go one better as he finished eighth.

Frank Arciero and Cal Wells III, co-owners of the second Toyota-backed team, at least had the advantage of beginning the season with a proven chassis. The team also benefited from the experience and wisdom of coordinator Bob Sprow and race engineer Gordon Coppuck, who quickly discovered one more fine asset in rookie driver Jeff Krosnoff.

The Californian endeared himself to everyone on the team with his trademark sense of humor and a superb work ethic. Together they worked steadily toward a competitive pace. Tragically, of course, due to a devastating accident in Toronto which also claimed the life of course worker Gary Avrin, we will never know how much Krosnoff could have achieved.

In auto racing, of course, the show must go on, heavy heart or no. The Arciero-Wells team wisely missed the race at M.I.S., but returned at Mid-Ohio with another rookie, Max Papis. The charismatic Italian, instantly impressive both in and out of the car, went a long way toward restoring the team's battered morale, especially following a steady drive to ninth in a drama-filled race at Road America.

Della Penna Motorsports

Base:	Campbell, Calif.
Driver:	Richie Hearn (R)
Sponsors:	Ralphs, Food 4 Less
Chassis:	Reynard 95I
Engines:	Ford/Cosworth XB
Tires:	Goodyear
Wins: 0; **Poles:** 0	
PPG Cup points: 3 (29th)	

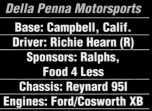

Team Scandia

Base:	Indianapolis, Ind.
Drivers:	Eliseo Salazar, Carlos Guerrero, Marco Greco, Michel Jourdain Jr. (R)
Sponsors:	Cristal, Copec, Mobil 1, Herdez, Perry Ellis, Alta Water, Int. Sports
Chassis:	Lola T96/00
Engines:	Ford/Cosworth XB
Tires:	Goodyear
Wins: 0; **Poles:** 0	
PPG Cup points: 3 – Salazar 2 (30th), Greco 1 (31st)	

John Della Penna took his first tentative steps toward a full-time PPG Cup program by entering talented protégé Richie Hearn in three races – at Long Beach, Toronto and Laguna Seca.

The entire 1995 Player's/Toyota Atlantic Championship-winning team, including crew chief Brendon Cleave, graduated en masse to the Indy Car series, but no one was under any illusions. They had prepared diligently and knew full well how tough the competition would be.

Race engineer David Cripps, who had spent the two previous years with Jimmy Vasser and Christian Fittipaldi, lent valuable experience to the tight-knit group, and together they made a favorable impression as Hearn kept out of trouble and drove to a most promising 10th-place finish on his debut in Long Beach.

Spurred on by an IRL victory at Las Vegas in September, the team can be expected to make solid gains in 1997.

Former IMSA sports car driver/entrant Andy Evans undertook a limited campaign of races after purchasing the team from former owner Dick Simon.

Brazilian Marco Greco and Mexican Carlos Guerrero began the season with a pair of new Lolas, but neither driver lasted more than three races, despite the fact that Greco earned a point for his 12th-place finish in the Rio 400. A series of accidents sealed Guerrero's fate, and he was duly replaced by unheralded 19-year-old countryman Michel Jourdain Jr., whose father had raced an Indy car when the series visited Mexico City in 1981 and whose uncle Bernard clinched Rookie of the Year honors in 1989. Jourdain did show some promise, despite a total lack of testing. Eliseo Salazar also contested four races and was similarly hamstrung by a lack of test time. The Chilean nevertheless scored a couple of points by finishing 11th in the Marlboro 500.

Project Indy

Base:	Brownsburg, Indiana
Driver:	Dennis Vitolo
Sponsor:	SmithKline Beecham
Chassis:	Reynard 95I
Engines:	Ford/Cosworth XB
Tires:	Goodyear
Wins: 0; **Poles:** 0	
PPG Cup points: 0	

Andreas Leberle, while unable to find the budget for a full-time entry in the IndyCar series, did make a welcome reappearance at Long Beach with the equally hard-trying Dennis Vitolo, who had procured sponsorship from the pharmaceutical giant, SmithKline Beecham.

Leberle, who had very little time to put the deal together, acquired a year-old Reynard chassis from Steve Horne – actually the car driven at Indianapolis in 1995 by Scott Goodyear – and received valuable assistance from the PacWest team as he converted the car to Ford/Cosworth specification. Veteran crew chief Walter Gerber also lent a hand to ready the car, whereupon Vitolo drove sensibly and was unfortunate to be hobbled by an electrical gremlin which narrowly prevented him from achieving his aim of making it to the finish line.

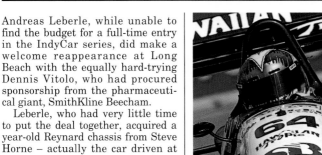

Photos: Michael C. Brown

79

Reynard

Production base: Bicester, England; U.S. base: Indianapolis, Ind.
Number of cars built in 1996: 33
Wins: 8 (Vasser 4, Zanardi 3, de Ferran 1);
Poles: 11 (Zanardi 6, Vasser 4, de Ferran 1)

After winning eight races, 13 poles and the PPG Cup championship in 1995, Reynard faced a tough task in improving its package for the new season. Nevertheless, Reynard's practical chief designer Malcolm Oastler and his staff produced another extremely effective car which, despite even tougher opposition, produced similarly impressive results, including another championship.

New aerodynamic regulations effectively cut the amount of downforce generated by the cars by as much as 30 percent, so, in common with its competition, Reynard spent a massive amount of time in the wind tunnel attempting to recoup the losses. The outcome was a slightly reprofiled composite monocoque tub. The windscreen was marginally lower than before, while a new engine cover proved more efficient. The most obvious changes were to the sidepods, which featured a distinctive, bulbous leading edge.

Suspension components were little changed from the 95I, although a new front anti-roll bar package permitted the use of a third shock, a third spring and bumpstop or any combination preferred by the individual teams. The rear pickup points were altered to suit a revised gearbox casing designed to provide more aerodynamic benefit to the new underbody. Reynard, in contrast to Lola and Penske, retained its use of a longitudinal layout, although different internals included a complete Xtrac system rather than the Reynard/Xtrac mechanism which proved troublesome in the early part of 1995. A refined oil scavenge system also was employed. (Incidentally, a new transverse box for the 1997 car was raced for the first time in Vancouver by Robby Gordon.)

The Reynard 96I proved especially effective when mated to Honda engines and Firestone tires. The Reynard-Mercedes option also seemed to work well, with Greg Moore, on Firestone tires, posting some excellent results in his rookie campaign. Team Rahal, on Goodyears, came on strong in the latter part of the season after taking advantage of some aerodynamic gains provided by new front wings and additional winglets on the rear end of the sidepods. Whether by coincidence or not, however, all of the teams employing a Reynard/Ford/Goodyear package – Brahma Sports Team, Walker Racing and the PacWest Racing Group (which used the older XB engines) – tended to struggle rather more.

The Lola Cars design team has undergone several changes during recent years. Most significantly, aerodynamicist Chris Saunders was spirited away from Williams Grand Prix Engineering in order to spearhead an extensive wind-tunnel program made even more critical by the rule changes introduced for 1996. Saunders' first task was to upgrade the Cranfield Institute facility (used exclusively for auto racing purposes by Lola) to allow the use of 40 percent scale models and provide more up-to-date instrumentation.

John Travis, meanwhile, who took charge of Indy Car design after Bruce Ashmore's defection to Reynard late in 1993, left the company shortly after the beginning of the season. He later found employment at Penske Cars.

In comparison to recent years, Lola founder Eric Broadley became more heavily involved in laying down specifications for the T96/00, joining Travis' team in an extensive redesign of the previous year's challenger.

The result was an extremely effective, well-engineered car which won three more races than in '95. New aerodynamics, refined following an estimated 1000 hours in the wind tunnel, were the most noticeable change, featuring longer and taller sidepods which offered substantially improved airflow. The profile of the sidepods was more akin to the Reynard 95I, tapering gradually from a high point almost level with the mirrors.

The T96/00 chassis featured, for the first time, composite internal bulkheads, which provided more overall stiffness. The suspension geometry front and rear also was altered, primarily in response to constant advancements being made by the tire companies. The transverse five-speed gearbox (with an option for six speeds, minus reverse, for the ovals) featured a lighter magnesium casing compared to the '95 car.

Three teams, featuring two different engines and both tire companies, achieved notable success with the latest Lola. Newman/Haas continued to be the benchmark, although Tasman added three more wins and Patrick Racing, with Scott Pruett, was unfortunate not to claim at least one of its own. Adrian Fernandez's win at Toronto, incidentally, represented Lola's landmark 100th Indy Car victory.

Lola

Production base: Huntingdon, England;
U.S. base: Indianapolis, Ind.
Number of cars built in 1996: 19
Wins: 8 (Andretti 5, Ribeiro 2, Fernandez 1);
Poles: 2 (Pruett 1, Ribeiro 1)

Photos: Michael C. Brown

Goldline Bearings Ltd

Proven Quality and Performance is our commitment to excellence

The suppliers of high quality bearings for high performance cars.

Ampep Goldline* generation of self-lubrication rod end and spherical bearings established in 1987 to meet the requirements of higher load rate, improved life and maintenance free features demanded by designers and operators of high performance cars.

To achieve these objectives the bearings have an aerospace pedigree and the designs have been based upon current state of the art aerospace materials technology applied to configurations and size ranges that have been well established in high performance racing car applications. 23 years of close development between Goldline Bearings and all disciplines of high performance car designs ensures our total commitment to excellence.

*Registered Trade Mark of SKF

U.S.A. DISTRIBUTOR:
CONTACT: Bob Long, Truechoice Inc
4180 Weaver Court, Hilliard, Ohio 43026
Tel No 614 8763483 / Fax No 614 8769292

24 Hour Delivery Worldwide Export Service

Goldline Bearings Ltd

CONTACT: Mike Jones, Ryan Currier, Richard Brunning
Stafford Park 17, Telford TF3 3BN, England.
Tel No 01952 292401 / Fax No 01952 292403

Penske

Production base: Poole, England; U.S. base: Reading, Pa.
Number of cars built in 1996: 7
Wins: 0; Poles: 3 (Tracy)

If Penske Racing thought it had a difficult time in 1995, that proved to be nothing in comparison with its travails in '96. In fact, for the first time since 1987, no Penske-built car won on the Indy Car circuit. To find the last time the *team* failed to record a victory, however, one had to go all the way back to 1976 (or 1974 if one counted John Watson's victory in the Austrian Grand Prix Formula 1 race with the Penske PC4).

Nevertheless, with even a modicum of good fortune, Penske could easily have nabbed at least three or four wins. At Homestead, for example, Paul Tracy had taken command of the race before jamming his car into gear after a pit stop and wrecking the transmission. Both one-mile oval races also seemed to be going Penske's way. Tracy, though, erred during a pit stop at Nazareth, collecting several crew members, while teammate Al Unser Jr. led convincingly on the Milwaukee Mile until a full-course caution in the late stages enabled Michael Andretti to make use of his softer tires. Finally, at Road America, Unser again was in charge until, unbelievably, his Mercedes engine blew itself apart less than a mile from the finish line.

Unser, furthermore, remained in contention for the PPG Cup championship until the final race at Laguna Seca. So what was the problem?

Nigel Bennett's Penske PC25 design featured a revised weight distribution and changes to the suspension geometry as a result of lessons learned in '95, when the PC24 proved not to make optimal use of the latest Goodyear tires. Initial impressions, indeed, following a test at Firebird Raceway, Ariz. in December, were extremely positive: 'You know when a car is good when it's fast right out of the box,' said Unser, 'and this one went pretty quick right away.'

Subsequent experience confirmed the car was very efficient on flat, smooth circuits – such as Firebird – where it was able to maintain a constant ride-height and attitude. Unfortunately, it proved overly pitch-sensitive, such that the car's balance tended to alter dramatically between the entry and exit of corners, which made it almost impossible to achieve an optimal setup and a consistent level of performance.

Eagle

Production base: Santa Ana, Calif.
Number of cars built in 1996: 3
Wins: 0; Poles: 0

Dan Gurney's All American Racers team made a welcome reappearance in 1996 following a 10-year absence from the Indy Car circuit. In all, 30 years have passed since AAR constructed its first Indy Car chassis. Its most recent success came in 1981, when Mike Mosley guided a Chevrolet/AAR-powered car to victory at Milwaukee. Incidentally, that was also the last win for a non-turbocharged motor.

The initial go-ahead to develop a new Eagle chassis was made in early 1993, whereupon Gurney's team began its development phase by learning lessons from a pair of '93 Lolas (and later a '94 car too), which had been acquired primarily as mobile test beds for the fledgling Toyota engine project.

The Eagle Mk.IV was designed, like the ultra-successful IMSA GTP Eagle Mk.III, by John Ward (who in fact parted company with AAR shortly before the end of the season), aerodynamicist Hiro Fujimori and chassis dynamics specialist Jim Hamilton. It involved a rather longer than expected gestation period but was ready for testing early in 1995. Soon thereafter, however, the IndyCar Technical Committee issued a substantial array of rule changes to be implemented in time for the 1996 season. So Ward & Co. went back to their respective drawing boards.

The AAR team has a well-equipped construction and test facility within its spacious premises in Santa Ana, Calif., including a 40 percent scale wind tunnel and fluid dynamics chamber, both of which saw extensive use while the Mk.V's design was finalized.

The all-composite tub, incorporating composite bulkheads for added rigidity, was constructed entirely in-house, while the transmission, designed in cooperation with Xtrac in England (which also produced customized work for Lola, Penske and Reynard), featured six forward gears mounted longitudinally.

The Mk.V was more often than not outpaced by the Arciero-Wells team's Reynard-Toyota, although not by a significant amount. Furthermore, AAR made steady gains as it learned more about the car from experience. The 1997 Mk.VI chassis, scheduled for completion in early January, was expected to offer a considerable improvement.

The Honda HRH Indy V8 *(below)* proved dominant in 1996, powering five different drivers to 11 wins in the 16 races.

The only other engine to record a victory was the Ford/Cosworth XD *(below right)*, Michael Andretti scoring five wins for Newman/Haas.

Photos: Michael C. Brown

Honda
**Production base:
Santa Clarita, Calif.
Wins: 11 (Vasser 4, Zanardi 3, Ribeiro 2, de Ferran and Fernandez 1);
Poles: 12 (Zanardi 6, Vasser 4, de Ferran and Ribeiro 1)**

Ford/Cosworth
**Production base:
Northampton, England;
Torrance, Calif.
Wins: 5 (Andretti);
Poles: 1 (Pruett)**

Mercedes-Benz
**Production base:
Brixworth, England;
U.S. base: Detroit, Mich.
Wins: 0;
Poles: 3 (Tracy)**

Toyota
**Production base:
Costa Mesa, Calif.
Wins: 0;
Poles: 0**

A mere 12 months after Bobby Rahal chose to give up on the fledgling Indy Car engine program at the conclusion of the 1994 season, Honda had made such substantial gains that the aluminum-block HRH engine was very much in demand. Over the winter of 1995/96, indeed, Hall Racing and Target/Chip Ganassi Racing opted to switch to Honda from Mercedes and Ford respectively. Together with Tasman Motorsports and Brix Comptech Racing they blazed the trail for other engine manufacturers to follow.

Incredibly, Alex Zanardi's very public blow-up while leading the U.S. 500 represented the first failure for the HRH during a race since its stunning debut exactly one year earlier at Indianapolis. It was also the first retirement for any Honda due to engine failure since Mid-Ohio in 1994.

Other breakages have occurred since then as the HRH was pushed closer to the edge of the envelope. Nevertheless, by the end of the 1996 season, the Honda was firmly entrenched as the engine of choice.

The bad news for 1997 is that Honda will not expand its customer base. The only change to the lineup will be a switch to Walker Racing following Jim Hall's retirement.

The new Ford/Cosworth XD engine, introduced at the beginning of the 1996 season and utilized by four teams – Brahma Sports Team, Newman/Haas Racing, Patrick Racing and Walker Racing – was generally perceived as being inferior to the Honda and Mercedes engines, both in terms of horsepower and reliability.

The smaller, lighter and supposedly more powerful XD certainly did suffer an inordinate amount of failures, but steady gains were made as the season progressed – except, perhaps, in terms of electrical components such as the crank trigger, which continued to break with monotonous regularity, especially on Raul Boesel's car. Nevertheless, the XD boasted five victories through the efforts of Michael Andretti. Christian Fittipaldi and Scott Pruett also were consistent front-runners.

The PacWest team posted some good results with the Series II development version of the older Ford/Cosworth XB, while Payton/Coyne Racing showed there was plenty of life left in the 'standard' XBs, especially at M.I.S. where Roberto Moreno was clocked at better than 230 mph toward the end of the U.S. 500.

The plan for '97 calls for every Ford customer to be equipped with an updated version of the XD.

Toward the end of the year, the common perception was that Ilmor Engineering, charged with development of the Mercedes-Benz IC108C motors, had done such a good job that Honda was under serious threat as the most powerful Indy Car powerplant. Speed trap figures certainly seemed to bear out that suggestion, which only served to heighten the surprise when Mercedes, like Penske, failed to win a race in 1996. It was the first time Ilmor had been shut out since claiming the first of its 104 Indy Car victories at Long Beach in 1987.

Paradoxically, while Ford won five races, Mercedes actually led significantly more laps (454 to 375) and won more poles (three to one) than Ford. Marlboro Team Penske, as already chronicled, might easily have won a handful of races, of which the most obvious was at Road America, where Al Unser Jr.'s engine broke almost within sight of the finish line. Team Rahal, through Bryan Herta, also came agonizingly close at Laguna Seca.

For 1997, production of a new IC108D engine is already in progress, and while Team Rahal has switched to Ford, the Mercedes strength should be maintained by the addition of the emerging PacWest team.

The folks at Toyota Racing Development knew they faced a tough challenge when they entered the Indy Car fray in 1996. Ford and Mercedes, of course, were already well established as the market leaders, while rival Japanese-based auto giant Honda was making great strides.

The learning curve began in 1993, with a motor designed by John Judd in England, but the definitive RV8A powerplant, developed jointly by teams of engineers in Japan and America, was ready only a few weeks before the start of the 1996 season. The initial signs were not too encouraging. It was clearly down on power in comparison to the opposition, and reliability wasn't anything to write home about either. Gradually, however, progress was made. The Nippondenso engine management underwent extensive development, leading to improved drivability, while rapid advances were made in terms of horsepower and engine longevity.

The first PPG Cup points came in Detroit, thanks to a virtuoso performance in the wet by P.J. Jones. More followed at Road America, where both Juan Fangio and Max Papis finished among the top 10. The tip of the iceberg had been uncovered.

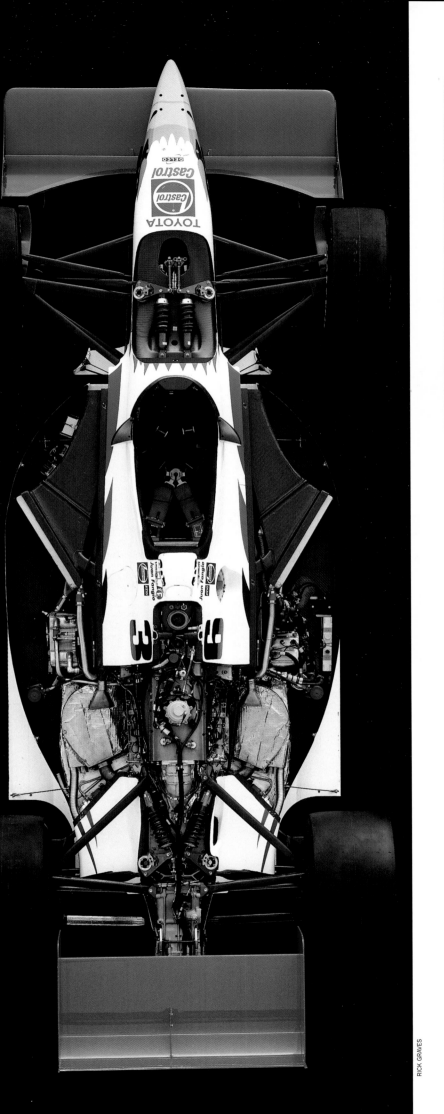
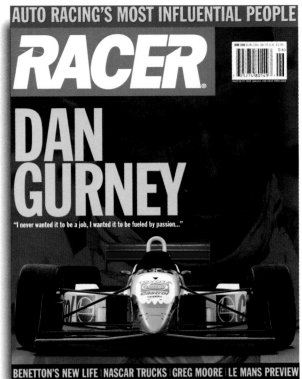

Scott Brayton, 1959–1996 • Jeff Krosnoff, 1964–1996 • Gary Avrin, 1952–1996

The close-knit world of Indy Car racing was hit twice by tragedy during the 1996 season. And as fate would have it, Scott Brayton, killed in a crash during practice at Indianapolis on May 17, and Jeff Krosnoff, who died along with course worker Gary Avrin in an accident shortly before the scheduled conclusion of the Molson Indy Toronto, were two of the sport's most well-liked characters.

The fact that Brayton lost his life while plying his trade in the rival Indy Racing League, rather than the PPG Indy Car World Series, transcended the oftentimes bitter feud that separated the two sanctioning bodies.

He might not have been among the most successful Indy Car drivers in history, at least in terms of results, yet Brayton's unbridled enthusiasm, his keen sense of humor and his infectious mood of optimism made him a popular figure throughout the auto racing world.

'This is hard for all of us to bear,' said John Menard, who had entered cars at Indy for Brayton since 1994, 'but if I know Scott, he'll probably be telling God a joke right now.'

Brayton, who was 37, began his career in karting at the age of 16. After progressing into Formula Ford with the Skip Barber Racing School, he chose to bypass the usual stepping stone categories and jumped directly into the Indy cars in 1981.

Brayton's father, Lee, who raced Indy cars in the 1960s, continued to wield a heavy influence in his son's racing career. In the early 1980s they worked together in developing the first Buick V6 stock-block engines for Indy Car competition, and in 1985 Scott rocked the establishment by qualifying in the middle of the front row at Indianapolis, alongside the similarly powered March 85C of Pancho Carter.

In all, Brayton contested exactly 150 Indy Car races, with a best finish of third at Milwaukee in 1992. He raced 14 times at Indianapolis, although only once, due to a variety of problems, did he complete all 200 laps. Nevertheless, his proudest moments in the sport came at Indy, most notably less than a week before his untimely death when he joined

an illustrious group comprising Ralph De Palma, Rex Mays, Duke Nalon, Eddie Sachs, Parnelli Jones, Mario Andretti, A.J. Foyt, Tom Sneva and Rick Mears as the only drivers to win back-to-back poles at Indianapolis.

Two months after the loss of Scott Brayton, the Indy Car community once again was in mourning after Jeff Krosnoff and Gary Avrin died following a multi-car crash at the end of Lakeshore Boulevard in Toronto.

Krosnoff, 31, from the La Canada-Flintridge area of California, was a rookie driver on the PPG Cup circuit. To all but the most ardent North American racing enthusiasts, he was also something of an unknown quantity having spent the majority of his career in Japan. Nevertheless, after joining the emerging Arciero-Wells team, Krosnoff quickly endeared himself both to the fans and to his fellow competitors for his cheerful demeanor and an almost

encyclopedic knowledge of the sport.

Krosnoff enrolled at the Jim Russell Racing Drivers' School at Laguna Seca in 1983 and was recognized by several North American magazines as a rising talent during the formative stages of his career. Yet after a partial season of Formula Atlantic in 1987 and a close second-place finish in the following year's SCCA Racetruck Challenge series, in which he won a season-high four races for Spencer Low's factory-backed Nissan team, Krosnoff was offered an opportunity to drive for SpeedStar Racing in the All-Japan Formula 3000 Championship.

Krosnoff at first envisaged the move as a step toward his ultimate goal of a future in Formula 1. His results were initially encouraging, with a best finish of third in his rookie season, although for a variety of reasons he never quite achieved the breakthrough he so desperately craved.

Still, Krosnoff carved a fine reputation in Japan. He competed regularly in F3000 and sports car events, and in 1994, driving for the factory-backed SARD-Toyota Group C team, Krosnoff led the Le Mans 24 Hours race comfortably with teammates Mauro Martini and Eddie Irvine until being hobbled by a transmission failure inside the final 90 minutes.

Krosnoff's connections led to Indy Car tests during the 1995/1996 off-season with both Target/Chip Ganassi Racing and Arciero-Wells Racing. He impressed both teams with his feedback and his amenable nature, and, to the surprise of many less well-informed 'insiders,' was invited to drive for Arciero-Wells.

His talents were masked at least to some extent by the slowly developing Toyota engine, but Krosnoff made steady progress. Toronto, indeed, provided his best qualifying effort of the season, 20th, as he worked inexorably closer to the front-running pace.

Krosnoff will be fondly remembered as one of the most likeable characters on the circuit. He lived life to the full, and during his time in Japan stood apart from the majority of his peers by taking a keen interest in the local culture. As an enthusiastic and accomplished writer, he also contributed an always insightful, regular column for *California Sports Car*, his local SCCA region's magazine. Away from the track he played drums for a small band, Mach V, which also comprised sometime Indy Car drivers Robbie Groff and David Kudrave. The group, indeed, had signed a recording contract for its first CD release just a few weeks before his untimely demise.

Gary Avrin, 44, a course worker positioned on the main Lakeshore Boulevard straightaway during the Molson Indy Toronto, died instantly when he was hit by Jeff Krosnoff's car which had vaulted over the safety wall.

Avrin, from Calgary, Alberta, was an engineer by profession, having

graduated from the University of Toronto in 1970. Avrin, who worked with TransCanada Pipelines before joining the Calgary-based Nova Corporation, held an almost life-long passion for auto racing and had lived his dream as a volunteer corner worker for many years. He was a popular and well-known figure around the Canadian race tracks, particularly at his home town's Race City Speedway where more than 200 friends, fellow marshals and family members gathered for a memorial service following a regular race meeting one week after his death.

TRIBUTES TO JEFF KROSNOFF

Frank Arciero, co-owner Arciero-Wells Racing: 'Every time I would see Jeff in the morning at the race track he would say to me, "Good morning, teacher," in Italian. It would mean a lot because I always enjoy when an American speaks to me in Italian. He was the nicest guy I have ever been associated with. He was gentle, honest, clean cut, and on top of it all, a great driver.'

Cal Wells III, co-owner Arciero-Wells Racing: 'Jeff was someone who in a short period of time you couldn't help but grow very close to. He was an individual that had a multitude of attributes that went beyond the fact he was a tremendous athlete. His intelligence, his humor and his education transcended his profession. Collectively, it provided a tremendous human being.'

Peter Scott, crew chief, Arciero-Wells Racing: 'Jeff was a true team player. Everyone on the crew would light up when Jeff showed up. He was always joking around with everyone and also took a genuine interest in what they were doing.'

TRIBUTE TO GARY AVRIN

Barry Green, owner, Brahma Sports Team: 'People like Gary provide the lifeblood of our sport. They stand out there close to the race track, come rain or shine, and they act almost as the eyes and ears of the drivers. They keep the drivers informed of any potential dangers up ahead on the road. And all these people are volunteers. They do it for the love of the sport.'

In memoriam:

Bill Cheesbourg, who drove a variety of sometimes peculiar cars at Indianapolis during his career in the 1950s and 1960s, passed away on November 6, 1995, at the age of 68. 'Big Bill' was best known for his exploits in stock cars, especially Fords, and also devoted much of his time to the Champion Highway Safety program, helping to promote safe-driving tips among high school children.

Larry Cannon also died November 6, 1995. 'Boom Boom' Cannon made a name for himself in the supermodified ranks, and in 1966 won a grueling 500-lap race on the famed Eldora Speedway in Ohio. Cannon competed in a wide variety of cars and in 1977 took over the car started by John Mahler to become the last relief driver ever utilized in the Indianapolis 500.

Howard Millican, 59, ace fabricator, machinist and general innovator around the Indy Car circuit for more than 30 years, died September 27, 1995 after a long illness. Millican, whose son, Ron Dawes, has served as crew chief/engineer for Hemelgarn Racing for several years, will perhaps best be remembered for developing a half-scale wind-tunnel in the 1980s just west of Indianapolis, which saw use by a wide variety of teams.

Position	Driver	Car	Tires	Homestead	Rio	Surfers Paradise	Long Beach	Nazareth	U.S. 500	Milwaukee	Detroit	Portland	Cleveland	Toronto	Michigan	Mid-Ohio	Road America	Vancouver	Laguna Seca	Points total
1	Jimmy Vasser (USA)	Target/Chip Ganassi Racing Reynard 96I-Honda	FS	1	8	p†1	1	7	p1	10	12	13	p10	8	p9	2	6	7	4	154
2	Michael Andretti (USA)	Newman/Haas Kmart/Texaco Havoline Lola T96/00-Ford XD	GY	9	22	19	7	†1	23	1	1	11	19	22	22	3	1	†1	9	132
3	*Alex Zanardi (I)	Target/Chip Ganassi Racing Reynard 96I-Honda	FS	24	p†4	21	24	13	†17	13	11	p†1	2	†2	21	p†1	p3	p†26	p†1	132
4	Al Unser Jr. (USA)	Marlboro Team Penske Penske PC25-Mercedes	GY	8	2	9	3	3	8	†2	22	4	4	13	4	13	†10	5	16	125
5	Christian Fittipaldi (BR)	Newman/Haas Kmart/Budweiser Lola T96/00-Ford XD	GY	6	5	5	21	9	12	6	†2	3	7	7	10	7	16	3	10	110
6	Gil de Ferran (BR)	Hall Racing Pennzoil Special Reynard 96I-Honda	GY	2	10	11	p†5	23	9	9	3	2	†1	18	19	17	25	4	25	104
7	Bobby Rahal (USA)	Team Rahal Miller Brewing Reynard 96I-Mercedes	GY	5	6	20	14	6	19	7	21	6	15	3	24	5	2	2	7	102
8	Bryan Herta (USA)	Team Rahal Shell Reynard 96I-Mercedes	GY	10	13	17	12	11	15	14	13	26	5	6	2	4	5	6	†2	86
9	*Greg Moore (CDN)	Forsythe Player's Ltd./Indeck Reynard 96I-Mercedes	FS	7	18	3	22	2	13	5	20	25	3	4	17	9	23	25	6	84
10	Scott Pruett (USA)	Patrick Racing Firestone Lola T96/00-Ford XD	FS	4	3	2	11	8	26	12	p10	23	8	10	13	21	7	20	3	82
11	Andre Ribeiro (BR)	Tasman Motorsports LCI International Lola T96/00-Honda	FS	16	1	8	27	12	4	8	24	7	20	p21	†1	8	19	21	19	76
12	Adrian Fernandez (MEX)	Tasman Tecate Beer/Quaker State Oil Lola T96/00-Honda	FS	11	14	23	6	10	NS	11	4	12	6	1	20	6	13	8	11	71
13	Paul Tracy (CDN)	Marlboro Team Penske Penske PC25-Mercedes	GY	p†23	19	22	4	p5	7	p3	17	27	9	5	NS	–	12	18	29	60
14	Mauricio Gugelmin (BR)	PacWest Racing Group Hollywood Reynard 96I-Ford XB	GY	26	25	4	15	15	2	15	16	16	21	12	3	26	21	24	5	53
15	Stefan Johansson (S)	Bettenhausen Alumax Aluminum Reynard 96I-Mercedes	GY	19	23	6	19	19	16	27	7	9	12	17	5	11	4	17	21	43
16	*Mark Blundell (GB)	PacWest Racing Group Hollywood/VISA Reynard 96I-Ford XB	GY	17	27	–	–	–	5	22	5	8	11	11	6	10	20	12	24	41
17	Parker Johnstone (USA)	Brix Comptech Motorola Reynard 96I-Honda	FS	NS	16	24	2	20	11	16	14	5	25	26	18	12	11	11	13	33
18	Robby Gordon (USA)	Walker Valvoline/Cummins/Craftsman Reynard 96I-Ford XD	GY	3	15	16	13	22	20	17	26	10	18	9	8	18	17	10	15	29
19	Emerson Fittipaldi (BR)	Hogan Penske Marlboro Latin America Penske PC25-Mercedes	GY	13	11	25	20	4	10	4	25	20	22	14	25	–	–	–	–	29
20	*Eddie Lawson (USA)	Galles Racing Delco Electronics Lola T96/00-Mercedes	GY	15	21	7	9	17	6	20	6	15	24	15	–	–	–	–	–	26
21	Roberto Moreno (BR)	Payton/Coyne Data Control/Mi-Jack Lola T96/00-Ford XB	FS	NS	9	12	8	24	3	25	23	19	14	23	23	23	22	27	12	25
22	Raul Boesel (BR)	Brahma Sports Team Reynard 96I-Ford XD	GY	14	7	13	16	21	24	26	8	28	26	24	7	22	14	23	20	17
23	Juan Manuel Fangio II (RA)	All American Racers Castrol Eagle Mk.V-Toyota	GY	21	17	15	25	25	22	19	18	14	13	28	14	20	8	19	28	5
24	*Jan Magnussen (DK)	Marlboro Team Penske Penske PC25-Mercedes	GY	–	–	–	–	–	–	–	–	–	–	–	–	14	–	–	–	
		Hogan Penske Marlboro Latin America Penske PC25-Mercedes	GY	–	–	–	–	–	–	–	–	–	–	–	–	–	26	22	8	5
25	Scott Goodyear (CDN)	Walker Valvoline DuraBlend Special Reynard 96I-Ford XB	GY	12	NS	–	–	–	–	–	–	–	–	–	19	–	–	9	18	5
26	*P.J. Jones (USA)	All American Racers Castrol Eagle Mk.V-Toyota	GY	–	–	–	–	–	–	24	9	24	23	20	16	25	18	13	27	4
27	*Max Papis (I)	Arciero-Wells Racing MCI Reynard 96I-Toyota	FS	–	–	–	–	–	–	–	–	–	–	–	–	24	9	–	22	4
28	Hiro Matsushita (J)	Payton/Coyne Panasonic/Duskin Lola T96/00-Ford XB	FS	18	24	10	28	26	14	28	19	21	17	27	15	19	15	15	23	3
29	*Richie Hearn (USA)	Della Penna Ralphs/Food 4 Less Reynard 95I-Ford XB	GY	–	–	–	10	–	–	–	–	–	–	–	–	25	–	–	17	3
30	Eliseo Salazar (RCH)	Team Scandia Cristal/Copec/Mobil 1 Lola T96/00-Ford XB	GY	–	–	–	–	–	21	–	18	–	–	–	–	11	15	–	–	2
31	Marco Greco (BR)	Scandia-Simon Int. Sports/Perry Ellis Lola T96/00-Ford XB	GY	25	12	–	–	–	–	–	–	–	–	–	–	–	–	–	–	1
32	Davy Jones (USA)	Galles Racing Delco Electronics Lola T96/00-Mercedes	GY	–	–	–	–	–	–	–	–	–	–	–	12	16	24	14	14	1
33	Carlos Guerrero (MEX)	Scandia-Simon Herdez Lola T96/00-Ford XB	GY	20	20	14	–	–	–	–	–	–	–	–	–	–	–	–	–	0
34	Mike Groff (USA)	Walker Valvoline DuraBlend Special Reynard 96I-Ford XB	GY	–	–	–	–	14	–	–	–	–	–	–	–	–	–	–	–	0
35	*Jeff Krosnoff (USA)	Arciero-Wells Racing MCI Reynard 96I-Toyota	FS	22	26	18	26	18	18	18	15	17	16	16	–	–	–	–	–	0
36	Teo Fabi (I)	PacWest Racing Group Hollywood/VISA Reynard 96I-Ford XB	GY	–	–	–	18	16	–	–	–	–	–	–	–	–	–	–	–	0
37	*Michel Jourdain Jr. (MEX)	Scandia-Simon Herdez Lola T96/00-Ford XB	GY	–	–	–	23	–	–	23	NS	22	–	–	–	–	–	16	26	0
38	Dennis Vitolo (USA)	Project Indy SmithKline Beecham Reynard 95I-Ford XB	GY	–	–	–	–	–	17	–	–	–	–	–	–	–	–	–	–	0
39	Gary Bettenhausen (USA)	Bettenhausen Alumax Aluminum Penske PC23-Mercedes	GY	–	–	–	–	–	21	–	–	–	–	–	–	–	–	–	–	0
40	*Fredrik Ekblom (S)	Walker Valvoline DuraBlend Special Reynard 96I-Ford XD	GY	–	–	–	–	–	25	–	–	–	–	–	–	–	–	–	–	0

Bold type indicates car still running at finish
* rookie
† led most laps
p pole position
NS did not start

Lap Leaders (Number of races led)

1	Alex Zanardi	610	(11)
2	Michael Andretti	281	(7)
3	Paul Tracy	214	(4)
4	Gil de Ferran	172	(4)
5	Andre Ribeiro	166	(3)
6	Jimmy Vasser	162	(8)
7	Al Unser Jr.	125	(3)
8	Christian Fittipaldi	80	(3)
9	Greg Moore	73	(4)
10	Bryan Herta	41	(1)
11	Parker Johnstone	35	(1)
12	Adrian Fernandez	17	(1)
13	Mauricio Gugelmin	12	(2)
	Scott Pruett	12	(3)
15	Robby Gordon	2	(1)
	Roberto Moreno	2	(1)
17	Bobby Rahal	1	(1)

Nations Cup

1	United States	282
2	Brazil	206
3	Italy	120
4	Canada	111
5	Mexico	71
6	Sweden	43
7	England	41
8	Argentina	5
	Denmark	5
10	Japan	3
11	Chile	2

Manufacturers Championship

1	Honda	271
2	Ford/Cosworth	234
3	Mercedes-Benz	218
4	Toyota	9

Constructors Championship

1	Reynard	276
2	Lola	260
3	Penske	139
4	Eagle	9

Jim Trueman Rookie of the Year

1	Alex Zanardi	132
2	Greg Moore	84
3	Mark Blundell	41
4	Eddie Lawson	26
5	Jan Magnussen	5
6	P.J. Jones	4
7	Max Papis	4
8	Richie Hearn	3
9	Jeff Krosnoff	0
10	Michel Jourdain Jr.	0
11	Fredrik Ekblom	0

We're not just here to chase checkered flags.

Even though it's Toyota's first year ever in IndyCar racing, the competition can't help but take notice.
Not just because of our winning reputation in the world of motorsports, but because of our reputation
in the "real" world, as well. That's why the rugged, reliable Toyota T100 is now the Official Truck of IndyCar.
Its proven performance will support every IndyCar team. You could say Toyota is so committed
to IndyCar racing, we'll even help the rest of the field get back on the track.

TOYOTA
motor *sports*

OUR MINDS ARE ALWAYS RACING

MARLBORO GRAND PRIX OF MIAMI, PRESENTED BY TOYOTA, METRO-DADE HOMESTEAD MOTORSPORTS COMPLEX   90

RIO 400, EMERSON FITTIPALDI SPEEDWAY   96

BARTERCARD INDY CAR AUSTRALIA, SURFERS PARADISE   102

TOYOTA GRAND PRIX OF LONG BEACH   108

BOSCH SPARK PLUG GRAND PRIX, NAZARETH SPEEDWAY   114

U.S. 500, MICHIGAN INTERNATIONAL SPEEDWAY   120

MILLER 200, THE MILWAUKEE MILE   126

ITT AUTOMOTIVE DETROIT GRAND PRIX   132

BUDWEISER/G.I. JOE'S 200, PRESENTED BY TEXACO/HAVOLINE, PORTLAND INTERNATIONAL RACEWAY   138

MEDIC DRUG GRAND PRIX OF CLEVELAND   144

MOLSON INDY TORONTO   150

MARLBORO 500, MICHIGAN INTERNATIONAL SPEEDWAY   156

MILLER 200, MID-OHIO SPORTS CAR COURSE   162

TEXACO/HAVOLINE 200, ROAD AMERICA   168

MOLSON INDY VANCOUVER   174

TOYOTA GRAND PRIX OF MONTEREY, FEATURING THE BANK OF AMERICA 300, LAGUNA SECA RACEWAY   180

ght: **Jimmy Vasser celebrates the first** ...n of his Indy Car career with his ...lighted pit crew.

...ck with Marlboro Team Penske, Paul ...acy *(below)* set the pace all weekend, ...t misfortune struck again as the race ...ared its climax.

HOMESTEAD

PPG INDY CAR WORLD SERIES • ROUND 1

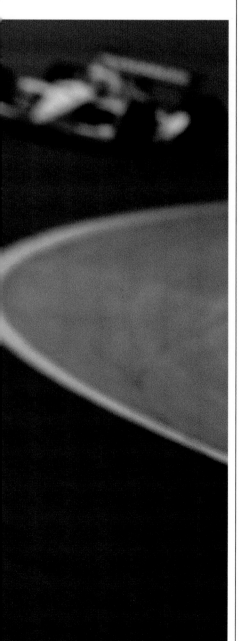

Michael C. Brown

1 – VASSER

2 – DE FERRAN

3 – GORDON

QUALIFYING

Michael C. Brown

Three topics of conversation were prevalent throughout practice and qualifying at Homestead. The first was the weather, which, by and large, was lousy; the second was the sheer speed of Paul Tracy; and the third was the track surface, to which had been applied a new sealing compound after it had shown signs of breaking up during the well-attended, week-long, preseason 'Spring Training' routine in early February.

Lap times during the first session on Friday were around a half-second slower than in testing, although the speeds gradually increased as more rubber was laid down and the grip level improved.

'The track's quite a lot different,' asserted Tracy, who topped the times in first practice with a best lap at 191.891 mph. 'You feel the bumps less in Turn Three and it's more slippery, but it doesn't really cause any problems. The car feels good. We're just fine-tuning.'

Tracy's name remained at the top of the speed charts. Indeed, his Penske was visibly quicker than any other car on the entry to Turns One and Three.

'He's on the top of his game right now,' said race engineer Nigel Beresford, who, like Tracy, had returned to the Penske fold after a one-year sabbatical – in his case with the Tyrrell Formula 1

team. 'The kid has just got the confidence to take the car deeper into the corner and pull it through. So it's a heck of a lot of fun working with him.'

Qualifying on Saturday afternoon was washed out by rain, but rather than rely simply on practice times to set the grid, IndyCar Director of Competition Wally Dallenbach bravely decided to reschedule the one-at-a-time session for Sunday morning.

Temperatures remained cool, but at least it was dry when, appropriately, Raul Boesel (above) took Barry Green's #1 Brahma Sports Reynard-Ford out onto the track to commence qualifying at 10.00 a.m. on Sunday. The Brazilian set the tone by posting a lap at 192.437 mph, more than 1.3 mph faster than his previous best, despite failing to improve on his second lap when the car bottomed out heavily in Turn Two.

Gil de Ferran, after working with his engineers to eliminate a loose condition earlier in the weekend, produced a sensational improvement of more than 8 mph to jump onto the provisional pole; but Tracy was up to the challenge. His final warmup lap, at 196.651, would have been good enough for second on the grid, and his two officially timed laps at 198.590 and 198.346 comfortably secured the pole.

Jimmy Vasser had grown tired of being referred to as 'the nearlyman' of Indy Car racing.

Three times in 1995 he qualified on the front row of the grid for Target/Chip Ganassi Racing, only to be beaten narrowly to the pole on each occasion. The 30-year-old Californian also enjoyed five podium appearances during his first four seasons of PPG Cup competition, including a pair of runner-up finishes. A victory, however, continued to elude him.

Now the record has been set straight. In the opening race of the new season, the Marlboro Grand Prix of Miami presented by Toyota, Lady Luck was riding with Vasser rather than against him.

After qualifying third, Vasser ran strongly throughout the 133-lap race. He had to play second fiddle to Paul Tracy for almost two-thirds of the race, but once the Canadian had succumbed to a broken transmission, Vasser was perfectly positioned to make a challenge for the lead. He soon overtook Gil de Ferran and never looked back.

'It feels great,' said a delighted Vasser. 'I planned on doing this. That's why I'm here – and hopefully this won't be my last.'

While Vasser celebrated his victory, the unfortunate Tracy was left to ponder the opposite end of the emotional spectrum. His #3 Marlboro Penske PC25-Mercedes had been fastest in every official session, including the warmup on race morning.

Tracy secured the pole with a record-setting average speed of 198.590 mph. The 27-year-old Canadian continued his domination in the race, although it took a considerable time before he was able truly to get into his stride.

The first delay came mere moments after IndyCar Starter Jim Swintal waved the green flag. Englishman Mark Blundell, making his Indy Car debut with the PacWest Racing Group, lost control of his Reynard-Ford/Cosworth while accelerating off the fourth turn and spun harmlessly. Cold tires were to blame. Farther back in the pack, fellow ex-Formula 1 racer Roberto Moreno also was caught out in Payton Coyne Racing's Data Control/Mi-Jack Lola-Ford. Moreno wasn't as fortunate. The Brazilian's car made contact with the outside retaining wall. His day was done.

The chastened Blundell reclaimed his grid position for the

restart, only for PacWest teammate Mauricio Gugelmin to bring out the caution flags again when he was clipped from behind by Michael Andretti on the exit of Turn Two. Gugelmin was able to continue, albeit with slightly rearranged rear suspension. He later spun out in Turn One. Andretti lost a lap while Tim Bumps and the crew replaced the shattered nose section on Newman/Haas Racing's Kmart/Texaco Havoline Lola-Ford.

Tracy jumped into a convincing lead once the green flags waved again. By lap 17, after only eight laps of racing, he was already six seconds clear of de Ferran. The Brazilian remained under pressure from Vasser, Scott Pruett and rookie Greg Moore, who already had dispensed with Bobby Rahal and Robby Gordon in the early stages.

Tracy's progress was interrupted once more on lap 18, this time when moisture was reported on the track surface. A fine drizzle had descended on the speedway as cool, unFlorida-like weather continued to blight the weekend. The cars circulated behind the pace car until the decision was made to display the red flag and park the cars in the hope that the weather would improve.

Service complete, Jimmy Vasser is waved away from his pit stall by crew chief Grant Weaver as race leader Paul Tracy cruises past in the background. The impressive main grandstand is typical of the first-class amenities offered by the superb new Homestead facility.

Exciting new venue joins PPG Cup schedule

Completion of the Metro-Dade Homestead Motorsports Complex represented the fulfillment of a long-held dream for South Florida race promoter Ralph Sanchez (below).

Having established an extremely successful property development business with a broad sphere of influence ranging to Haiti and Belize, the Cuban-born Sanchez's initial foray into motorsports was not nearly so lucrative. In fact, it almost brought about his financial downfall when a huge storm virtually washed out his initial Miami Grand Prix IMSA sports car venture in 1983. Sanchez, unbowed, fought back. The event became a major success, soon drawing large crowds and inestimable prestige to the downtown area.

Sanchez spread his wings by bringing Indy Car racing to another circuit, in Tamiami Park, between 1985 and 1988, when scheduling conflicts brought the relationship to a temporary halt. Meanwhile, he continued to devote his considerable energy to the Bicentennial Park venue, and in 1995 the Indy cars were back in South Florida, attracting a capacity crowd of more than 90,000 to the final event to be held on the downtown race track.

All along, however, Sanchez's goal had been to construct a permanent facility. Several potential venues were considered, including Homestead, and, ironically, it was the devastation caused by Hurricane Andrew in August 1992 which guided the project toward fruition. Officials from the city of Homestead, Dade County and, of course, Sanchez's Miami Motorsports concern worked long and hard in thrashing out the details. Finally, on the weekend of November 3–5, 1995, the dream became a reality as the new complex hosted its first event for NASCAR Busch Grand National stock cars.

The Homestead facility, constructed on almost 344 acres, features both a 1.527-mile oval, its four corners banked at eight degrees, and a 2.21-mile infield road course. A state-of-the-art pit/garage/hospitality complex ensures a magnificent environment for teams and sponsors alike, while the imposing main grandstand, rising eight stories, comprises 20 luxury skyboxes and seats for more than 65,000 spectators.

The venue represents an exciting addition to the PPG Indy Car World Series schedule, and one that is likely to play an important role in American motorsports for many years to come.

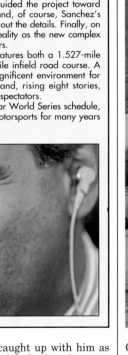

Photos: Michael C. Brown

The teams were allowed to refuel and change tires during the stoppage, and after a half-hour delay the status quo was restored as Tracy once again moved clear of the pack. This time, though, after jumping out to an early lead in excess of four seconds over de Ferran, the gap soon began to stabilize.

'I had a misfire early in the race,' declared de Ferran, 'so the red flag was really a blessing for us. The battery plug had worked loose and the crew was able to repair it during the red flag.'

Some interesting battles began to develop throughout the field as the race reached one-third distance. Moore, for example, took advantage of some slower traffic to pass Pruett for fourth place on lap 50. A couple of laps later, the young Canadian's inexperience caught up with him as he found himself balked inadvertently by Juan Manuel Fangio II's under-powered Eagle-Toyota. In a flash, Moore lost three places to Pruett, Al Unser Jr., who had moved stealthily into a challenging position after a lackluster performance in qualifying, and Gordon.

Unser's hopes of a top finish were dashed soon afterward when he tangled with the lapped car of Carlos Guerrero in Turn Three. Unser lost a lap while a damaged nose section was replaced. Moore also fell a lap behind when he was assessed a stop-and-go penalty for passing Fangio during a caution period.

Tracy continued to lead strongly through the middle of the race, leaving de Ferran, Vasser and Pruett embroiled in their battle for second.

Gordon and Rahal also were scrapping mightily over fifth place, while Andre Ribeiro moved up into contention with Steve Horne's LCI International Lola-Honda before having his nose clipped by Gordon as the pair jostled for position off the fourth turn on lap 82.

The resulting caution for debris gave everyone the opportunity to take on service. But as Tracy accelerated out of the pits, his dreams of victory were shattered by a broken gearbox.

'Obviously I'm extremely disappointed with the way our race ended, since I really feel we were the class of the field this weekend,' said Tracy with remarkable sangfroid. 'The car was really hooked up and we were looking strong but we had a failure, plain and simple.'

A strong debut oval appearance for Alex Zanardi also came to an end under the caution. The likeable Italian had moved up to a promising seventh, only for the left-rear wheel to part company with his Target Reynard immediately following a pit stop. Heavy contact with the wall was the inevitable result.

Tracy's demise enabled de Ferran to take up the running in Jim Hall's Pennzoil Reynard-Honda. His time in the lead was extended by yet more light precipitation, which delayed the restart until lap 102, but right away afterward he was passed by Vasser, who had loomed large in his mirrors all afternoon.

'We knew we were faster than de Ferran,' proclaimed Vasser's race engineer, Julian Robertson. 'He was holding us up in the first part [of the

race]. Jimmy said the car was under-steering a bit, so we tweaked it during the pit stop. A little bit of extra front wing helped.'

Slower cars immediately in front of the leaders at the restart also played a crucial role: 'I decided to go around the outside of Raul [Boesel] in Turn Four, because it seemed like the best way to get a sling-shot on the traffic,' said de Ferran. 'But when I moved out, the guy in front of him [Jeff Krosnoff] went high as well, so I was kind of boxed in. Jimmy just flew by me on the inside like I was stopped.'

Vasser, once into the lead, was able to maintain a healthy advantage throughout the remainder of the race.

'My car was incredibly consistent,' related Vasser. 'My Firestone tires were unbelievable. It's the first time I've raced with them and they were everything I hoped they would be. My Honda engine was great. The only guy I couldn't blow past was Gil – and he had an "H" on the side of his car as well.'

De Ferran was unable to challenge Vasser in the closing stages. Instead, as slower traffic continued to pose problems, he came under increasing pressure from Pruett, Rahal and Gordon, who exchanged positions several times in the closing stages.

Pruett, having overtaken Rahal for third on lap 115, was mere inches behind de Ferran as the pair swept into Turn Four for the final time. Gordon and Rahal, too, were close behind.

'We had some great racing today,' said Pruett after losing out to Gordon by just 0.004 seconds at the finish line. 'On that last lap I thought I had a chance to get de Ferran. There was a bunch of us going into Turn Four and de Ferran came down in front of me. He was just taking his line but I had to back off. Robby got a run on me at that point. He did a good job.'

Rahal was equally pleased to finish fifth: 'That's the best oval car I've had since 1992, when we won the championship,' he noted. 'It was fun today.'

Christian Fittipaldi also posted a good performance, rising from 15th on the grid to sixth in his Kmart/Budweiser Lola. Moore, meanwhile, was simply sensational in the closing stages as he came from mid-pack to pass everyone, including Vasser, during a charge which elevated him from a lapped 13th prior to the final restart to seventh, just over 20 seconds behind the race winner. Along the way he executed several breathtaking outside-line passes.

'There's no doubt my car was the fastest out there once Paul [Tracy] was out,' said Moore, who proved the veracity of his statement by posting the fastest lap of the race just two tours from the finish. 'It's too bad I couldn't have won the race for the Player's/Forsythe team.'

That honor, of course, went instead to Target/Chip Ganassi Racing, as well as Vasser, Reynard, Honda and Firestone. But perhaps the story line would have been different if Tracy's gearbox had held together . . .

The joy of winning

A maiden victory is always sweet, yet for Jimmy Vasser the win at Homestead held a special significance as a result of the rollercoaster of emotion he experienced following the race at Portland in 1995. Vasser, after finishing a distant second to Al Unser Jr., was declared the winner later in the evening after Unser's car failed post-race inspection. Three months later, the decision was overturned upon appeal. The win was returned to Unser.

'I was never happy about the circumstances of the "win" at Portland, so there was no emotion in losing it,' said Vasser. 'Today was very exciting because I had the opportunity to bring the Target/Chip Ganassi car across the line first – and as I put my fist in the air, I glanced over at my team and they were all jumping up and down off the wall. It was a great feeling.'

Vasser became the 220th driver to win an Indy Car race. He achieved the feat in his 56th start.

'One for 56 doesn't sound too good,' he noted, 'but a lot of the time I haven't been with a proper effort and team. I've always believed in myself, and the biggest thing for me is that I have been able to grow with Chip's Target team. I've been with this team for a year now and we did a lot of testing over the winter. When you do that, you gain more speed and more confidence in your team and your car, and that in turn leads to more confidence in yourself.

'I remember the feeling when I was winning a lot of races in the lower formulae, when I was coming up through the ranks, and it is a bit of a reality check when you break into Indy Car, especially with a team that is not a front-running team. And let's face it, I have not won a race in four years so it feels pretty darn good. I hope and intend to win many more races.'

Photos: Michael C. Brown

SNIPPETS

• The only manufacturers not represented toward the front of the field were Toyota and Eagle, both of which were making their Indy Car debuts. Neither of the Toyota-powered cars – the Reynard of **Jeff Krosnoff** (above) and the Eagle of Juan Manuel Fangio II – reached the finish, although both the Arciero-Wells and All American Racers teams were adopting a positive approach: 'In racing you're either winning or you're improving,' said Krosnoff, 'and we're improving.'

• One of the most intriguing aspects of the opening race of the new season was the apparent equality among competing equipment suppliers. Each one of the first eight finishers relied upon a different combination of chassis, engine and tires.

• The [Brix Comptech] team was forced to miss the race after Parker Johnstone sustained a slight concussion in a heavy crash during practice on Saturday morning.

• Payton-Coyne Racing performed a minor miracle in providing a brand-new Lola T96/00 for **Roberto Moreno**. The Brazilian had concluded a last-minute deal to join the team and his car arrived at Miami airport, direct from the Lola factory in England, on Tuesday. Team manager Bernie Myers first located an all-night paint shop, then arranged for the car to be stripped down to its bare essentials. The newly liveried tub was delivered to Homestead at noon on Wednesday and, incredibly, was completed in time for first practice Friday morning!

• **Barry Green**'s pair of Brahma Sports Team Reynard 96I chassis are numbered 007 and 021. The crew quickly, and appropriately, assigned the nicknames 'craps' and 'blackjack' to the respective cars. Incidentally, Raul Boesel relied upon 'craps' for the majority of the weekend.

• Opinions were divided with regard to the predominantly black color scheme on Michael Andretti's **Kmart/Texaco Havoline Lola**. Andretti, though, had no doubts: 'I think it looks mean, intimidating – kind of Dale Earnhardt-ish,' he said, a gleam in his eye. 'I think it'll look fairly frightening in the mirrors.'

• **Mark Blundell** (below) endured an action-packed Indy Car baptism, including a brake failure as he prepared to make a pit stop during the Sunday morning warmup. That was just the beginning. 'I've experienced the whole spectrum,' he said with a rueful smile after finishing a disappointed 17th. 'I spun at the start, I stalled in the pits, and I got black-flagged for passing the pace car. It can only get better!' Little did he know . . .

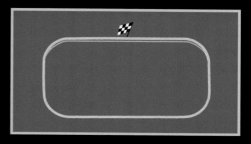

PPG INDY CAR WORLD SERIES • ROUND 1
MARLBORO GRAND PRIX OF MIAMI, PRESENTED BY TOYOTA

METRO-DADE HOMESTEAD MOTORSPORTS COMPLEX, HOMESTEAD, FLORIDA

MARCH 3, 133 laps – 203.091 miles

Place	Driver (Nat.)	No.	Team Sponsors Car-Engine	Tires	Q Speed	Q Time	Q Pos.	Laps	Time/Status	Ave.	Pts.
1	Jimmy Vasser (USA)	12	Target/Chip Ganassi Racing Reynard 96I-Honda	FS	196.622	27.958s	3	133	1h 51m 23.100s	109.399	20
2	Gil de Ferran (BR)	8	Hall Racing Pennzoil Special Reynard 96I-Honda	GY	197.830	27.787s	2	133	1h 51m 26.256s	109.348	16
3	Robby Gordon (USA)	5	Walker Valvoline/Cummins/Craftsman Reynard 96I-Ford XD	GY	194.946	28.199s	7	133	1h 51m 26.840s	109.338	14
4	Scott Pruett (USA)	20	Patrick Racing Firestone Lola T96/00-Ford XD	FS	196.571	27.965s	4	133	1h 51m 26.844s	109.338	12
5	Bobby Rahal (USA)	18	Team Rahal Miller Brewing Reynard 96I-Mercedes	GY	196.315	28.002s	5	133	1h 51m 27.468s	109.328	10
6	Christian Fittipaldi (BR)	11	Newman/Haas Kmart/Budweiser Lola T96/00-Ford XD	GY	193.335	28.434s	15	133	1h 51m 39.764s	109.127	8
7	*Greg Moore (CDN)	99	Forsythe Player's Ltd./Indeck Reynard 96I-Mercedes	FS	195.958	28.053s	6	133	1h 51m 43.760s	109.062	6
8	Al Unser Jr. (USA)	2	Marlboro Team Penske Penske PC25-Mercedes	GY	193.520	28.406s	13	132	Running		5
9	Michael Andretti (USA)	6	Newman/Haas Kmart/Texaco Havoline Lola T96/00-Ford XD	GY	194.549	28.256s	10	132	Running		4
10	Bryan Herta (USA)	28	Team Rahal Shell Reynard 96I-Mercedes	GY	194.526	28.259s	11	131	Running		3
11	Adrian Fernandez (MEX)	32	Tasman Tecate Beer/Quaker State Oil Lola T96/00-Honda	FS	193.178	28.457s	16	131	Running		2
12	Scott Goodyear (CDN)	15	Walker Valvoline DuraBlend Special Reynard 96I-Ford XB	GY	189.894	28.949s	22	131	Running		1
13	Emerson Fittipaldi (BR)	9	Hogan Penske Marlboro Latin America Penske PC25-Mercedes	GY	194.261	28.298s	12	131	Running		
14	Raul Boesel (BR)	1	Brahma Sports Team Reynard 96I-Ford XD	GY	192.437	28.566s	17	131	Running		
15	*Eddie Lawson (USA)	10	Galles Racing Delco Electronics Lola T96/00-Mercedes	GY	190.317	28.885s	20	131	Running		
16	Andre Ribeiro (BR)	31	Tasman Motorsports LCI International Lola T96/00-Honda	FS	194.599	28.249s	9	130	Running		
17	*Mark Blundell (GB)	21	PacWest Racing Group VISA Reynard 96I-Ford XB	GY	190.741	28.820s	19	129	Running		
18	Hiro Matsushita (J)	19	Payton/Coyne Panasonic/Duskin Lola T96/00-Ford XB	FS	186.752	29.436s	23	124	Running		
19	Stefan Johansson (S)	16	Bettenhausen Alumax Aluminum Reynard 96I-Mercedes	GY	190.959	28.787s	18	115	Transmission		
20	Carlos Guerrero (MEX)	22	Scandia-Simon Herdez Lola T96/00-Ford XB	GY	190.231	28.897s	21	112	Running		
21	Juan Manuel Fangio II (RA)	36	All American Racers Castrol Eagle Mk.V-Toyota	GY	177.401	30.987s	26	108	Fuel		
22	*Jeff Krosnoff (USA)	25	Arciero-Wells Racing Reynard 96I-Toyota	FS	184.519	29.792s	25	102	Engine		
23	Paul Tracy (CDN)	3	Marlboro Team Penske Penske PC25-Mercedes	GY	198.590	27.681s	1	84	Transmission		2
24	*Alex Zanardi (I)	4	Target/Chip Ganassi Racing Reynard 96I-Honda	FS	193.382	28.427s	14	83	Accident		
25	Marco Greco (BR)	7	Scandia-Simon Int. Sports/Perry Ellis Lola T96/00-Ford XB	GY	185.395	29.651s	24	64	Electrical		
26	Mauricio Gugelmin (BR)	17	PacWest Racing Group Hollywood Reynard 96I-Ford XB	GY	194.627	28.245s	8	53	Accident		
NS	Roberto Moreno (BR)	34	Payton/Coyne Data Control/Mi-Jack Lola T96/00-Ford XB	FS	no speed	no time	27	0	Accident		
NS	Parker Johnstone (USA)	49	Brix Comptech Motorola Reynard 96I-Honda	FS	no speed	no time	–	–	Accident in practice		

* denotes Rookie driver

Caution flags: Laps 1–4, accident/Moreno; laps 6–8, accident/Gugelmin; laps 17–34, light rain; laps 35–38, restart after red flag; laps 53–56, spin/Gugelmin; laps 58–60, debris; laps 82–101, accident/Ribeiro and Gordon/then light rain. **Total:** seven for 56 laps.

Lap leaders: Paul Tracy, 1–83 (83 laps); Gil de Ferran, 84–101 (18 laps); Jimmy Vasser, 102–133 (32 laps). **Totals:** Tracy, 83 laps; Vasser, 32 laps; de Ferran, 18 laps.

Fastest race lap: Greg Moore, 28.385s, 193.665 mph, on lap 131.

Championship positions: 1 Vasser, 20; **2** de Ferran, 16; **3** Gordon, 14; **4** Pruett, 12; **5** Rahal, 10; **6** C. Fittipaldi, 8; **7** Moore, 6; **8** Unser, 5; **9** Andretti, 4; **10** Herta, 3; **11** Fernandez and Tracy, 2; **13** Goodyear, 1.

Official Information Technology Provider **EDS**

RIO

PPG INDY CAR WORLD SERIES • ROUND 2

1 – RIBEIRO

2 – UNSER

3 – PRUETT

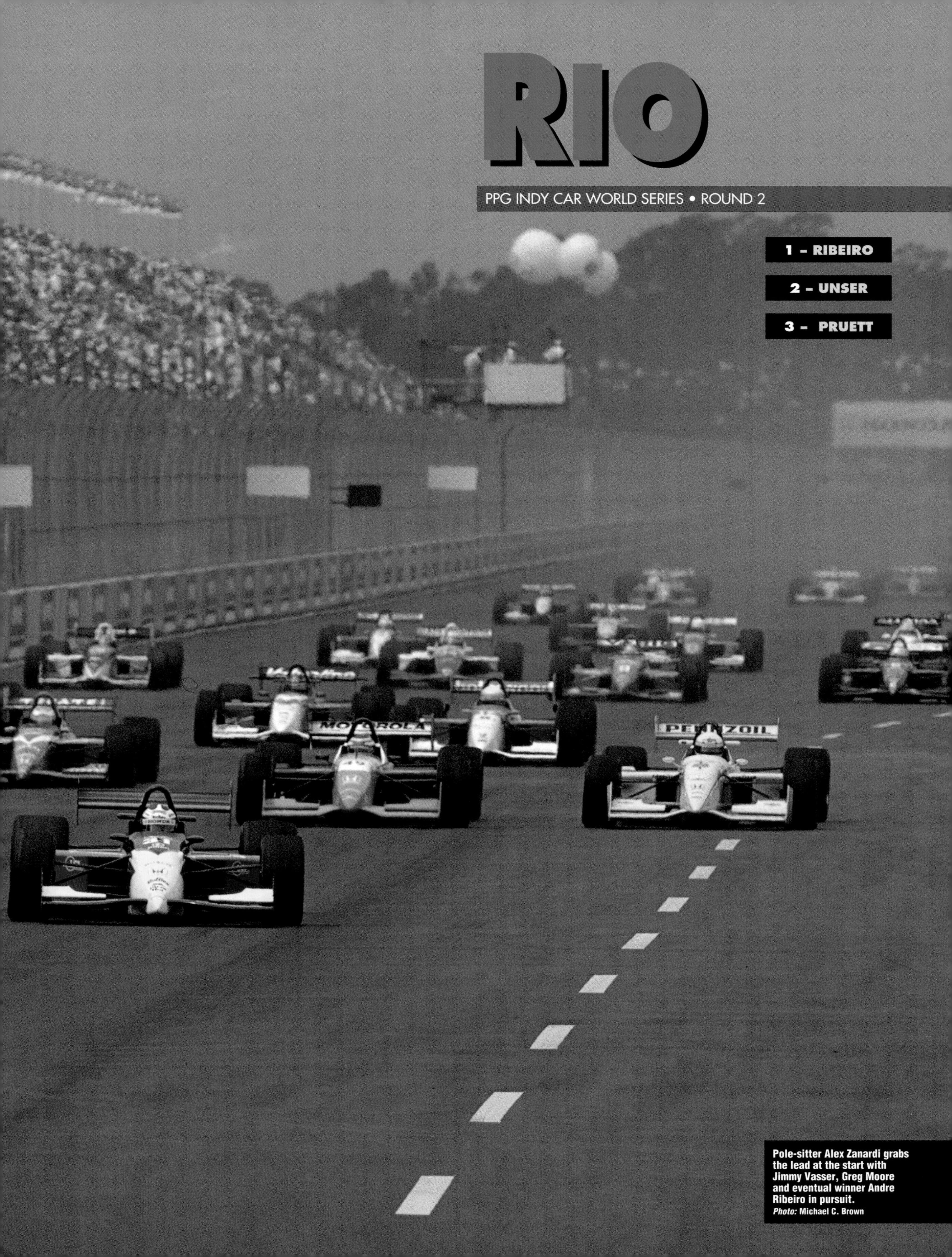

Pole-sitter Alex Zanardi grabs the lead at the start with Jimmy Vasser, Greg Moore and eventual winner Andre Ribeiro in pursuit.
***Photo:* Michael C. Brown**

Michael C. Brown

QUALIFYING

Brazil's newest auto racing hero, Andre Ribeiro, elevated himself to the brink of superstar status in his homeland by scoring a hugely popular victory in the Rio 400. The good-looking, impeccably mannered young man from Sao Paulo was con-tent to play a waiting game in the early stages of the 133-lap, 400-kilometer race around the Emerson Fittipaldi Speedway, set within the grounds of the Autodromo Nelson Piquet on the outskirts of Rio de Janeiro. And when impressive rook-ie Greg Moore encountered an electrical problem with just 18 laps to go, Ribeiro was perfectly poised to take the lead in his LCI International Lola T96/00-Honda. The fiercely patriotic crowd was on its feet, waving flags and throwing hats high into the air as Ribeiro sped beneath the checkered flag just over two seconds clear of Al Unser Jr.'s Marlboro Penske-Mercedes.

'This is great,' said Ribeiro, close to tears after being mobbed by an army of well-wishers. 'It's so exciting. I feel so happy for all these people who came to watch because they deserve this. They're a great crowd. They're so enthusiastic. It's a fantastic day for me and the Tasman team.'

Ribeiro's triumph represented the second straight win for both Honda and Firestone, whose apparent superiority had been outlined in qualifying as the two Target/Chip Ganassi Reynards of Alex Zanardi and Jimmy Vasser occupied the front row of the grid. Nevertheless, Mercedes and Goodyear also displayed front-running potential. Moore led handsomely in his Mercedes-powered Player's Reynard, while Gil de Ferran showed there was nothing wrong with the Goodyear tires as he, too, ran up front in the Pennzoil Reynard-Honda.

Zanardi took advantage of his pole position to claim the lead at the start. Ribeiro tucked in behind on the long run down to the first corner, with Vasser slipping into third ahead of Moore and the similar Goodyear-tired Miller/Team Rahal Reynard-Mercedes of Bobby Rahal.

After an early yellow flag to remove Juan Manuel Fangio II's recalcitrant Castrol Eagle-Toyota, which had stalled due to an electrical malfunction, the leaders became embroiled in some exciting wheel-to-wheel action. The crowd went into a frenzy on lap seven as Ribeiro drove around the outside of Zanardi in Turn Four, after the Italian had vainly attempted to block the inside line. Nice move. Down into Turn One, however, Zanardi returned the favor with an equally well-judged pass on the inside.

Next time around, Moore executed a brave maneuver to displace Vasser on the outside into Turn One. The youngster almost immediately took over second place when Ribeiro slid sideways under hard acceleration off Turn Four.

The combination of two long straightaways, with the cars reaching speeds in excess of 200 mph, a couple of flat-out kinks and a pair of tight, third- or fourth-gear corners ensured plenty of opportunities for overtaking. Drafting became of paramount importance.

On lap 11, however, the excite-

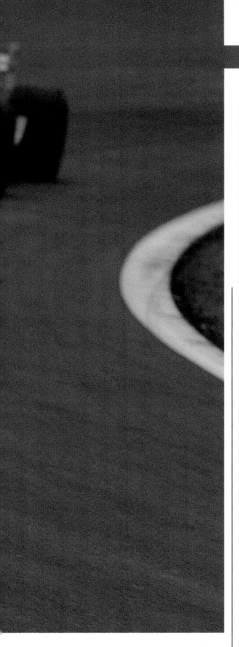

Flying start

The inaugural Rio 400 was declared a huge success by the enthusiastic Brazilian media as well as the estimated 70,000 spectators. Ribeiro's victory ensured massive exposure throughout the country, including front page stories in more than 80 newspapers on Monday morning.

Less than a month earlier, however, the event seemed to be in some jeopardy following an inspection of the newly constructed Emerson Fittipaldi Speedway by IndyCar Vice President, Competition Kirk Russell. A poor paving job led to Russell declaring the circuit 'unusable,' and he left the organizers with an extensive list of problems to be corrected.

A vast workload remained even as the Indy Car teams began to arrive in Rio less than a week before the race. Grandstands were still to be built. A huge complex of hospitality suites, which extended beyond the length of the pit lane, consisted of little more than a pile of scaffolding poles. Air-conditioned temporary huts for the individual teams were far from ready.

Miraculously, the race went on with nary a hitch. The track was bumpy, but none of the drivers complained unduly. Most, indeed, praised the circuit's uniquely challenging nature.

'That's one of the great things about Indy Car racing,' said Ribeiro. 'You don't always have the same kind of tracks. Every one is different. This place adds a new dimension.'

Even the region's traditionally capricious weather cooperated. Ominous dark clouds obscured the nearby mountains for much of the day, but, thankfully, while the action-packed race was held in hot, steamy conditions, the inevitable rain storm held off until most of the crowd had long since departed for home.

Far left: Indy Car racing's Brazilian contingent fared well in their home race, all but one finishing in the points. Andre Ribeiro leads Gil de Ferran and the lapped Marco Greco.

Mark Blundell *(below)* was lucky to escape a horrifying 195 mph crash with relatively minor injuries after his PacWest Reynard suffered brake failure.

maintained the upper hand when they pitted again under yellow on lap 61.

De Ferran, Ribeiro and Vasser elected not to make another pit stop at this juncture, and so, to the crowd's delight, two Brazilians headed the pack for the restart. Sadly, de Ferran's optimism turned to anguish on lap 80 when his Pennzoil Reynard ground to a halt on the back straightaway.

'We think we may have had a problem with the fuel pickup, because the fuel gauge still indicated we had five gallons left when the engine stalled,' related a disappointed de Ferran, who lost two laps in being towed back to the pits.

Divergent pit strategies enabled Moore to gain the lead for the first time. He was followed by Michael Andretti, Robby Gordon and Rahal as most of the other front-runners, including Ribeiro, Unser, Zanardi and Scott Pruett, chose to take on service.

Andretti's hopes went up in smoke, quite literally, when his Ford/Cosworth XD engine expired

soon afterward. Moore, though, led until being called in for his third pit stop, once again under caution, on lap 97. Crucially, Zanardi and Gordon both remained out on the track as all the other contenders grasped the opportunity to top up with fuel and fit fresh tires.

Yet another incident on the restart brought the yellows out once more on lap 102. This time, while Gordon's Walker Racing crew elected to gamble on being able to run the rest of the distance, Mo Nunn and Ganassi's team preferred to err on the side of caution by calling Zanardi into the pits for fuel and tires. The stop relegated Zanardi to 10th – last among those remaining on the lead lap.

The restart saw Ribeiro charge past Gordon in Turn One. Moore followed him through, and took over the lead in Turn Four when Ribeiro left his braking a fraction too late. With 25 laps remaining, Moore extended his margin over Ribeiro to around one second, but there it stayed as the Brazilian steadied himself in preparation for a final challenge.

ment turned to horror as Mark Blundell suffered a massive accident in Turn Four. The Englishman had moved up four places from the start and was running directly behind Hollywood/PacWest teammate Mauricio Gugelmin when his brake pedal went to the floor. Blundell pitched his Reynard to the left in a desperate attempt to scrub off speed, but to no avail. The car merely skimmed over the grass before careening back across the track and slamming headlong into the outside retaining wall at unabated speed.

Miraculously, Blundell clambered unaided from the wreckage, although he collapsed on the ground in pain just a few yards away.

'Frankly, I was lucky to get away with that one,' reflected Blundell, who was forced to sit out the next three races as he nursed three broken bones in his right foot and severe bruising. 'I want to say I have nothing but compliments for Reynard for the strength of their chassis. I think, under the circumstances, I made out quite well for a crash with such a heavy impact.'

The ensuing lengthy caution allowed Zanardi some respite from the attentions of Moore, who continued to shadow the leader once the race was restarted. Their duel was interrupted only briefly by pit stops under caution on lap 40. Zanardi

Michael C. Brown

Local boy makes good. Andre Ribeiro thrilled the enthusiastic Brazilian crowd with a home win. Third-place finisher Scott Pruett is about to receive a soaking from the joyful victor.

Michael C. Brown

It was never needed. On lap 116, Moore's engine abruptly lost power.

'It's too bad,' said Moore with remarkable composure. 'We were strong all day. I thought that this was our race – again! I guess we just don't have the luck we had last year [when he won 10 out of 12 Indy Lights races].'

A fine drive by Parker Johnstone, who ran as high as third in the Motorola Reynard-Honda, also came to an end at virtually the same time, due to a faulty fuel pickup.

The latest caution period briefly suspended a spectacular seven-car battle for second place between Unser, Gordon, Pruett, Rahal, Christian Fittipaldi (who had worked steadily into contention after starting from the back of the grid due to a crash during practice), Raul Boesel and Zanardi.

The crowd, however, was oblivious. All the fans were concerned about was the fact a Brazilian was in the lead!

Ribeiro appeared to have matters under control as he quickly moved away from Unser at the restart. But then the caution lights flashed on once again after Gordon, who had been fighting to keep pace with the leaders and at the same time conserve fuel, lost the unequal struggle and speared into the Turn One wall.

An action-filled afternoon there-

Local hero

South America has amassed a glorious history in auto racing. Argentina's Juan Manuel Fangio led the way by claiming a record five Formula 1 World Championship titles in the 1950s. Later, after a period of domination by European drivers in Formula 1, a string of supremely talented Brazilians sprung to the forefront of international competition. Emerson Fittipaldi earned a pair of titles in the early 1970s, while countrymen Nelson Piquet and Ayrton Senna continued the winning tradition into the 1980s and '90s.

Fittipaldi, after a brief hiatus from the sport in the early '80s, rekindled his competitive desires during a one-off drive in the Miami Grand Prix sports car event in 1984. He jumped into the Indy cars shortly afterward and rejuvenated his career with another long string of accomplishments including two Indianapolis 500 crowns and one PPG Indy Car World Series title.

Fittipaldi's feats uncovered a rich seam of previously untapped enthusiasm for Indy Car racing, which eventually translated into a fresh breed of young South American drivers seeking to emulate his achievements.

Andre Ribeiro is one such. In 1994, after three years in Europe, Ribeiro realized there were precious few opportunities to achieve his goal of graduating into Formula 1. Instead he set his sights on America. Ribeiro joined Steve Horne's Tasman Motorsports Group and competed in the burgeoning PPG-Firestone Indy Lights Championship. He won four races in his first year and easily claimed Rookie of the Year honors.

The next logical step, both for Tasman and Ribeiro, was the PPG Cup series. Initially the plan comprised the use of Lola chassis and Mercedes engines, although a subsequent approach from Honda led to a late switch both to the Japanese engines and Reynard chassis. The new combination was almost immediately successful, with Ribeiro claiming his maiden victory – from the pole – in the New England 200 at New Hampshire International Speedway. The Brazilian win, however, represented a new high point in his career.

'This is the first time that everyone – my family, friends, sponsors and the people working with me – have all been together for a race, so I cannot say how much this win means to me,' he said proudly. 'And to win here in Brazil is incredible.'

fore boiled down to a four-lap dash to the checkered flag. Ribeiro, despite feeling the pressure from a deliriously happy crowd, was up to the job. He even set his fastest lap of the race with just one lap remaining.

'One of the things I have learned in racing is that the best drivers learn how to control their emotions,' said an elated Ribeiro. 'I tell you, for me today it was tough. During the last yellow I caught a glimpse of the

crowd in the grandstands and they were all standing up and waving. I knew they were waving at me. It was very hard to keep my concentration because I was so excited as well.'

Unser was content to finish second in a car that truly didn't behave like a front-runner, while Pruett j-u-s-t held off a last-ditch passing attempt from Zanardi.

'I'm a little disappointed because we had a very good car,' said the impressive Italian. 'It was a fantastic feeling to lead the race, but things didn't quite work out for us today.'

The 'battle of the beers' fell in favor of Budweiser, thanks to the efforts of Christian Fittipaldi, who narrowly beat Rahal (Miller) and Boesel (Brahma) to the finish line. Vasser claimed eighth, having lost a lap shortly after halfway due to a tire mix-up in his pit. Rio-born Roberto Moreno posted a solid performance to finish ninth in Payton-Coyne's Data Control/Mi-Jack Lola-Ford.

Incredibly, the three remaining Brazilians – de Ferran, Emerson Fittipaldi and Marco Greco – also finished among the PPG Cup points after the unfortunate Bryan Herta was obliged to make an unscheduled stop to affix a loose wheel just three laps from the end of a most extraordinary race.

SNIPPETS

• The staff at **Penske Cars** and gearbox specialists Xtrac combined to produce a new, stronger selector mechanism following the failure experienced at Homestead by Paul Tracy. 'To be honest, the part that broke hadn't caused any problems in three years,' said Tracy's race engineer Nigel Beresford. 'Paul almost stalled the engine when he left the pits and then he jammed it into gear. It was really an induced problem, but the Xtrac guys really did a good job to beef up the parts, just to make sure.'

• Eight Brazilian drivers among the 27-car field ensured massive interest among the local fans and media. Much of it was centered upon national super-hero **Emerson Fittipaldi**, who was instrumental in

bringing the PPG Indy Car World Series to his homeland – and after whom the new 1.8-mile oval had been named. Fittipaldi, however, struggled for most of the weekend. He ran as high as 10th, whereupon his hopes of a strong finish were thwarted when he ran out of fuel and had to be towed back to the pits.

• Some drivers were using third gear for Turns One and Four, while others preferred fourth. 'Most of the time I am using third gear,' said **Alex Zanardi** (below)

on Thursday, 'because yesterday I made a bet with Jimmy [Vasser]. He said it would be fourth gear; I said it would be third. I won $5.'

• An oversight by the Scandia-Simon team led to fifth and sixth gears being transposed in **Marco Greco**'s (above) gearbox on Satur-

day morning. As a result, the Ford/Cosworth XB engine was 'buzzed' to what was believed to be a new record 15,800 rpms.

• A rumor began circulating in Brazil to the effect that **Carl Haas**, co-owner with actor Paul Newman of Newman/Haas Racing and for many years the North American distributor for Lola Cars, had concluded a deal for Swift Engineering to design and construct a new Indy car for 1997. No one at Swift Engineering was prepared to comment on the subject, while Haas himself said simply: 'I can't give you any quote on it.'

• **Scott Goodyear** (right) suffered a fractured vertebra and was unable to race after crashing heavily during practice on Saturday. The unfortunate Canadian

had just left the pits in Walker Racing's Valvoline DuraBlend Reynard-Ford, intent upon experimenting without the second element of the rear wing in a bid to improve his car's straight-line speed. He made it only as far as Turn Two before losing control. Goodyear spent the weekend in a local hospital before being airlifted (via Federal Express) to his home in Indiana.

Photos: Michael C. Brown

PPG INDY CAR WORLD SERIES • ROUND 2

RIO 400

EMERSON FITTIPALDI SPEEDWAY, AUTODROMO NELSON PIQUET, RIO DE JANEIRO, BRAZIL

MARCH 17, 133 laps – 247.912 miles (398.97 km)

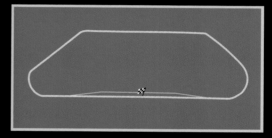

Place	Driver (Nat.)	No.	Team Sponsors Car-Engine	Tires	Q Speed	Q Time	Q Pos.	Laps	Time/Status	Ave.	Pts.
1	Andre Ribeiro (BR)	31	Tasman Motorsports LCI International Lola T96/00-Honda	FS	166.758	40.240s	3	133	2h 06m 08.100s	117.927	20
2	Al Unser Jr. (USA)	2	Marlboro Team Penske Penske PC25-Mercedes	GY	163.824	40.961s	12	133	2h 06m 10.241s	117.894	16
3	Scott Pruett (USA)	20	Patrick Racing Firestone Lola T96/00-Ford XD	FS	164.344	40.831s	10	133	2h 06m 10.832s	117.884	14
4	*Alex Zanardi (I)	4	Target/Chip Ganassi Racing Reynard 96I-Honda	FS	167.084	40.162s	1	133	2h 06m 10.867s	117.884	14
5	Christian Fittipaldi (BR)	11	Newman/Haas Kmart/Budweiser Lola T96/00-Ford XD	GY	no speed	no time	28	133	2h 06m 11.640s	117.872	10
6	Bobby Rahal (USA)	18	Team Rahal Miller Brewing Reynard 96I-Mercedes	GY	165.514	40.543s	6	133	2h 06m 12.152s	117.864	8
7	Raul Boesel (BR)	1	Brahma Sports Team Reynard 96I-Ford XD	GY	no speed	no time	26	133	2h 06m 13.210s	117.847	6
8	Jimmy Vasser (USA)	12	Target/Chip Ganassi Racing Reynard 96I-Honda	FS	166.952	40.194s	2	132	Running		5
9	Roberto Moreno (BR)	34	Payton/Coyne Data Control/Mi-Jack Lola T96/00-Ford XB	FS	163.282	41.097s	14	132	Running		4
10	Gil de Ferran (BR)	8	Hall Racing Pennzoil Special Reynard 96I-Honda	GY	165.208	40.618s	7	131	Running		3
11	Emerson Fittipaldi (BR)	9	Hogan Penske Marlboro Latin America Penske PC25-Mercedes	GY	163.439	41.058s	13	131	Running		2
12	Marco Greco (BR)	7	Scandia-Simon Int. Sports/Perry Ellis Lola T96/00-Ford XB	GY	156.380	42.911s	23	131	Running		1
13	Bryan Herta (USA)	28	Team Rahal Shell Reynard 96I-Mercedes	GY	163.083	41.147s	16	131	Running		
14	Adrian Fernandez (MEX)	32	Tasman Tecate Beer/Quaker State Oil Lola T96/00-Honda	FS	164.895	40.695s	8	126	Running		
15	Robby Gordon (USA)	5	Walker Valvoline/Cummins/Craftsman Reynard 96I-Ford XD	GY	163.931	40.934s	11	124	Accident		
16	Parker Johnstone (USA)	49	Brix Comptech Motorola Reynard 96I-Honda	FS	165.518	40.542s	5	118	Out of fuel		
17	Juan Manuel Fangio II (RA)	36	All American Racers Castrol Eagle Mk.V-Toyota	GY	152.249	44.075s	24	118	Running		
18	*Greg Moore (CDN)	99	Forsythe Player's Ltd./Indeck Reynard 96I-Mercedes	FS	165.525	40.540s	4	116	Electrical		
19	Paul Tracy (CDN)	3	Marlboro Team Penske Penske PC25-Mercedes	GY	no speed	no time	25	102	Accident		
20	Carlos Guerrero (MEX)	22	Scandia-Simon Herdez Lola T96/00-Ford XB	GY	161.834	41.465s	17	95	Engine		
21	*Eddie Lawson (USA)	10	Galles Racing Delco Electronics Lola T96/00-Mercedes	GY	161.568	41.533s	19	87	Drive-line		
22	Michael Andretti (USA)	6	Newman/Haas Kmart/Texaco Havoline Lola T96/00-Ford XD	GY	163.136	41.134s	15	86	Engine		
23	Stefan Johansson (S)	16	Bettenhausen Alumax Aluminum Reynard 96I-Mercedes	GY	159.385	42.102s	21	61	Overheating		
24	Hiro Matsushita (J)	19	Payton/Coyne Panasonic/Duskin Lola T96/00-Ford XB	FS	160.880	41.711s	20	53	Header		
25	Mauricio Gugelmin (BR)	17	PacWest Racing Group Hollywood Reynard 96I-Ford XB	GY	164.500	40.793s	9	49	Brakes		
26	*Jeff Krosnoff (USA)	25	Arciero-Wells Racing Reynard 96I-Toyota	FS	158.732	42.275s	22	37	Engine		
27	*Mark Blundell (GB)	21	PacWest Racing Group Hollywood/VISA Reynard 96I-Ford XB	GY	161.678	41.505s	18	10	Accident		
NS	Scott Goodyear (CDN)	15	Walker Valvoline DuraBlend Special Reynard 96I-Ford XB	GY	no speed	no time	–	–	Accident in practice		

*denotes Rookie driver

Caution flags: Laps 4–5, tow in/Fangio; laps 11–22, accident/Blundell; laps 40–44, accident/Fernandez; laps 61–63, tow in/E. Fittipaldi; laps 80–83, tow in/de Ferran; laps 86–89, blown engine/Andretti; laps 96–99, fire/Guerrero; laps 101–103, accident/Tracy and Greco; laps 116–118, Moore slow on course; laps 119–120, tow in/Johnstone; laps 124–128, accident/Gordon. **Total:** 11 for 47 laps.

Lap leaders: Alex Zanardi, 1–6 (6 laps); Andre Ribeiro, 7 (1 lap); Zanardi, 8–60 (53 laps); Gil de Ferran, 61–80 (20 laps); Greg Moore, 81–97 (17 laps); Zanardi, 98–102 (5 laps); Robby Gordon, 103–104 (2 laps); Moore, 105–115 (11 laps); Ribeiro, 116–133 (18 laps). **Totals:** Zanardi, 64 laps; Moore, 28 laps; de Ferran, 20 laps; Ribeiro, 19 laps; Gordon, 2 laps.

Fastest race lap: Gil de Ferran, 40.120s, 167.260 mph, on lap 79.

Championship positions: 1 Pruett, 26; **2** Vasser, 25; **3** Unser, 21; **4** Ribeiro, 20; **5** de Ferran, 19; **6** Rahal and C. Fittipaldi, 18; **8** Gordon and Zanardi, 14; **10** Moore and Boesel, 6; **12** Andretti and Moreno, 4; **14** Herta, 3; **15** Fernandez, E. Fittipaldi and Tracy, 2; **18** Goodyear and Greco, 1.

Official Information Technology Provider **EDS**

1 – VASSER

2 – PRUETT

3 – MOORE

SURF

Marlboro

Opposite page: The field snakes toward the first chicane on the opening lap with Vasser leading Pruett and Tracy.

Following pages: Pressured by Gil de Ferran, Greg Moore leans into a corner in his Player's Reynard. The Canadian rookie, making only the third start of his Indy Car career, scored his first podium finish.

ERS PARADISE

Any lingering doubts about the potency of Jimmy Vasser as a serious contender for the 1996 PPG Indy Car World Series were well and truly dispelled by his dominant performance at Bartercard IndyCar Australia. Vasser, winner of the opening round in Florida, first of all laid claim to his very first Indy Car pole – the first for Honda on a street course – then took full advantage by leading all but five laps in Chip Ganassi's Target Reynard-Honda.

'I gotta tell you, that's the best race car I've ever had,' he declared. 'I wanted to keep going it was so nice.'

The only minor hiccup for Vasser came during his first scheduled pit stop when a problem with the refueling system prevented him from taking on a full load of methanol. Vasser was obliged to make an extra stop. In the event, it mattered little. His nearest challenger, Scott Pruett, wasn't able to capitalize on the opportunity due to concerns over his Ford/Cosworth XD engine's fuel consumption. So Vasser was able to continue on his merry way.

Pruett was reasonably content after emerging with his third consecutive top-four finish for Firestone/Patrick Racing, while Greg Moore once again underlined his status as a sensationally promising rookie by securing his first Indy Car podium appearance in only his third start for Jerry Forsythe.

Pruett, after falling behind Vasser only in the final moments of qualifying, piled on the pressure by setting quick time in the final warmup session on Sunday morning. Vasser, realizing the importance of a good start, actually made rather too good a getaway at the first time of asking. The pole-sitter's advantage as he approached the stripe did not win the approval of IndyCar Starter Jim Swintal, who responded with a shake of the head as he steadfastly kept his green flags furled. The entire field would have to make one more complete lap before the race was under way.

This time Vasser timed his acceleration to perfection. Pruett dutifully tucked into second, while Paul Tracy muscled his Marlboro Penske-Mercedes ahead of Alex Zanardi in the second Target Reynard-Honda. The Newman/Haas Lola-Fords of Michael Andretti and Christian Fittipaldi maintained their third row starting positions, fifth and sixth, with Parker Johnstone (Motorola Reynard-Honda), Moore (Player's/Indeck Reynard-Mercedes) and the two

QUALIFYING

Jimmy Vasser had to overcome a tenacious challenge from Scott Pruett on the Gold Coast. Pruett, indeed, was fastest in every session except the crucial one, final qualifying, when Vasser nipped in front by a scant 0.017 seconds on his very last lap. Crew chief Grant Weaver was impressed.

'At the start of the session I went up to [race engineer Julian Robertson] and I said, "We need two seconds, Jules; where are we going to find two seconds?"' related Weaver. 'Jimmy's amazing. He just sucked it in and went for it.'

'We'd been having some problems with the brakes,' explained Vasser. 'I spun three times on Friday, but we made the car better and I figured now was the time to push a little harder. I went out for the last time with three minutes to go. My first flying lap was a [1m] 38.2 and that was taking it a little bit easy, so I knew there was more to come.'

Sure enough, with the seconds ticking away in the session, Vasser turned in his fastest lap, a new record 1m 35.265s, when it mattered most.

Pruett had to be content with second, while Alex Zanardi underlined the potency of Ganassi's Reynard/Honda/Firestone combination by moving up to third on the grid. Zanardi's effort was all the more impressive as he was plagued by all manner of dramas during practice, including a gearbox problem, a broken fuel pump and a leaking oil tank.

'The car is handling well,' said Zanardi. 'Probably there was more to come but it's very difficult with all the walls to get a good lap.'

Paul Tracy posted what he described as a 'banzai' lap to be comfortably fastest of the Goodyear contingent, with Michael Andretti, the previous track record holder, surprisingly more than 0.7 seconds slower.

'Realistically, that was one of those laps you hardly ever pull off,' said a wide-eyed Tracy. 'We're really about a second and a half away from the Firestones. They just have so much grip, it's like watching a slot car.'

Herta escapes fire

The most dramatic incident during yet another exciting Gold Coast IndyCarnival weekend occurred when a scheduled pit stop for Bryan Herta went drastically awry.

Herta, who had fought an ill-handling Shell/Team Rahal Reynard-Mercedes all weekend, had moved up from 17th place to seventh before making a routine stop during a full-course caution on lap 40.

'I came into the pits in good shape,' said Herta. 'I hit my marks in the pit and to be quite honest I'm not really sure what happened next. I thought I saw [right-front tire changer] Cole [Selva] wave me out. I started to go and the next thing I know I hear this loud whoosh! and then [general manager] Scott [Roembke] is yelling at me to get out [of the car].'

Herta braked quickly to a halt but the damage already had been done. The fuel hose had not been detached from the car and the initial, brief, throttle application was enough to tear the pit-side fuel tank from its mounting.

The resultant conflagration was doused with remarkable speed and agility by crew members both from his own team and the adjacent pit of teammate Bobby Rahal. Thankfully, no one was injured by the fire, although crewmen Larry Ellert and Mike Hofmeister were treated for minor abrasions.

Tasman Lola-Hondas of Adrian Fernandez and Andre Ribeiro completing the top 10.

Pruett pushed Vasser hard for the first few laps, before the leader began to inch away. No one else could keep pace with the two Firestone-shod cars. By lap 10, Tracy, still in third, had slipped more than six seconds adrift.

Then came the first full-course caution when Johnstone made a mistake and nosed into the tire wall at the Queensland Chicane. It was his second such incident of the day, having damaged the other front corner of his Motorola Reynard in a similar incident during the warmup.

'It was one of those situations where it was an inch too much, and I paid the price,' reflected Johnstone.

Right away after the restart, Gil de Ferran misjudged his attempt to pass Fernandez and rudely punted the Mexican into retirement. Andretti showed how a pass should be made as he relieved Zanardi of fourth place, although three laps later, having closed rapidly on Tracy, Andretti also made a blatant error as he locked up his brakes and rammed into the rear of the Penske at Conrad Jupiters Corner.

'I knew I was quicker than him out of the [preceding] quick chicane and I just went to the inside line to see what it was like,' claimed Andretti, who continued in third place as an irate Tracy remained stationary on the exit of the blind turn. 'I was gonna test the left side [of the road] and maybe have a look there the next time, but [my car] just bottomed out on the bumps, [the brakes] locked up and I just went into him. My fault. The worst part is I wasn't even going to try to pass him.'

Tracy wasn't impressed.

'We were just pacing ourselves and trying to save the car and everything was going great,' related the Canadian. 'Then all of a sudden Michael pulled a typical move. It was textbook Andretti 101; he locks up his brakes, goes into a corner totally out of control, hits me from behind and then keeps on going.'

Ironically, the incident also cost Andretti's teammate, Fittipaldi, dearly, as the Brazilian was forced to a complete halt in the melee. He resumed a lap down in 20th.

Everyone took the opportunity to make their first pit stops under the ensuing caution – everyone, that is, except Al Unser Jr., who had qualified poorly, 16th, but had already topped up with fuel during the earlier

Photos: Michael C. Brown

Beneficiaries of the attrition which hit the leaders included Christian Fittipaldi *(left)*, Eddie Lawson *(below far left)* and Stefan Johansson *(below left)*.

Bottom: Mauricio Gugelmin lifted his spirits (and those of his team) with a fine fourth place for PacWest.

caution. The strategy enabled Unser to jump up to third for the restart.

Pruett once again kept pace with Vasser for a few laps, although this time the leader turned in a string of fast times and quickly began to pull clear. By lap 34, the gap had grown to more than nine seconds.

'We had a fuel consumption problem all weekend,' explained Pruett. 'We ran hard the first 10 laps and then we had to be careful. We just had to conserve, conserve, conserve.'

Vasser appeared to be sailing away into the distance. But he, too, had a problem.

'I had made my stop and I was jammin',' said the laid-back Californian, 'and all of a sudden they told me I gotta come in [to the pits] again. I was pissed.'

Vasser made his second stop on lap 36, although excellent work by Grant Weaver and the crew enabled the #12 Target car to maintain second place. His cause was aided by the fact Unser pitted for fuel and tires on the same lap.

Pruett inherited a huge lead. And when the caution lights flashed on just four laps later, the opportunity to make a pit stop under yellow appeared to cement his advantage. However, the Patrick team's concerns over fuel consumption meant that he was unable to capitalize. According to the telemetry data, if Pruett stopped then, on lap 40, he would not have quite enough fuel to

make it to the finish. The call was made for Pruett to complete one more lap before taking on service.

'I was coming in,' said a rueful Pruett. 'At the last minute I could just hear someone yell, "Stay out, stay out, stay out!" '

The decision was costly. Everyone else, including Vasser, made their stops on lap 40. So when Pruett came in, alone, next time around, after one extra lap behind the pace car, he fell to fifth place in the lineup.

But all was not yet lost. Almost immediately after the restart, Unser made a rare error as he attempted to outbrake de Ferran into the Marlboro Chicane. Both cars slid sideways after making contact, and a close-following Moore was forced into evasive action. Pruett slipped past them all. Suddenly he was back up into second place!

A couple more brief caution periods served to ease most teams' concerns about fuel, whereupon Vasser

maintained a brisk pace to cement an accomplished victory.

'I was giving it all I had,' he said. 'I didn't want [Scott] to get around me, so I was driving with everything I had to stay in front.'

Vasser extended his margin to more than 12 seconds before easing off in the closing stages. His eventual margin of victory was 7.748 seconds. Moore followed in third.

'At the end I was really pushing hard to try and catch Scott,' said the Canadian, 'but it was kind of a Catch-22. As soon as I got close, my brakes started to go away. I was third, there was no one chasing me, so I just started cruising.'

Raul Boesel also drove a fine race for Barry Green's Brahma Sports Team, rising from 15th to fourth, only to be hit by the same refueling snafu that almost caught out Vasser. Boesel wasn't so lucky. His Reynard-Ford ran dry five laps from the finish.

Mauricio Gugelmin inherited the position after a truly gutsy performance aboard Bruce McCaw's Hollywood Reynard-Ford. The Brazilian had been worried all weekend by chronic brake problems and began the race with his confidence at a very low ebb. A spin on lap 24 didn't help his cause, dropping him from eighth to 19th, but his recovery to fourth place represented an excellent effort.

'I was so mad after the spin because I made a mistake,' admitted Gugelmin. 'I was lucky it was in a slow-speed corner because I didn't flat-spot the tires. But the team did a great job of calling the pit stops and getting me some positions free of charge. Fourth place, I'm pretty happy.'

De Ferran's eventful afternoon ended when he, too, ran out of fuel with less than two laps remaining. Christian Fittipaldi's excellent comeback therefore was rewarded with useful fifth-place points, with Stefan Johansson also performing yeoman work for Tony Bettenhausen's Alumax team by claiming sixth.

Rookie Eddie Lawson benefited similarly from the attrition in Rick Galles' Delco Electronics Lola-Mercedes, while Ribeiro endured a long afternoon, hobbled almost from the start by a broken, crucial, second gear. His persistence was repaid with eighth ahead of Unser, first of the lapped cars after his spin.

Michael C. Brown

SNIPPETS

Photos: Michael C. Brown

• The Firestone engineers were justifiably elated after claiming the top three places and leaving Goodyear firmly in their wheel tracks. 'We are going to remember Surfers Paradise for a long, long time,' said Bridgestone/Firestone motorsports manager **Al Speyer** *(above)*. 'This is what we came here for – to show the world we were as good on a street course as we have been on oval tracks.'

• **Adrian Fernandez** didn't have much luck in the race but he was happier in love after announcing his engagement to Australian girlfriend Tania Leigh. The couple met during a PR function prior to IndyCar Australia in 1993.

• The first sign of fuel gurgling into the vent hose during a pit stop is generally regarded as the signal that the car has been fully replenished. But **Jimmy Vasser**'s team was not alone in obtaining a false reading during the race. 'It seems to be a problem with the Reynards,' confided Vasser. 'Several cars had problems this afternoon and I was probably lucky not to run out of fuel, like a couple of the other guys did. We thought we had a full load of fuel on board, but obviously we didn't.'

• **Carlos Guerrero** looked set for a solid top-10 finish in the Scandia/Simon team's Herdez Lola before crashing just 17 laps from the finish. The Mexican also had damaged his car during qualifying on Friday.

• **Mark Blundell**, still extremely stiff and sore as a result of his crash in Rio, took the trouble to fly halfway around the world to Surfers Paradise, even though he was not fit enough to drive his PacWest Reynard. 'It was a hell of a long flight from London but it was definitely worth it to come here and show support for the team,' said the Englishman.

• **Christian Fittipaldi** was delighted to finish fifth, having overcome adversity for the third straight race.

'My tires were completely shot,' he said. 'I couldn't fight with the other guys but I'm happy because it puts us third in the championship. Hopefully I can have an uneventful run next time and perhaps I'll be able to finish in the top three. It'll be good to have a nice, quiet race for a change!'

• **Hiro Matsushita** *(below)* earned a feather in his cap during Saturday morning practice when he set 17th best time, ahead of such illustrious names as Al Unser Jr. and Emerson Fittipaldi. Sadly, a wiring loom problem prevented the Japanese driver from displaying his true mettle during final qualifying.

PPG INDY CAR WORLD SERIES • ROUND 3
BARTERCARD INDY CAR AUSTRALIA

SURFERS PARADISE STREET CIRCUIT, QUEENSLAND, AUSTRALIA

MARCH 31, 65 laps – 181.610 miles

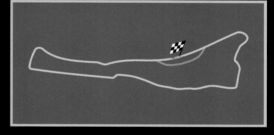

Place	Driver (Nat.)	No.	Team Sponsors Car-Engine	Tires	Q Speed	Q Time	Q Pos.	Laps	Time/Status	Ave.	Pts.
1	Jimmy Vasser (USA)	12	Target/Chip Ganassi Racing Reynard 96I-Honda	FS	105.583	1m 35.265s	1	65	2h 00m 46.856s	90.218	22
2	Scott Pruett (USA)	20	Patrick Racing Firestone Lola T96/00-Ford XD	FS	105.565	1m 35.282s	2	65	2h 00m 54.605s	90.122	16
3	*Greg Moore (CDN)	99	Forsythe Player's Ltd./Indeck Reynard 96I-Mercedes	FS	103.667	1m 37.026s	8	65	2h 00m 59.172s	90.065	14
4	Mauricio Gugelmin (BR)	17	PacWest Racing Group Hollywood Reynard 96I-Ford XB	GY	103.363	1m 37.311s	11	65	2h 01m 07.074s	89.967	12
5	Christian Fittipaldi (BR)	11	Newman/Haas Kmart/Budweiser Lola T96/00-Ford XD	GY	103.842	1m 36.863s	6	65	2h 01m 13.706s	89.885	10
6	Stefan Johansson (S)	16	Bettenhausen Alumax Aluminum Reynard 96I-Mercedes	GY	101.111	1m 39.479s	20	65	2h 01m 31.081s	89.671	8
7	*Eddie Lawson (USA)	10	Galles Racing Delco Electronics Lola T96/00-Mercedes	GY	99.929	1m 40.655s	22	65	2h 01m 53.246s	89.399	6
8	Andre Ribeiro (BR)	31	Tasman Motorsports LCI International Lola T96/00-Honda	FS	103.522	1m 37.162s	9	65	2h 02m 31.916s	88.929	5
9	Al Unser Jr. (USA)	2	Marlboro Team Penske Penske PC25-Mercedes	GY	102.439	1m 38.189s	16	64	Running		4
10	Hiro Matsushita (J)	19	Payton/Coyne Panasonic/Duskin Lola T96/00-Ford XB	FS	97.730	1m 42.921s	25	64	Running		3
11	Gil de Ferran (BR)	8	Hall Racing Pennzoil Special Reynard 96I-Honda	GY	103.349	1m 37.325s	12	63	Out of fuel		2
12	Roberto Moreno (BR)	34	Payton/Coyne Data Control/Mi-Jack Lola T96/00-Ford XB	FS	101.662	1m 38.940s	19	61	Running		1
13	Raul Boesel (BR)	1	Brahma Sports Team Reynard 96I-Ford XD	GY	102.837	1m 37.809s	15	60	Out of fuel		
14	Carlos Guerrero (MEX)	22	Scandia-Simon Herdez Lola T96/00-Ford XB	GY	100.105	1m 40.478s	21	48	Accident		
15	Juan Manuel Fangio II (RA)	36	All American Racers Castrol Eagle Mk.V-Toyota	GY	98.707	1m 41.902s	23	46	Out of fuel		
16	Robby Gordon (USA)	5	Walker Valvoline/Cummins/Craftsman Reynard 96I-Ford XD	GY	102.957	1m 37.695s	14	45	Electrical		
17	Bryan Herta (USA)	28	Team Rahal Shell Reynard 96I-Mercedes	GY	102.199	1m 38.420s	17	40	Pit fire		
18	*Jeff Krosnoff (USA)	25	Arciero-Wells Racing Reynard 96I-Toyota	FS	98.557	1m 42.056s	24	38	Accident		
19	Michael Andretti (USA)	6	Newman/Haas Kmart/Texaco Havoline Lola T96/00-Ford XD	GY	103.994	1m 36.721s	5	36	Electrical		
20	Bobby Rahal (USA)	18	Team Rahal Miller Brewing Reynard 96I-Mercedes	GY	103.013	1m 37.642s	13	33	Transmission		
21	*Alex Zanardi (I)	4	Target/Chip Ganassi Racing Reynard 96I-Honda	FS	105.269	1m 35.549s	3	31	Transmission		
22	Paul Tracy (CDN)	3	Marlboro Team Penske Penske PC25-Mercedes	GY	104.789	1m 35.987s	4	16	Accident		
23	Adrian Fernandez (MEX)	32	Tasman Tecate Beer/Quaker State Oil Lola T96/00-Honda	FS	103.486	1m 37.195s	10	14	Accident		
24	Parker Johnstone (USA)	49	Brix Comptech Motorola Reynard 96I-Honda	FS	103.670	1m 37.023s	7	10	Accident		
25	Emerson Fittipaldi (BR)	9	Hogan Penske Marlboro Latin America Penske PC25-Mercedes	GY	102.025	1m 38.588s	18	8	Engine		

* denotes Rookie driver

Caution flags: Lap 1, yellow start; laps 10–12, accident/Johnstone; laps 18–20, accident/Tracy; laps 39–41, accident/Krosnoff; laps 42–44, accident/Unser and de Ferran; lap 49, accident/Guerrero. **Total:** six for 14 laps.

Lap leaders: Jimmy Vasser, 1–36 (36 laps); Scott Pruett, 37–41 (5 laps); Vasser, 42–65 (24 laps). **Totals:** Vasser, 60 laps; Pruett, 5 laps.

Fastest race lap: Jimmy Vasser, 1m 37.854s, 102.790 mph, on lap 25.

Championship positions: 1 Vasser, 47; **2** Pruett, 42; **3** C. Fittipaldi, 28; **4** Ribeiro and Unser, 25; **6** de Ferran, 21; **7** Moore, 20; **8** Rahal, 18; **9** Gordon and Zanardi, 14; **11** Gugelmin, 12; **12** Johansson, 8; **13** Boesel and Lawson, 6; **15** Moreno, 5; **16** Andretti, 4; **17** Herta and Matsushita, 3; **19** Fernandez, E. Fittipaldi and Tracy, 2; **22** Goodyear and Greco, 1.

Official Information Technology Provider **EDS**

LONG BEACH

Michael C. Brown

Michael C. Brown

Gil de Ferran's luck was out once more. The Brazilian dominated the race until his Honda engine lost power in the closing laps, relegating him to fifth place.

Below: Paul Tracy chases Jimmy Vasser out of the hairpin in the early stages of the race. The Californian went on to record his third win from four starts.

The victory was all but in the bag. Less than five laps remained and Gil de Ferran appeared to be cruising toward a well-deserved success aboard Jim Hall's Pennzoil Reynard-Honda.

De Ferran had been the class of the field in the 22nd annual Toyota Grand Prix of Long Beach. He qualified squarely on the pole and gave up the lead only briefly while making his first routine pit stop. Cruelly, however, midway around lap 101, suddenly his Honda engine failed to respond as it had on every other occasion he had pinned his right foot to the pedal bulkhead. A hose-clamp securing the wastegate exhaust pipe had failed, robbing the engine of vital turbocharger boost pressure and the vast majority of its horsepower.

'This beats Rio as the biggest disappointment in my career,' said a distraught de Ferran. 'The car was running perfectly. I had no indication ahead of time.'

The engine continued to run cleanly, but without anything close to the same alacrity that had allowed de Ferran to leave the remainder of the field in his wake. It was only a matter of time before his hard-earned advantage was eroded. Sure enough, as de Ferran limped down Seaside Way, alongside the Convention Center, a surprised Jimmy Vasser simply motored on past.

'I couldn't believe it,' said Vasser, who had been more than eight seconds adrift before de Ferran hit trouble. 'I came around the corner and there's this yellow car going slow.'

Vasser rode his good fortune to take the checkered flag comfortably clear of Parker Johnstone, who enjoyed by far the most satisfying result of his career.

'I feel bad for Gil but we'll certainly take the win,' said Vasser. 'Lady Luck smiled on us today.'

Vasser's first slice of good fortune came on lap four, when the right-front tire on his Target Reynard came into stout contact with Paul Tracy's Marlboro Penske-Mercedes as the pair jostled for position into Turn One. Vasser, having lost out to Tracy under braking for the same corner on the opening lap, had taken advantage of his Honda's straightline speed, as well as a useful aerodynamic tow, and was attempting to redress the balance. Tracy, though, had the inside line covered. So Vasser tried the long way around, only for contact to be made as the Canadian squeezed his rival out toward the wall.

The impact was enough to momentarily rip the steering wheel from Vasser's grip, although fortunately no lasting damage was incurred by either car or driver.

Vasser wisely tucked in behind, and his patience was rewarded on lap 10 when Tracy locked up his brakes in the same location and performed a quick 360-degree spin. 'Thank you very much,' said Vasser as he scooted past into third place.

The leading duo, de Ferran and Vasser's teammate, Alex Zanardi, continued to run close together at the front of the field after maintaining their grid positions since the

QUALIFYING

A Honda-powered Reynard occupied pole position for the third time in four races, but unlike in Brazil and Australia, where Chip Ganassi's pair, Zanardi and Vasser, took the honors in their Firestone-tired Target cars, this time it was de Ferran, Pennzoil, Hall Racing and Goodyear which combined to scoop the $10,000 Marlboro Pole Award.

'We are using a similar setup to the one we ran in Australia and the car is working quite well,' said de Ferran after securing the provisional pole on Friday with a new track record of 52.283 seconds (109.482 mph). 'I kind of went berserk a little bit [on the last lap], but it paid off.

'Put it this way, I don't think I could have gone a lot faster – I don't even think there was another tenth [of a second] in the car.'

Sure enough, even with more rubber laid on the track for the final session on Saturday afternoon – and with several drivers inching closer to the ultimate pace – de Ferran eked out a mere 0.075. But it was enough for his second career Indy Car pole.

'I have to give a lot of credit to Goodyear,' he said. 'They came up with a new tire that is an improvement from what we had in Australia. They have a wealth of experience and they're putting a lot of effort into their tires.'

The usual frenzied activity in the closing minutes of the session was negated when Robby Gordon's Valvoline Reynard-Ford suffered a blown engine, spreading a liberal dose of lubricant on the racing surface. Nevertheless, Zanardi already had done enough to clinch the outside front row position ahead of Vasser.

Paul Tracy, whose progress on Friday was interrupted by a couple of minor altercations with the omnipresent walls, improved to fourth on the grid in the final session ahead of Scott Pruett and the impressive Parker Johnstone.

Below: Paul Tracy leads sparring partner Michael Andretti. The Canadian scored his first finish of the year but his former teammate was under fire from all sides.

Bottom: Christian Fittipaldi leaves Greg Moore in no doubt about his feelings after the pair's collision at Turn Seven. The Brazilian's angry outburst earned him a $5000 fine.

Jubilant Johnstone

Parker Johnstone just might have been the happiest man in Long Beach following his sensational second-place finish for Brix Comptech Racing. And justifiably so. In fact, Johnstone began the weekend with a stern warning from team co-owner Doug Peterson to the effect that due to severe financial constraints any further damage to the car could result in a drastically foreshortened season.

Furthermore, the team had been restructured following a dismal visit to Australia, with young Shad Huntley being newly promoted to the position of overall crew chief.

Johnstone refused to allow the distractions to affect his concentration. Instead he worked hard on perfecting the setup of his Motorola Reynard-Honda with race engineer Ed Nathman and technical supervisor Steve Conover.

'The problem that we suffer is that we don't have the resources to do much testing,' noted Johnstone. 'Everybody else has been pounding around all week since returning from Australia, and we have to do our testing over the race weekend.'

Progress, though, was swift. Johnstone, who qualified 14th on the provisional grid Friday, vaulted to sixth on Saturday afternoon. He then drove a thoughtful, consistent, error-free race and was rewarded by his best finish to date in an Indy car.

'I came to this track for the first time in 1979 to watch a Formula 1 race,' recalled an emotional Johnstone. 'I cut school and came with my childhood sweetheart – and now wife – Sharon. That race ignited me like no other single event to become a race car driver. Here we are, 17 years later, and I am sharing a podium with the Emperor of Long Beach, Al Unser Jr. [who finished third after winning six of the previous eight races on the California streets]. To be racing with the best in the world, this is what it's all about. For us, today, second is as good as a victory. This will be something to tell my grandchildren!'

start. Tracy's error allowed Scott Pruett to move into fourth with Pat Patrick's Firestone Lola-Ford/Cosworth. Tracy resumed fifth ahead of Johnstone in the Brix Comptech team's Motorola Reynard-Honda.

Greg Moore had overtaken Robby Gordon in the early stages, only to fall from seventh to 11th due to an electrical glitch on lap five. Moore, though, was soon charging back into the picture. Michael Andretti was his first victim, on lap nine, followed four laps later by the other Newman/Haas Lola-Ford of Christian Fittipaldi. Moore also found a way past Al Unser Jr.'s Penske-Mercedes before coming up once again behind Gordon, who this time refused to acquiesce quite so easily.

The leading positions remained unchanged until the end of lap 39, when de Ferran peeled into the pit lane for service. Zanardi took over in the lead, but only as far as Turn One where a misunderstanding with Bobby Rahal, who was about to be lapped, saw the Italian's day ended prematurely against the wall.

'I was following Bobby Rahal for two laps and the blue flags were out,'

related a disappointed Zanardi. 'He braked early and I thought he was going to let me by – but he didn't.'

At almost the same moment, Gordon's day took on a whole new perspective when his car lurched forward momentarily as he engaged first gear during an otherwise routine pit stop. The miscue was enough for the refueling nozzle to become jammed, causing some fuel to be spilled. A brief fire ensued. Gordon was forced to evacuate the car, although before long he was being rebuckled and sent on his way.

A full-course caution, due to Zanardi's crash, ensured that Gordon lost only one lap due to the pit lane melee, although as if he hadn't already experienced enough excitement for one day, Gordon later became entangled with both Team Rahal cars, in separate incidents, as well as outbraking himself and spending some time parked against the tire wall in Turn Six.

'I had a terrible day,' he summarized. 'It's one of the worst days I've had in a long time.'

De Ferran, meanwhile, resumed in the lead once everyone else had

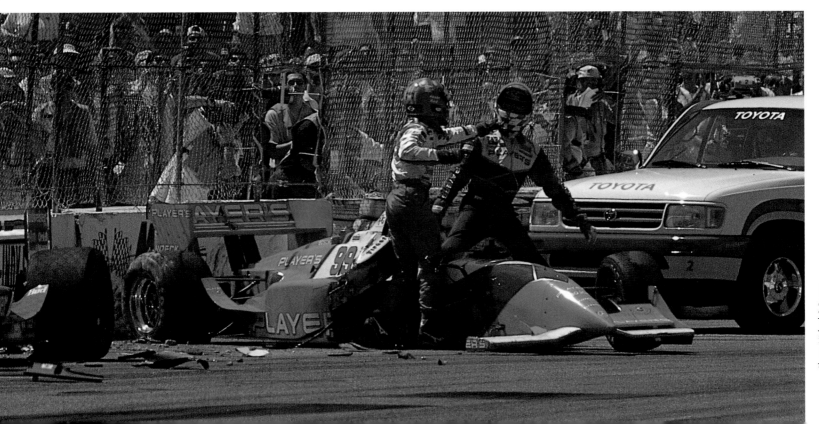

Michael C. Brown

An action-filled few days for Michael Andretti began during a test session at Michigan International Speedway on Wednesday, when he crashed heavily after experiencing an engine failure.

'It was a hard hit,' recounted Andretti at Long Beach on Friday, 'but I feel OK apart from a few bumps and bruises. It says a lot for the current chassis regulations.'

Andretti struggled to find a good balance for his car during practice in California, and it wasn't until switching to the spare chassis that he was able to eradicate a persistent oversteer characteristic. Andretti was more confident as he entered final qualifying, only for his efforts to be thwarted firstly by an uncooperative Paul Tracy and then by an oily track, after Robby Gordon suffered a massive engine failure in the closing minutes. Andretti, the erstwhile track record holder, qualified a disappointing 12th.

Later, during the regular drivers' meeting, Andretti was aggrieved when several rivals, including Tracy, with whom he had collided during the previous race in Australia, plus Mauricio Gugelmin and Robby Gordon, appeared clad in specially produced T-shirts bearing the legend 'Michael Andretti's Racing School for the Blind – If you can't beat 'em, hit 'em!'

Andretti was not amused.

'It's so childish,' he said. 'I apologized to Paul after I hit him in Australia but he refuses to accept my apology. Then, in qualifying this afternoon, he deliberately held me up – twice. It's uncalled for and totally unprofessional. He's like a big kid. It's about time he grew up.'

The following day, Andretti drew yet more criticism after being involved in collisions with both of the PacWest drivers, Gugelmin and Teo Fabi, who was standing in for the injured Mark Blundell. This time IndyCar Chief Steward Wally Dallenbach felt compelled to act, fining Andretti $5000 and placing him on probation for an indefinite period as a result of what were described as 'numerous driving infractions, including three separate incidents with PacWest cars and one with Paul Tracy.'

The Newman/Haas and PacWest teams also were assessed fines following a brief altercation between crew members in the pit lane after the race. The IndyCar coffers were bolstered by a further $5000, courtesy of Christian Fittipaldi, who earned his fine for remonstrating with Greg Moore after their incident in Turn Seven. Moore, to his immense credit, merely ignored his rival's protestations and made his way back to his pit.

---

taken the opportunity to make their first pit stops. Vasser ran second ahead of Tracy, who made up some time with a superfast stop by Jon Bouslog's crew. Next up were Johnstone, Pruett, Moore and Christian Fittipaldi.

The latter pair created the next drama. Fittipaldi first of all pulled off a brave maneuver by outbraking Moore into the tight Turn Eight hairpin on lap 46. Two laps later, when Fittipaldi was squeezed to the inside as he attempted to outbrake Pruett into Turn Six, Moore audaciously repassed the Brazilian on the outside line. It was a cleanly executed pass. Fittipaldi, however, carried a little extra momentum coming off the turn and briefly nosed ahead on the short run up to the left-handed Turn Seven. He then turned in to the corner, oblivious to the fact the nose of Moore's Reynard was already there. The result was predictable: The cars came into contact and careened heavily into the wall on the opposite side of the track.

The flow of the race was interrupted again as the cleanup crews went to work, although the status quo remained as de Ferran took off once more at the restart, pursued by Vasser and Tracy. Behind, Pruett displayed his determination by passing Johnstone neatly in Turn One. His satisfaction was short-lived. On lap 68, Pruett's Ford/Cosworth engine began to misfire. A broken coil was to blame. Pruett lost two laps in the pits while the offending item was replaced.

The yellow flags waved again on lap 73, as a result of Gordon's error in Turn Six. The hiatus was perfectly timed, allowing everyone to make their second, final pit stops under caution. The only change of position among the top 10 saw Adrian Fernandez move ahead of Andretti for sixth as the Newman/Haas team applied surgery to the Kmart/Texaco Lola's nose, which had been damaged in an earlier incident with the lapped PacWest Reynard of Teo Fabi.

As the pack approached Turn Eight in readiness for the restart, Andretti tangled with the other PacWest car of Mauricio Gugelmin, who, apart from an unscheduled pit stop on lap 57, had driven steadily and was running contentedly in eighth place.

Caution flags remained at the hairpin while Gugelmin's car was refired, but they were unheeded by Tracy, who seized his opportunity to pass Vasser on the following lap. The moment's inattentiveness cost him dear. Tracy fell to sixth after being assessed a mandatory stop-and-go penalty.

The remainder of the race was largely uneventful, save for de Ferran's cruel injustice. The only real excitement was provided by Tracy, who turned up the wick dramatically in a bid to gain a place on the podium. He passed Fernandez on lap 87, and in the closing 18 laps reduced the deficit to teammate Unser from more than 11 seconds to less than one.

'All in all, today was a great day for the team because we finally got some points and were able to go from 21st to 10th in the standings,' concluded Tracy after finishing fourth. 'My crew really worked hard. We had the fastest lap of the race. Now we've got some momentum and we're on our way.'

The hobbled de Ferran salvaged fifth place from his heartbreaking end to the day, while Fernandez took sixth despite never really being happy with the handling of his Tecate/Quaker State Lola-Honda. Andretti fell a lap off the ultimate pace, thanks to an extra pit stop in the closing stages, but he still finished clear of Roberto Moreno, who deservedly finished among the points for the third straight time in Payton/Coyne's Data Control/Mi-Jack Lola-Ford.

Vasser, meanwhile, had now won three races out of four, padding his PPG Cup lead to 23 points over Pruett, who benefited from the high attrition and regained 11th place after his delay in the pits.

'Obviously it wasn't really our race today,' noted Vasser. 'We didn't have the car to beat Gil. He was really hooked up and I was just trying to be consistent. I was just going to bring the car home and get the points [for second place]. Then I saw the yellow car slow down . . .

'They say in this business sometimes it's better to be lucky than good. Today we were lucky and good.'

SNIPPETS

• **Carl Haas** confirmed during the Long Beach weekend that locally based Swift Engineering will develop and build a new chassis in time for the 1997 season. The car will be designed by a team headed by Swift's David Bruns and Newman/Haas race engineers Peter Gibbons and Brian Lisles.

• Reigning Toyota Atlantic champion **Richie Hearn** (below) guided John Della Penna's ex-Hiro Matsushita Reynard-Ford 95I to a solid finish on his Indy Car debut. 'I did pretty much what I wanted to do,' said Hearn, 'which was to finish the race and finish in the top 10. It was a long race but I learned a lot. It was a great experience.'

• **Alex Zanardi** offered fulsome praise for his Target/Chip Ganassi teammate, Jimmy Vasser, after qualifying on the front row of the grid for the second time in four races. 'I have to be very pleased with my performance,' said Zanardi, 'and I have to thank Mr. Vasser because he has been a great help to me. I hope that doesn't stop!'

• Sponsorship from Pittsburgh-based corporation SmithKline Beecham, manufacturers of a vast range of consumer health-care products including Aquafresh toothpaste, Contac cold medicines and Tums anti-acids, enabled **Dennis Vitolo** to return to Indy Car competition at the wheel of Project Indy's ex-Scott Goodyear/Andre Ribeiro Reynard 95I. Andreas Leberle took delivery of the car only 10 days previously and his small team worked wonders to install a Ford/Cosworth engine in time. Vitolo seemed set to finish until the electrical system quit in the late stages.

• **Juan Manuel Fangio II**'s All American Racers Eagle-Toyota sported a bold new paint scheme (below center) for the team's home race, featuring the head of a Bald Eagle on the nose of the Castrol-backed car.

• Mexico's **Michel Jourdain** Jr. made a promising Indy Car debut with Team Scandia. The 19-year-old, who graduated via the Mexican Formula 2 Championship, replaced countryman Carlos Guerrero in the Herdez Lola-Ford (below) but promptly crashed during a midweek test at Firebird Raceway in Arizona. Jourdain bounced back well, however, and gradually picked up his pace until being forced out of the race due to a water leak.

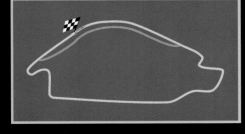

Photos: Michael C. Brown

TOYOTA GRAND PRIX OF LONG BEACH

LONG BEACH STREET CIRCUIT, CALIFORNIA

APRIL 14, 105 laps – 166.950 miles

Place	Driver (Nat.)	No.	Team Sponsors Car-Engine	Tires	Q Speed	Q Time	Q Pos.	Laps	Time/Status	Ave.	Pts.
1	Jimmy Vasser (USA)	12	Target/Chip Ganassi Racing Reynard 96I-Honda	FS	109.310	52.365s	3	105	1h 44m 02.363s	96.281	20
2	Parker Johnstone (USA)	49	Brix Comptech Motorola Reynard 96I-Honda	FS	108.715	52.651s	6	105	1h 44m 05.911s	96.228	16
3	Al Unser Jr. (USA)	2	Marlboro Team Penske Penske PC25-Mercedes	GY	108.417	52.796s	9	105	1h 44m 06.772s	96.213	14
4	Paul Tracy (CDN)	3	Marlboro Team Penske Penske PC25-Mercedes	GY	108.985	52.521s	4	105	1h 44m 07.363s	96.204	12
5	Gil de Ferran (BR)	8	Hall Racing Pennzoil Special Reynard 96I-Honda	GY	109.639	52.208s	1	105	1h 44m 34.436s	95.789	12
6	Adrian Fernandez (MEX)	32	Tasman Tecate Beer/Quaker State Lola T96/00-Honda	FS	108.214	52.895s	13	105	1h 44m 38.685s	95.724	8
7	Michael Andretti (USA)	6	Newman/Haas Kmart/Texaco Havoline Lola T96/00-Ford XD	GY	108.264	52.871s	12	104	Running		6
8	Roberto Moreno (BR)	34	Payton/Coyne Data Control/Mi-Jack Lola T96/00-Ford XB	FS	107.555	53.219s	18	104	Running		5
9	*Eddie Lawson (USA)	10	Galles Racing Delco Electronics Lola T96/00-Mercedes	GY	105.822	54.091s	24	104	Running		4
10	*Richie Hearn (USA)	44	Della Penna Ralph's/Food 4 Less Reynard 95I-Ford XB	GY	107.125	53.433s	22	103	Running		3
11	Scott Pruett (USA)	20	Patrick Racing Firestone Lola T96/00-Ford XD	FS	108.910	52.557s	5	103	Running		2
12	Bryan Herta (USA)	28	Team Rahal Shell Reynard 96I-Mercedes	GY	107.620	53.187s	17	100	Running		1
13	Robby Gordon (USA)	5	Walker Valvoline/Cummins/Craftsman Reynard 96I-Ford XD	GY	108.504	52.754s	7	98	Running		
14	Bobby Rahal (USA)	18	Team Rahal Miller Brewing Reynard 96I-Mercedes	GY	107.268	53.362s	21	98	Running		
15	Mauricio Gugelmin (BR)	17	PacWest Racing Group Hollywood Reynard 96I-Ford XB	GY	108.278	52.864s	11	97	Running		
16	Raul Boesel (BR)	1	Brahma Sports Team Reynard 96I-Ford XD	GY	107.947	53.026s	16	90	Running		
17	Dennis Vitolo (USA)	64	Project Indy Smith Klein Beecham Reynard 95I-Ford XB	GY	102.489	55.850s	28	87	Electrical		
18	Teo Fabi (I)	21	PacWest Racing Group Hollywood/VISA Reynard 96I-Ford XB	GY	107.551	53.221s	19	86	Clutch		
19	Stefan Johansson (S)	16	Bettenhausen Alumax Aluminum Reynard 96I-Mercedes	GY	107.306	53.343s	20	50	Engine		
20	Emerson Fittipaldi (BR)	9	Hogan Penske Marlboro Latin America Penske PC25-Mercedes	GY	108.168	52.917s	14	48	Accident		
21	Christian Fittipaldi (BR)	11	Newman/Haas Kmart/Budweiser Lola T96/00-Ford XD	GY	108.396	52.807s	10	47	Accident		
22	*Greg Moore (CDN)	99	Forsythe Player's Ltd./Indeck Reynard 96I-Mercedes	FS	108.490	52.761s	8	47	Accident		
23	*Michel Jourdain Jr. (MEX)	22	Scandia-Simon Herdez Lola T96/00-Ford XB	GY	102.566	55.808s	27	46	Radiator		
24	*Alex Zanardi (I)	4	Target/Chip Ganassi Racing Reynard 96I-Honda	FS	109.535	52.257s	2	39	Accident		
25	Juan Manuel Fangio II (RA)	36	All American Racers Castrol Eagle Mk.V-Toyota	GY	104.934	54.549s	26	29	Oil leak		
26	*Jeff Krosnoff (USA)	25	Arciero-Wells Racing Reynard 96I-Toyota	FS	106.151	53.923s	23	23	Engine		
27	Andre Ribeiro (BR)	31	Tasman Motorsports LCI International Lola T96/00-Honda	FS	108.100	52.951s	15	4	Accident		
28	Hiro Matsushita (J)	19	Payton/Coyne Panasonic/Duskin Lola T96/00-Ford XB	FS	105.332	54.343s	25	1	Electrical		

* denotes Rookie driver

Caution flags: Laps 39–44, accident/Zanardi and Rahal; laps 48–53, accident/C. Fittipaldi and Moore; laps 71–74, accident/Gordon. **Total:** three for 16 laps.

Lap leaders: Gil de Ferran, 1–38 (38 laps); Alex Zanardi, 39 (1 lap); de Ferran, 40–101 (62 laps); Jimmy Vasser, 102–105 (4 laps). **Totals:** de Ferran, 100 laps; Vasser, 4 laps; Zanardi, 1 lap.

Fastest race lap: Paul Tracy, 53.482s, 107.027 mph, on lap 99.

Championship positions: 1 Vasser, 67; **2** Pruett, 44; **3** Unser, 39; **4** de Ferran, 33; **5** C. Fittipaldi, 28; **6** Ribeiro, 25; **7** Moore, 20; **8** Rahal, 18; **9** Johnstone, 16; **10** Gordon, Zanardi and Tracy, 14; **13** Gugelmin, 12; **14** Fernandez, Lawson, Andretti and Moreno, 10; **18** Johansson, 8; **19** Boesel, 6; **20** Herta, 4; **21** Matsushita and Hearn, 3; **23** E. Fittipaldi, 2; **24** Goodyear and Greco, 1.

1 – ANDRETTI

2 – MOORE

3 – UNSER

Michael Andretti put a difficult start to the season firmly behind him with a commanding hometown victory.

Left: Andretti savors his success with sponsor Earl Segerdahl and team owners Paul Newman and Carl Haas.
Photos: Michael C. Brown

NAZARETH

QUALIFYING

Paul Tracy's speed on the tricky, downhill entrance to Turn Three was simply awesome, especially during qualifying when he dug deep into his reserves of bravery and became the first driver ever to lap beneath the 19-second barrier at Nazareth.

'It's all him,' praised race engineer Nigel Beresford after Tracy had clinched the pole at a sensational 18.874 seconds (190.737 mph). 'All you have to do is give him a semi-decent car and he does the rest. He's just incredibly committed and confident, especially on the entry to the corners, which is where he makes up most of his time compared to [Penske teammates] Emerson [Fittipaldi] and Al [Unser Jr.]. He's amazing.'

Tracy, typically, took the pole in his stride, although he did pause to dedicate his efforts to the memory of his uncle Jim, who died of cancer earlier in the week.

'Track conditions are perfect,' reflected Tracy. 'I knew after the first session yesterday we were capable of getting in the 18s. But we've still got some work to do. The trick is to keep the car consistent through the whole race.'

Fittipaldi was almost as impressive, annexing second on the grid and displaying his most competitive form since the corresponding race at Nazareth one year earlier. The veteran Brazilian was only a little over one-tenth slower at 18.998.

Unser, who is habitually more conservative in qualifying, nevertheless was delighted to record his fastest ever lap of the track, 19.274, which remained good for sixth on the 26-car grid.

Jimmy Vasser extended his string of top-three qualifying efforts, third in Chip Ganassi's Target Reynard-Honda, narrowly edging out Scott Pruett (Firestone Lola-Ford) and an optimistic Michael Andretti.

'Everything seems to be coming together,' said Andretti. 'We have a good race car – maybe the best package we've had this year. We should be tough in the race. We've got to come away from here with some points. At the minimum, we need to come away with a podium finish.'

Prophetic words.

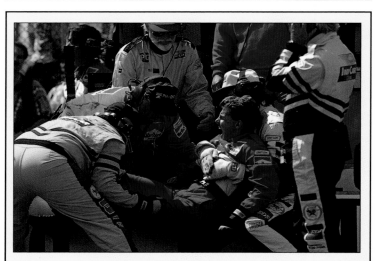

Photos: Michael C. Brown

Penske pit drama

Paul Tracy appeared to have a virtual lock on the Bosch Spark Plug Grand Prix. The 27-year-old Canadian was fastest in every official session and was evidently driving with supreme confidence. He fought off the advances of Emerson Fittipaldi during the early stages of the race and by one-quarter distance, 50 laps, had extended his lead to almost 4.5 seconds. Nothing, it seemed, could stop him from romping away to his 11th Indy Car victory.

But not everything was quite as it seemed.

'I blistered the right-side tires before the first stop, so we were getting into a little bit of trouble toward the end of the run,' related Tracy. 'When I saw some traffic up ahead, I realized I was going to have a tough time getting past, so I radioed in and said I was coming in [to the pits] next lap.

'I was fairly quick coming in, but with all the blisters on the tires and the lack of grip, I couldn't stop that well, and the last 10 feet I locked up the fronts and the [tire] stagger just drove the car over toward the wall.'

Tracy's Penske collected the left-rear tire changer, Matt Johnson, as well as air-jack operator John Whiteman and refueler Matt Burns, all of whom were bowled over against the pit wall.

The trio were treated at the IndyCar Medical Center and released with a variety of bumps, strains and bruises.

Tracy himself was deeply upset by the incident, which he acknowledged as his own fault.

'All I could think about was the look on Matt's face on the ground,' he said. 'It was horrible. I really couldn't get motivated after that because I felt so bad.

'I kept radioing in to [team manager] Chuck [Sprague], but nobody knew how Matt was, because he had been taken to the hospital. Eventually, one of the crew guys ran down to the medical center and he was propped up in a chair with a can of Coke and a bag of chips and he was watching the race on TV! Matt then got on the radio and told me he was OK and to get after it.'

A greatly relieved Tracy pressed hard after his final pit stop. His progress was hindered slightly by a broken front wing, but the resultant understeer was infinitely preferable to the oversteer characteristic which plagued many of his rivals in the closing stages. Consequently, Tracy managed to reclaim fifth place from Bobby Rahal.

'It's just disappointing,' concluded Tracy, 'because I made some mistakes today and we weren't able to capitalize on how good the car was.'

Right: Greg Moore burns rubber as he rejoins the race after a routine pit stop. The young Canadian snatched second place with a stunning late-race charge.

Al Unser Jr. *(below)* finished third for Penske to move into second place in the PPG Cup point standings.

Michael Andretti was facing intense and mounting pressure prior to the Bosch Spark Plug Grand Prix at Nazareth Speedway. Most obviously, his challenge for the PPG Indy Car World Series crown already was looking somewhat precarious, having amassed only 10 points from the season's first four races. And as if that wasn't bad enough, following the previous race at Long Beach, Andretti had been placed on probation by IndyCar Chief Steward Wally Dallenbach. Any further incidents might easily result in a substantial fine – or even a ban.

Andretti, however, bounced back in style, answering his critics with a magnificent drive to victory in front of an appreciative hometown crowd.

'This is the best medicine you can have,' said a delighted Andretti, who lives virtually within earshot of the quirky three-cornered oval. 'And to have it happen right here at home just makes it even more special.'

A thrilling climax to the 200-lap race saw rookie driver Greg Moore forge past two of the most accomplished oval track veterans, Emerson Fittipaldi and Al Unser Jr., inside the final eight laps. Unser,

meanwhile, not to be outdone, usurped Fittipaldi from third place with an equally audacious pass on the very last lap.

The Penskes, based in nearby Reading, Pa., have always performed well at Nazareth. Indeed the third member of Roger Penske's triumvirate, Paul Tracy, seemed to have the measure of the entire field until his #3 Marlboro Penske-Mercedes was involved in a frightening accident during a pit stop on lap 82.

Tracy, comfortably fastest throughout practice and qualifying, led the 26-car field toward the start at a fast pace before bolting confidently into the first corner ahead of Fittipaldi. Scott Pruett pounced around the outside of fellow second row qualifier Jimmy Vasser to take third place on the opening lap, pursued by old rivals Andretti and Unser. The rest of the top dozen contenders followed in grid order, with Robby Gordon next ahead of Bobby Rahal, Alex Zanardi, Christian Fittipaldi, Raul Boesel and Bryan Herta.

Tracy was obliged to run hard in order to stay ahead of the resurgent Fittipaldi, emerging from almost a year in the shadows to mount a strong challenge to the Canadian's dominance. Pruett couldn't quite match their pace but he was able to

maintain third ahead of Vasser and Andretti. The local hero was content to bide his time in the early stages.

'It's easy to be patient when you have a car like I did this weekend,' said Andretti.

The first incident occurred after 16 laps, when minor contact between Juan Manuel Fangio II and Hiro Matsushita led to a brief full-course caution. Both cars were able to continue.

Andretti took advantage of the restart to charge past Vasser. Eleven laps later he passed Pruett for third, then latched onto the tail of Fittipaldi, whom he relegated on lap 69.

Tracy by then was some eight seconds to the good, most of his advantage gained as he disposed of traffic with almost clinical efficiency. But then, as he prepared to make a routine pit stop, Tracy allowed his concentration to lapse for a moment. Before he knew it his car was sliding out of control. Three crew members were sent flying, although, miraculously, no one was seriously hurt.

'I really couldn't get motivated after that, because I felt so bad about what had happened,' said Tracy, who lost a lap while making two extra stops before service could be completed on his car by a hastily rearranged crew.

Andretti also survived a miscue in

the pits when he stalled the engine. 'Fortunately, I've been there before and my crew's been there, so they were ready for it,' said Andretti with a wry smile. 'They got me going real quick. I think we only lost around five seconds, so I was lucky.'

Fittipaldi wasn't immune either, experiencing a slight delay due to a broken air-jack. Andretti was therefore able to gain the lead once the stops had been completed. Unser took advantage of the various dramas to rise up to second, followed by the impressive Moore, who once again handled Jerry Forsythe's Player's/Indeck Reynard-Mercedes with considerable aplomb after qualifying conservatively in 13th. Fittipaldi rejoined in fourth.

Bobby Rahal, running fifth in his Miller Genuine Draft Reynard-Mercedes, was lapped by Andretti just after half-distance, but held onto the position until just two laps from the finish when he was repassed by the resurgent Tracy.

'I'm a little disappointed, especially after losing out on fifth place on the last lap,' related Rahal. 'I could run with the leaders in the middle of the race but I got a lap down. Playing catchup isn't what you want.'

Andretti made full use of his good fortune to extend a useful advantage

U.S. 500

The Vanderbilt Cup

North America's newest auto racing tradition, the U.S. 500, forged a link with the past due to a special recreation of the famous Vanderbilt Cup.

Instituted in 1904 by wealthy railroad magnate William K. Vanderbilt, who raced with some success in Europe and briefly held the world speed record by achieving 92.2 mph in a 90 hp Mercedes, the Vanderbilt Cup became one of the most sought-after prizes in the pioneer days of the sport.

Vanderbilt's aim was to raise the profile of the American automobile industry, which at the time lagged far behind its European counterparts.

The inaugural race, held over 10 laps of a 28.4-mile road course on Long Island, N.Y., attracted 18 starters and was won by the American, George Heath, in a French Panhard. Four years later, George Robertson's victory in a Locomobile represented the first time the trophy had been won aboard an American-built car.

The increasing hostilities in Europe effectively brought the event to its knees in 1916. Another 20 years would pass before it was reincarnated by the founder's nephew, George Vanderbilt. Once more, however, after victories in 1936 and 1937 by legendary Europeans Tazio Nuvolari and Bernd Rosemeyer, the onset of World War II signalled the end of the Vanderbilt Cup . . . until 1996, when the Vanderbilt family granted permission for a replica of the famous silver trophy to be commissioned, as was the original, from Tiffany & Co.

PPG INDY CAR WORLD SERIES • ROUND 6

1 – VASSER

2 – GUGELMIN

3 – MORENO

Photos: Michael C. Brown

Opposite: We're number one! Jimmy Vasser and the Target/Chip Ganassi Racing team enjoy their historic victory in the inaugural U.S. 500.

More than a dozen cars were damaged in a frightening pileup at the start.
Below left: Barry Green's crew work to repair Raul Boesel's Brahma Reynard.

Target/Chip Ganassi Racing dominated the story-lines before, during and after the inaugural U.S. 500 at Michigan International Speedway.

The vast majority of attention was focused upon PPG Cup leader Jimmy Vasser, who took the Marlboro Pole Award, was involved in a massive pileup prior to the start and then guided his backup Reynard-Honda to victory in the restarted 250-lap race. The combined feat earned him an impressive $1,157,750 in purse and contingency prizes as well as the glorious Vanderbilt Cup. Vasser also padded his lead in the PPG Cup standings to 36 points over distant eighth-place finisher Al Unser Jr.

Teammate Alex Zanardi joined in the spree by outpacing Vasser in the opening stages. The Italian bolted into a commanding lead before being halted by a rare – but massive – Honda engine failure.

Parker Johnstone and Andre Ribeiro, driving for the Brix Comptech and Tasman teams respectively, took turns out in front following Zanardi's demise, only to run into difficulties during the closing stages. Vasser, having taken much of the race to properly dial in his spare chassis, took full advantage by scoring his fourth win in just six starts.

'All the credit goes to my team,' said a grateful Vasser. 'At one point I fell back to fifth or sixth and I couldn't run in traffic at all. It was terrible. I could only do 225 [mph laps], and at the end of the race I could do 231, 232, no problem. These guys did a heck of a job. We worked on the car at every pit stop to make it a little bit better. We fought all day long and we came back and won.'

Brazil's Mauricio Gugelmin matched his career best by finishing second for Bruce McCaw's PacWest Racing Group, while countryman Roberto Moreno produced a sensational run to the final podium position – a first both for himself and the tightly budgeted Payton/Coyne team – in his Data Control Lola-Ford.

Morning rain gave way to clearing skies as the 1 p.m. start time approached, and when Paul Newman pulled the pace car onto pit road, right on schedule, the field appeared to be lined up cleanly in anticipation of the green flag. Vasser, Adrian Fernandez and Bryan Herta comprised the front rank of the three-by-three formation, but just as Vasser, the pole-sitter, began to accelerate through Turn Four,

QUALIFYING

Cool, breezy conditions and even a few snow flurries greeted the Indy Car teams during their extended weekend of practice and qualifying May 9–12. Not that Jimmy Vasser seemed to notice as he set a hot pace and extended his sequence of top-three starting positions by claiming the special $100,000 Marlboro Pole Award.

'All of our hard work last winter is beginning to pay off,' said Vasser. 'We did a lot of testing and we just have a really good combination with the Reynard chassis, Honda engine and Firestone tires.'

Adrian Fernandez also relied upon Honda horsepower and Firestone grip as he took advantage of the cool conditions on Saturday morning to turn a fastest-ever hot lap at M.I.S. of 235.608 mph with Steve Horne's Tecate Beer/Quaker State Lola-Honda. The likeable Mexican couldn't quite repeat it in qualifying, running on his own and without the benefit of a draft, but he did post a 231.108 to clinch a position in the middle of the front row.

'To be honest, we thought we could beat 232,' said Fernandez. '[But] conditions changed a little bit for qualifying. The sun came out just before we went out. It was a little bit warmer.'

Bryan Herta, first to run in the single-car lineup, interrupted the Honda parade by taking third on the grid with Team Rahal's Shell Reynard-Mercedes *(above)*.

'That was a great run for us,' said a delighted Herta. 'I told my engineer, Ray Leto, there's not one thing I can think of to make the car any quicker. I don't think I've ever said that before – even when I was on pole.'

Alex Zanardi, in Chip Ganassi's second Target Reynard-Honda, was joined on row two by Al Unser Jr., fastest of Roger Penske's Marlboro Penske-Mercedes contingent, and Andre Ribeiro in a second Tasman Lola-Honda.

suddenly his car veered to the right, apparently after making light contact with Fernandez. Chaos ensued. Vasser and Herta both slammed into the outside retaining wall. Fernandez spun into the infield. There was mayhem behind, too, as drivers searched desperately for a piece of unoccupied race track.

When the dust had settled, 10 cars were immobile. The red flags signified a stoppage even before the race had begun.

'I don't know what happened,' said Vasser. 'I was rolling on the power to come down to the green and I think I got hit in the rear or something and the car just turned around on me.'

The general consensus was that the front row trio had been bunched rather too closely together – and

that perhaps Vasser had paced the field a little too slowly. Vasser disagreed: 'That's my prerogative. I'm the pole-sitter and I get to set the speed. If someone wants to go faster, let them put it on pole and then they can set the pace!'

The cars of Vasser, Herta, Ribeiro, Fredrik Ekblom and Jeff Krosnoff were too badly damaged to continue. The respective crews instead hustled to race-prepare their backup machines – or, in Ekblom's case, install him in teammate Robby Gordon's backup Valvoline Reynard. All were present and correct when the grid was reformed almost an hour later. So, too, were Johnstone, Gugelmin, Raul Boesel, Eddie Lawson, Gil de Ferran, Emerson Fittipaldi and Juan Manuel Fangio II,

who reclaimed their grid positions after their teams had repaired varying degrees of damage.

Fernandez wasn't so fortunate. The Tasman team had been under the impression his car was repairable, but when their Lola finally was brought back to the pit lane, almost 40 minutes after the accident, it quickly became apparent that rather more work was required. Ed Daood and the crew simply ran out of time to prepare the Mexican's spare chassis.

The restart, thankfully, was clean. The Target cars of Vasser and Zanardi jumped immediately into the lead, followed by Unser, Emerson Fittipaldi and Scott Pruett, who began the race in an optimistic mood after topping the speed charts at 232.985 mph during the final warmup session on Saturday.

'This week has gone without a hitch,' said Pruett. 'We've run at the top of the track and the bottom and we've been able to run in traffic. The car and the tires have been terrific.'

The previously perceived lack of power from the Ford/Cosworth XD engine also appeared to have been overcome. But not the reliability problems. On lap three, Pruett's day ended amid a vast cloud of smoke, engine blown.

Ekblom's similar XD powerplant expired shortly afterward. Walker Racing teammate Gordon was out inside 100 laps with yet another failure. Ditto Raul Boesel's Brahma Sports Reynard-Ford XD. The Newman/Haas team had its own troubles, Michael Andretti ousted by a constant velocity joint failure and Christian Fittipaldi hobbled by a misfire in the closing stages.

Most of the leading contenders took the chance to make their first pit stops during the third caution of the afternoon, on lap 25. The PacWest team decided otherwise. Gugelmin and Mark Blundell thereby moved to the front of the pack from their midfield positions – and, to the surprise of many, stayed there for the remainder of the race. Moreno also eschewed a pit stop at that early juncture. He even enjoyed a couple of laps in the lead before settling back into a more comfortable pace.

Zanardi soon reemerged from the pack and proceeded to take control of the race. He was never headed between laps 37 and 163, despite making three routine pit stops, and seemed set for victory until his engine suffered a catastrophic failure in front of the pits on lap 175.

121

Above: There was mayhem at the start, triggered when the Reynard of pole-sitter Jimmy Vasser lurched to the right after making contact with Fernandez's Lola. With wreckage strewn across the track, out came the red flags.

Forced to rely on his backup car for the restart, Vasser was unable to match the pace of his teammate, Alex Zanardi, who is first to complete routine service *(left).* The Italian appeared to have victory within his grasp until his engine erupted in a plume of smoke *(right),* allowing Vasser to surge past. *Far right:* Andre Ribeiro looked set to inherit the win until he was obliged to make a late stop for fuel.

Astute pit strategy allowed the PacWest Reynards of Mauricio Gugelmin (leading) and Mark Blundell to get among the leaders. While the Brazilian took second place at the finish, Blundell had to settle for fifth after an unluckily timed stop.

Roberto Moreno gave the modestly funded Payton/Coyne team a tremendous boost with a superb run to third place.

his Miller Reynard-Mercedes. Team-mate Herta had moved into a challenging fourth before suffering an engine meltdown with 34 laps remaining.

Johnstone was another mechanical casualty. After his crew had repaired extensive damage from the initial carnage, the 1995 Marlboro 500 pole-sitter moved up rapidly from 16th on the grid and was leading just shy of the 400-mile mark when a miscalculation on the fuel saw him coast to a halt in Turn Four. The error cost Johnstone several laps. He was eventually sidelined by a gearbox failure.

The drama-filled race boasted spectacular wheel-to-wheel action virtually from start to finish, although high attrition saw only 11 of the 26 starters still running at the finish. Indeed, following Ribeiro's late problem, Vasser was assured a clear run to the finish with only Gugelmin remaining on the lead lap.

'In the beginning the car wasn't good in traffic,' noted Gugelmin, 'but we made some good calls in the pits and in the end we could run wide open all the way around. So I'm pretty pleased with second place.'

Moreno was equally delighted, especially after running laps in excess of 230 mph during the closing stages as he chased after Vasser. The hot pace enabled Moreno to pass the stricken Ribeiro for third place on the very last lap.

'It's a great result for this team,' declared an ecstatic Moreno. 'At the last pit stop I told my team to keep on the same set of tires because they were so good. They were amazed, but it was the right call. I was even catching Jimmy at the end. It's great to know that I can run that quick on a superspeedway.'

Ribeiro salvaged fourth ahead of Blundell, who ran as high as second before being obliged to make a pit stop under green with 43 laps remaining. The unfortunate Englishman fell a lap behind and was unable to overcome the deficit.

Vasser also lost a lap by pitting at the same time as Blundell. The championship leader, however, had Lady Luck on his side and managed to regain the lead lap by virtue of some perfectly timed cautions. 'That's the thing about this business,' declared Vasser. 'You just never give up.'

Several drivers were forced almost to a complete stop by a seemingly impenetrable smoke-screen. Incredibly, it was the first blow-up for Honda in a race since Rahal suffered a somewhat less conspicuous fate at Mid-Ohio in 1994.

'There are no words to describe how I feel,' said the crestfallen Zanardi. 'I suppose I'll receive one point for the most laps led, but it's a poor consolation for our effort. The car was perfect, simply beautiful. It's a shame.'

Greg Moore also was out of luck following another brilliant effort in his Player's Ltd./Indeck Reynard-Mercedes. The youngster qualified only 17th but moved rapidly into contention. He was among the top five by lap 24 and remained there

until his demise, due to yet another engine failure, on lap 225.

Along the way, Moore somehow survived an amazing spin coming off the banking in Turn Two as he attempted to hold off Ribeiro for second place on lap 161. 'It worked . . . for a while,' claimed Moore with a broad smile.

Ribeiro, despite being troubled from the restart by a malfunctioning telemetry system on his backup Lola, moved to the front as the race entered its final 100 miles. Ultimately, a worsening fuel pickup problem caused him to make an additional pit stop in the closing stages, costing him all hope of the win.

A promising day for Bobby Rahal ended when he brushed the wall on lap 130, damaging the suspension on

New restart procedure finds favor

IndyCar introduced a new double-file restart procedure for the U.S. 500. The system included a few minor glitches, which were ironed out for subsequent races, but by and large it received entirely positive reviews from fans, teams and drivers alike.

'I think it worked very well,' said Tasman Motorsports Group team owner Steve Horne. 'There are bound to be a few sticking points when a new procedure is introduced, but I think it makes the race more understandable for the fans, which is exactly what we should be doing.'

On ovals, the rule changes take effect the moment a full-course caution is instigated. As soon as the yellow caution lights are illuminated, the pit lane is closed (indicated at the pit entrance by a red flag with a black 'P') until the pace car has picked up the race leader. Next time around, only cars on the lead lap are allowed to make a pit stop. All others have to wait one more lap before being serviced.

Any competitor already committed to a pit stop when the flag is displayed has the option of proceeding through the pits without stopping or completing the stop and then taking up position at the back of the longest line prior to the restart.

If the car has passed the pit entry before the flag is displayed, the driver may complete the stop without penalty. Crossed green and yellow flags prior to the restart provide the signal for the field to split into two rows. Cars on the lead lap line up on the outside groove, with all remaining lapped traffic to the inside. (The alignment was switched for the following week's race on The Milwaukee Mile, where passing was deemed rather more difficult than on the M.I.S. superspeedway.)

There was some confusion during the U.S. 500 when Vasser, having lost a lap immediately prior to the caution on lap 209, after making a pit stop under green, was able to line up ahead of race leader Ribeiro at the restart. However, everyone else on the lead lap had made a pit stop during the caution, which effectively allowed Vasser to regain the lead lap. He was therefore permitted to take the restart on the outside groove, ahead of Ribeiro. Vasser maintained his position at the restart, and when the caution lights flashed on again a couple of laps later, he was able to go around to the rear of the main group.

Again, for subsequent races, the apparent anomaly was resolved by a rules clarification demanding that all cars on the lead lap but ahead of the race leader be waved past the pace car in order to take up position behind the line of cars on the lead lap. Thus, for the restart, the race leader is always at the head of the pack.

For road courses meanwhile, where a double-file restart often is impractical, the entire field is realigned in true race order behind the pace car.

SNIPPETS

• **Mark Blundell**, racing for the first time since Rio, was involved in the melee before the start and was fortunate to escape injury when his helmet was struck by an errant wheel. Despite a headache, Blundell produced a stunning drive and looked to be in contention for the win until losing a lap in the late stages.

• Sweden's **Fredrik Ekblom** (*below*) impressed the Walker team after being invited to drive the injured Scott Goodyear's #15 Valvoline DuraBlend Reynard. Ekblom, despite running the older, less powerful Ford/Cosworth XB engine, was consistently within one or two mph of team leader Robby Gordon's XD car.

• After displaying a good turn of speed during practice and qualifying, none of the three **Penskes** was nearly so competitive in the race. Nevertheless, they persevered to score valuable PPG Cup points by finishing seventh (Paul Tracy), eighth (Al Unser Jr.) and 10th (Emerson Fittipaldi).

• **Gil de Ferran**'s luck does not seem to improve. His hopes of qualifying on the pole were thwarted by a rare Honda engine failure during his warmup laps, while in the race (*above*) he lost five laps with a reprise of the broken hose clamp that cost him victory in Long Beach.

• **Arciero-Wells Racing** proudly unveiled a new sponsor for Jeff Krosnoff's Reynard-Toyota on the eve of the race, thanks to telecommunications giant MCI having made a commitment to the team after a lengthy courtship.

• 'The money's great and the Vanderbilt Cup is great,' said **Jimmy Vasser** after scooping the considerable spoils of victory, 'but the championship points, that's the number one thing. We don't go racing for just one race; we go racing for the season. All the hard work is for the ultimate goal, the PPG Cup championship, so the points we earned today, hands down, is the most important thing for me.'

• Veteran **Gary Bettenhausen** (*below*) was the only 'second weekend' qualifier, having been invited to drive one of his brother Tony's Alumax Penskes. His race ended against the wall on lap 80, apparently after sustaining a puncture.

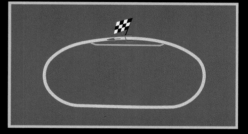

Photos: Michael C. Brown

PPG INDY CAR WORLD SERIES • ROUND 6
U.S. 500
MICHIGAN INTERNATIONAL SPEEDWAY, BROOKLYN, MICHIGAN
MAY 26, 250 laps – 500.000 miles

Place	Driver (Nat.)	No.	Team Sponsors Car-Engine	Tires	Q Speed	Q Time	Q Pos.	Laps	Time/Status	Ave.	Pts.
1	Jimmy Vasser (USA)	12	Target/Chip Ganassi Racing Reynard 96I-Honda	FS	232.025	31.031s	1	250	3h 11m 48.712s	156.403	21
2	Mauricio Gugelmin (BR)	17	PacWest Racing Group Hollywood Reynard 96I-Ford XB	GY	225.625	31.911s	14	250	3h 11m 59.707s	156.254	16
3	Roberto Moreno (BR)	34	Payton/Coyne Data Control Lola T96/00-Ford XB	FS	221.447	32.513s	20	249	Running		14
4	Andre Ribeiro (BR)	31	Tasman Motorsports LCI International Lola T96/00-Honda	FS	229.710	31.344s	6	249	Running		12
5	*Mark Blundell (GB)	21	PacWest Racing Group VISA Reynard 96I-Ford XB	GY	221.487	32.508s	19	249	Running		10
6	*Eddie Lawson (USA)	10	Galles Racing Delco Electronics Lola T96/00-Mercedes	GY	221.618	32.448s	18	249	Running		8
7	Paul Tracy (CDN)	3	Marlboro Team Penske Penske PC25-Mercedes	GY	228.980	31.444s	7	248	Running		6
8	Al Unser Jr. (USA)	2	Marlboro Team Penske Penske PC25-Mercedes	GY	230.213	31.275s	5	246	Running		5
9	Gil de Ferran (BR)	8	Hall Racing Pennzoil Special Reynard 96I-Honda	GY	225.957	31.864s	13	245	Running		4
10	Emerson Fittipaldi (BR)	9	Hogan Penske Marlboro Latin America Penske PC25-Mercedes	GY	227.816	31.604s	8	241	Running		3
11	Parker Johnstone (USA)	49	Brix Comptech Motorola Reynard 96I-Honda	FS	224.372	32.090s	16	236	Gearbox		2
12	Christian Fittipaldi (BR)	11	Newman/Haas Kmart/Budweiser Lola T96/00-Ford XD	GY	226.246	31.824s	12	232	Engine		1
13	*Greg Moore (CDN)	99	Forsythe Player's Ltd./Indeck Reynard 96I-Mercedes	FS	224.025	32.139s	17	225	Engine		
14	Hiro Matsushita (J)	19	Payton/Coyne Panasonic/Duskin Lola T96/00-Ford XB	FS	216.048	33.326s	25	217	Running		
15	Bryan Herta (USA)	28	Team Rahal Shell Reynard 96I-Mercedes	GY	230.774	31.199s	3	216	Engine		
16	Stefan Johansson (S)	16	Bettenhausen Alumax Aluminum Reynard 96I-Mercedes	GY	219.081	32.865s	22	195	Engine		
17	*Alex Zanardi (I)	4	Target/Chip Ganassi Racing Reynard 96I-Honda	FS	230.751	31.202s	4	175	Engine		1
18	*Jeff Krosnoff (USA)	25	Arciero-Wells Racing MCI Reynard 96I-Toyota	FS	217.341	33.128s	24	143	Engine		
19	Bobby Rahal (USA)	18	Team Rahal Miller Brewing Reynard 96I-Mercedes	GY	225.464	31.934s	15	130	Accident		
20	Robby Gordon (USA)	5	Walker Valvoline/Cummins/Craftsman Reynard 96I-Ford XD	GY	220.877	32.597s	21	94	Engine		
21	Gary Bettenhausen (USA)	26	Bettenhausen Alumax Aluminum Penske PC23-Mercedes	GY	208.607	34.515s	27	79	Accident		
22	Juan Manuel Fangio II (RA)	36	All American Racers Castrol Eagle Mk.V-Toyota	GY	209.476	34.371s	26	69	Engine		
23	Michael Andretti (USA)	6	Newman/Haas Kmart/Texaco Havoline Lola T96/00-Ford XD	GY	226.602	31.774s	11	67	c.v. joint		
24	Raul Boesel (BR)	1	Brahma Sports Team Reynard 96I-Ford XD	GY	227.561	31.640s	10	54	Electrical		
25	*Fredrik Ekblom (S)	15	Walker Valvoline DuraBlend Special Reynard 96I-Ford XD	GY	218.501	32.952s	23	11	Engine		
26	Scott Pruett (USA)	20	Patrick Racing Firestone Lola T96/00-Ford XD	FS	227.718	31.618s	9	3	Engine		
NS	Adrian Fernandez (MEX)	32	Tasman Tecate Beer/Quaker State Oil Lola T96/00-Honda	FS	231.108	31.154s	2	0	Did not start – accident		

* denotes Rookie driver

Caution flags: Laps 3–6, blown engine/Pruett; laps 11–14, blown engine/Ekblom; laps 23–27, debris; laps 47–53, tow/Fangio; laps 84–96, accident/Bettenhausen; laps 128–137, accident/Rahal; laps 147–152, fluid on course; laps 160–166, spin/Moore; laps 175–182, blown engine/Zanardi; laps 209–214, tow/Johnstone; laps 217–220, tow/Herta; laps 224–227, blown engine/Moore. **Total:** 12 for 78 laps.

Lap leaders: Jimmy Vasser, 1–18 (18 laps); Alex Zanardi, 19–25 (7 laps); Mauricio Gugelmin, 26–28 (3 laps); Roberto Moreno, 29–30 (2 laps); Gugelmin, 31–36 (6 laps); Zanardi, 37–163 (127 laps); Greg Moore, 164–165 (2 laps); Parker Johnstone, 166–199 (34 laps); Vasser, 200–206 (7 laps); Johnstone, 207 (1 lap); Andre Ribeiro, 208–240 (33 laps); Vasser, 241–250 (10 laps). **Totals:** Zanardi, 134 laps; Vasser and Johnstone, 35 laps; Ribeiro, 33 laps; Gugelmin, 9 laps; Moreno and Moore, 2 laps.

Fastest race lap: Alex Zanardi, 30.836s, 233.493 mph, on lap 18.

Championship positions: 1 Vasser, 94; 2 Unser, 58; 3 Pruett, 49; 4 Ribeiro, 38; 5 de Ferran, 37; 6 Moore, 36; 7 C. Fittipaldi, 33; 8 Andretti and Tracy, 31; 10 Gugelmin, 28; 11 Rahal, 26; 12 Moreno, 24; 13 Johnstone and Lawson, 18; 15 E. Fittipaldi, 17; 16 Zanardi, 15; 17 Gordon, 14; 18 Fernandez, 13; 19 Blundell, 10; 20 Johansson, 8; 21 Boesel and Herta, 6; 23 Matsushita and Hearn, 3; 25 Goodyear and Greco, 1.

Official Information Technology Provider **EDS**

MILWAUKEE

QUALIFYING

Paul Tracy set a hot pace throughout each of the practice sessions, his #3 Marlboro Penske-Mercedes turning significantly faster speeds on the new ultra-smooth surface than would ever have been possible prior to the winter repaving.

'The track is grippier and faster but it still has the same characteristics as before,' said Tracy. 'We have a mid-corner to exit push and it eats up the tires. We tried both [Goodyear compounds]. There's not much in it in lap times and they both go off after about 40 laps. After that you're hanging on. The problem is, we need to go 65 laps . . .'

Qualifying, sadly, was cancelled due to persistent rain, which began after only seven cars had completed their two-lap runs. The grid instead was determined according to practice times. Tracy duly started on the pole, although he was not awarded either the bonus PPG Cup point or an opportunity to draw a key for the end-of-season chance to win a brand-new Mercedes.

The Canadian was followed by a pair of Fittipaldis, with uncle Emerson again showing well on the short ovals to usurp nephew Christian, for whom third on the grid represented his best starting position since joining the Indy Car ranks in 1995.

Bryan Herta (above, on left, with Rahal) posted a fine effort, fourth fastest in Team Rahal's Shell Reynard-Mercedes, despite experiencing the same characteristics as pole-sitter Tracy.

'The car's got some mid-corner understeer and it's loose on exit – much the same as everyone, I think,' said Herta astutely. 'We're just trying to find a happy balance for the race. The track's still a bit slippery because the weather hasn't really been warm enough for the new surface to cure. I'm sure it'll be a lot faster next year.'

Michael Andretti lined up fifth, with Al Unser Jr. back in 11th after concentrating on running the harder of the two available Goodyear tires.

Capitalizing on the extra grip offered by Goodyear's 'option' compound tires, Michael Andretti *(above)* snatched victory from old rival Al Unser Jr. at a restart with six laps left to run.

Center left: Brazilian veteran Emerson Fittipaldi once again produced a strong performance on a short oval to take fourth place.

Quickest in practice, Paul Tracy *(left)* finished third after a spirited battle with Penske teammate Unser in the closing stages.

Moore the merrier

Greg Moore *(left)* was in no way concerned about having to start Jerry Forsythe's Player's/Indeck Reynard-Mercedes from 18th on the starting grid.

'I think you could see the Goodyears fade and the Firestone cars come on strong,' he forecast. 'The same thing happened at Nazareth.'

The youngster was right, to a degree, although in the closing stages he encountered just a little too much understeer, which prevented him from offering a serious challenge to the leaders. Nevertheless, when the caution lights came on with just 10 laps to go, team manager Tony Brunetti made a shrewd decision by calling Moore into the pits. Under the new restart procedure, Moore, even after his stop, would be able to retake his position immediately behind the other four cars on the lead lap.

'We knew we weren't going to pass those guys with a big understeer,' declared race engineer Steve Challis, 'so we put some more front wing in the car. It was a great call by Tony. Unfortunately, I blew it. I was a bit too aggressive and we gave him a bit too much [wing angle].'

Immediately after the restart, Moore suddenly found himself battling oversteer as the front of the car was virtually pinned to the pavement. He spun in Turn Four and was fortunate to avoid contact. Moore, though, gathered up the car to finish fifth.

'We had to go for it,' said Challis. 'We had a chance for the win. No guts, no glory.'

Tire choice proved to be a crucial factor in determining the outcome of the Miller 200. In the final analysis, Lady Luck also played a prominent role.

The most important decision regarding tires was, in effect, already beyond the control of the participants. It had been made prior to the start of the season, when the teams had to make a straight choice: Goodyear or Firestone, one or the other.

For the most part, the two corporate giants have proven remarkably closely matched since Firestone took on the established might of Goodyear by rejoining the Indy Car marketplace in 1995 after a 21-year sabbatical. Individual examples of one tire company holding a significant advantage over the other have been rare. Milwaukee, however, was one such, as all the leading contenders – with the notable exception of top rookie protagonist Greg Moore, who produced another stunning drive in Jerry Forsythe's Player's Ltd./Indeck Reynard-Mercedes – were equipped with Goodyear Eagles.

Michael Andretti joined the majority of Goodyear runners in choosing to concentrate upon the slightly softer 'option' compound, which offered a little more grip than the 'primary' tires. Al Unser Jr., by contrast, after sampling both alternatives during practice, reckoned his best chance of victory lay with the primary tires.

The two lifelong friends and rivals waged a spirited battle around the recently repaved Milwaukee Mile, and as the 200-lap race drew toward its conclusion it appeared that Unser's choice had been typically astute. He had taken control of the proceedings and held a clear lead in his familiar red-and-white Marlboro Penske-Mercedes. But a couple of late caution periods not only erased his advantage, they also changed the complexion of the race entirely. Andretti's sinister black Kmart/Texaco Havoline Lola-Ford/Cosworth was suddenly back in the picture.

Softer tires made the difference as Andretti produced a stunning outside-line pass to grasp the lead at a restart with just six laps remaining. Unser fought back, but Andretti wasn't to be denied. He held on to win by a scant 0.146 seconds.

'It was a fun race,' said a jubilant Andretti after breaking his tie with Unser by scoring the 32nd victory of his Indy Car career. 'It's always fun running with Al. We've had some great races in the past and I feel that I can run side by side with him all day if we have to.'

Blue sky and a comfortable temperature greeted contestants for the beginning of practice on Friday morning, and happily, after a passing rainstorm had washed out qualifying on Saturday afternoon, the picture-perfect conditions were restored on raceday.

Paul Tracy, starting from the pole, held off the advances of an on-form Emerson Fittipaldi at the first corner. Behind the two Penskes, a fast-starting Gil de Ferran moved smartly from sixth to third with a bold move around the outside line in Turns One and Two.

'I figured everybody would squeeze down to the inside,' reasoned de Ferran, correctly, 'and I just got by [Bryan] Herta on the outside.'

Andretti also passed Herta's Shell Reynard-Mercedes on the opening lap, diving through cleanly on the inside into Turn Three. Then, before any further shuffling could occur, the yellow lights flashed on as Parker Johnstone performed a quick pirouette in Turn Two. Miraculously, Johnstone managed to avoid contact with anything solid. In fact, he continued after losing only two positions!

The race was restarted with five laps in the books, and once again Tracy held station at the head of the field ahead of E. Fittipaldi, de Ferran and Christian Fittipaldi in the second Newman/Haas Lola-Ford. Teammate Andretti, uncharacteristically, lost a couple of positions at the green, although he was soon to regain his stride.

Andretti displaced de Ferran on lap 22, then set his sights on the two leaders, Tracy and the elder Fittipaldi. Inside 10 laps, Andretti had whittled a deficit of almost five seconds to less than a car length. Eight laps later, Andretti had passed both of the Penskes and was through into the lead.

Unser, meanwhile, after starting 11th, had moved to sixth by lap 21. He next passed de Ferran, whose Pennzoil Reynard-Honda had developed a dangerous loose condition, then became embroiled in a battle with the younger Fittipaldi for several laps before being able to assert his authority. Unser's decision to concentrate on the more durable Goodyear rubber was already beginning to pay off, as most of the other serious contenders began to slip and slide as their softer tires lost their original effectiveness.

'We made a big change on the car this morning, after the warmup, because the car went loose,' related

129

Photos: Michael C. Brown

Michael Andretti *(above)* and Al Unser Jr. *(below)* have been friends and/or rivals virtually since birth. The sons of two of Indy Car racing's most popular and enduring stars grew up, quite literally, in a racing environment as their respective families traveled around the race tracks of North America in the 1960s and '70s. There was never any real doubt they would one day follow in their fathers' footsteps – nor that they would be ultimately successful.

The first race, one could say, was won by Unser, who was born in April 1962, some six months before Andretti. Since then their lives have been inextricably linked, even though they pursued disparate routes during the formative stages of their careers.

Unser, like his father, Al, and uncle Bobby, who between them claimed seven Indianapolis 500 victories and five National Championships, raced primarily on dirt ovals, the traditional training ground for Indy Car drivers. Andretti, whose father, Mario, numbers the 1978 Formula 1 World Championship and three Indy Car titles among his many accomplishments, displayed his European heritage by establishing a background in road racing. Each was successful.

Unser made the switch from sprint cars to Super Vee in 1980. He won the championship for Rick Galles the following year and added the SCCA Can-Am title in 1983 before graduating into the Indy Car ranks. Andretti, after a grounding in Formula Ford, won the Super Vee title in 1981, one year after Unser, and the Formula Mondial/Atlantic crown in '83.

Whether by happenstance or design, the second-generation racers had rarely competed against each other prior to entering the Indy Car fray. That all changed in 1984, when Andretti joined Maury Kraines' Kraco Racing team on a full-time basis.

Unser enjoyed a one-year head-start on Andretti, yet they have remained amazingly closely matched in terms of career credits. Each finished second in the PPG Cup point standings during his third full season. Unser won the championship for the first time in 1990, while Andretti snared the title in 1991. Prior to the Miller 200 they had won 31 Indy Car races apiece, tied for most among active drivers on the PPG Cup circuit.

Tracy. 'I was expecting it to do that in the race, so we dialed in some push but it just stayed that way all race.'

Unser passed his teammate – none too easily, it must be said – on lap 55, then took advantage of a slightly faster scheduled pit stop to move ahead of Andretti once the first round of service had been completed.

The status quo remained through the middle stages, as Unser maintained a small but appreciable advantage over Andretti. Not too far behind, Tracy and E. Fittipaldi fought a protracted battle for third. C. Fittipaldi couldn't maintain the leaders' pace and slipped a lap behind Unser on lap 108, having fallen prey shortly beforehand to the impressive Moore. The young Canadian stood alone among the Firestone contingent in being able to come even close to the front-running pace. By this stage Scott Pruett's Patrick Lola-Ford and the two Tasman Lola-Hondas of Andre Ribeiro and Adrian Fernandez were already two laps behind.

The frantic pace was interrupted on lap 134, when Raul Boesel crashed his Brahma Sports Reynard-Ford in Turn Two after making contact with series debutant P.J. Jones' Castrol Eagle-Toyota. Boesel was uninjured but a lengthy caution ensued while the debris was cleared.

The leaders all took the opportunity to make their second pit stops under yellow. This time Andretti's crew was able to redress the balance, although it took Unser only a handful of laps to regain the advantage once the race was restarted just after three-quarter distance.

Andretti maintained a close pursuit until, shortly after the 175-lap mark, Unser suddenly extended his lead to almost five seconds.

'Traffic is what made the difference,' declared Andretti. 'On our own, I felt we were pretty even, but as soon as we got into traffic he'd pull away a bit.'

Then came Andretti's salvation – when Mark Blundell, who had been running 14th in his VISA Reynard, glanced the wall in Turn Three and brought out the caution flags one more time.

The restart came with just six laps remaining. This time Andretti held the trump card with his slightly softer rubber: 'I saw Al couldn't take it in [to Turn One] as deep as I could, and I saw his car give a little wiggle,' related Andretti. 'I knew I had to do it now or never. So I just went for it. My car stuck and his didn't.'

In a flash, Andretti went around Unser on the outside line. The crowd roared its approval. Tracy, coincidentally, swept past E. Fittipaldi in an identical maneuver, then attempted to do the same to Unser in Turn Three. Even louder roar! Unser rebuffed that challenge but wasn't able to hold off the Canadian into Turn One. Unser had fallen from first place to third inside little more than 20 seconds. But he wasn't done. Unser fought back in Turn Three, repassing Tracy with a similarly gutsy move on the outside. This was Indy Car racing at its absolute finest.

Unfortunately, the excitement waned as Moore lost control of his fifth-placed Reynard on the exit of Turn Four on lap 196. Incredibly, as with Johnstone at the start, Moore didn't hit a thing, but the yellows flashed on again. Moore calmly gathered his wits, drove through the pit lane and resumed in fifth, still a lap clear of C. Fittipaldi, who complained afterward of a general lack of grip.

Bobby Rahal (Miller Reynard-Mercedes) and Ribeiro (LCI International Lola-Honda) were a further two laps behind, followed by de Ferran, who never regained his early speed but did salvage ninth place by nipping past a disgruntled PPG Cup leader Jimmy Vasser on the very last lap.

'I can't believe what my car did,' said Vasser, who battled all weekend to find a consistent balance on his Target Reynard-Honda. 'I've been fighting push all weekend and it went loose!'

The focus of the record 48,000-strong crowd, however, was at the front of the field. After the yellow there was time for only a one-lap sprint to the finish. Unser tried his darnedest but Andretti was far too experienced to allow himself to be outfumbled at that stage in the proceedings. Tracy and Fittipaldi, whose Hogan Penske car developed oversteer in the closing stages, also were within 1.5 seconds as they sped beneath the checkered flag.

'If I was in Al's shoes, I'd be a little upset right now,' said Andretti magnanimously. 'He dominated the race and just got passed in the last couple of laps because of the yellow. He made the right choice in tires and his car was working better. It just came down to luck. But that's the way it goes. It was certainly a fun race and I'm pretty sure the crowd enjoyed it.'

Rapturous applause during the podium ceremony confirmed the veracity of Andretti's statement.

Unser, of course, desperately needed the maximum points to boost his own challenge for the PPG Cup championship, but as ever, he accepted his fate gracefully.

'We really worked hard as a team this weekend and it showed,' said Unser. 'The Marlboro car was the one to be in. Michael had the softer tires and they came in quicker than mine on the last restart, and that was the big difference. My car was set up for the long run. It wasn't set up for a trophy dash, and today's race came down to a trophy dash.'

SNIPPETS

• **Penske Cars** confirmed that John Travis, chief Indy Car design engineer at Lola for the past four years, had instead switched across to the Penske camp and would work in concert with Nigel Bennett and race/design engineers Nigel Beresford and Tom Brown on production of the 1997 chassis.

• Milwaukee Mile promoter **Carl Haas** (below) earned prodigious praise not only

for the quality of the resurfacing work but also the last-minute installation of a warmup lane on the inside of Turns One and Two. The work was recommended by several drivers following a test session less than two weeks prior to the race.

• An accident in the pit lane prior to the final warmup session on Sunday morning left Tasman Motorsports Group mechanic **Howard**

Minckler with two broken bones in his left leg and Honda engineer **Kazuhiko Imamura** with damaged ligaments in his right ankle.

• **Alex Zanardi** continued along his steep learning curve on the short ovals by crashing heavily in Turn Four immediately before commencing a qualifying run. 'We need to calm the Latin temperament a bit,' commented race engineer Morris Nunn. A sore Zanardi took to his backup car for the race and finished 13th, hindered throughout by oversteer.

• **The new restart rules**, introduced at the U.S. 500, were modified slightly for Milwaukee, with all unlapped cars lining up on the inside and lapped traffic on the outside. The change was made in anticipation of overtaking being more difficult on the one-mile oval than on the wide-open M.I.S. superspeedway.

'I must admit, I was one of the main opponents of

the new restart rule,' said race winner Michael Andretti, 'but I have to say it's working well. It certainly makes for a great show for the fans.'

• The newly renamed Team Scandia reappeared with its

pair of '96 Lolas (above) for **Eliseo Salazar** and **Michel Jourdain Jr.** 'It's good to be back and the car has potential,' said Salazar. 'I normally do quite well on the short ovals but I don't have enough time in the car, so I just have to learn.'

Photos: Michael C. Brown

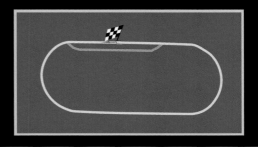

PPG INDY CAR WORLD SERIES • ROUND 7
MILLER 200

THE MILWAUKEE MILE
WISCONSIN STATE FAIR PARK, WEST ALLIS, WISCONSIN

JUNE 2, 200 laps – 200.000 miles

Place	Driver (Nat.)	No.	Team Sponsors Car-Engine	Tires	Q Speed	Q Time	Q Pos.	Laps	Time/Status	Ave.	Pts.
1	Michael Andretti (USA)	6	Newman/Haas Kmart/Texaco Havoline Lola T96/00-Ford XD	GY	173.102	20.797s	5	200	1h 33m 32.649s	128.282	20
2	Al Unser Jr. (USA)	2	Marlboro Team Penske Penske PC25-Mercedes	GY	171.201	21.028s	11	200	1h 33m 32.795s	128.278	17
3	Paul Tracy (CDN)	3	Marlboro Team Penske Penske PC25-Mercedes	GY	176.058	20.448s	1	200	1h 33m 33.589s	128.260	**14
4	Emerson Fittipaldi (BR)	9	Hogan Penske Marlboro Latin America Penske PC25-Mercedes	GY	174.456	20.636s	2	200	1h 33m 34.100s	128.249	12
5	*Greg Moore (CDN)	99	Forsythe Player's Ltd./Indeck Reynard 96I-Mercedes	FS	168.599	21.352s	18	200	1h 33m 57.229s	127.722	10
6	Christian Fittipaldi (BR)	11	Newman/Haas Kmart/Budweiser Lola T96/00-Ford XD	GY	173.903	20.701s	3	199	Running		8
7	Bobby Rahal (USA)	18	Team Rahal Miller Brewing Reynard 96I-Mercedes	GY	170.802	21.077s	13	197	Running		6
8	Andre Ribeiro (BR)	31	Tasman Motorsports LCI International Lola T96/00-Honda	FS	170.128	21.160s	16	197	Running		5
9	Gil de Ferran (BR)	8	Hall Racing Pennzoil Special Reynard 96I-Honda	GY	172.848	20.828s	6	196	Running		4
10	Jimmy Vasser (USA)	12	Target/Chip Ganassi Racing Reynard 96I-Honda	FS	170.687	21.091s	14	196	Running		3
11	Adrian Fernandez (MEX)	32	Tasman Tecate Beer/Quaker State Oil Lola T96/00-Honda	FS	169.245	21.271s	17	196	Running		2
12	Scott Pruett (USA)	20	Patrick Racing Firestone Lola T96/00-Ford XD	FS	170.355	21.132s	15	196	Running		1
13	*Alex Zanardi (I)	4	Target/Chip Ganassi Racing Reynard 96I-Honda	FS	172.523	20.867s	7	195	Running		
14	Bryan Herta (USA)	28	Team Rahal Shell Reynard 96I-Mercedes	GY	173.782	20.716s	4	195	Running		
15	Mauricio Gugelmin (BR)	17	PacWest Racing Group Hollywood Reynard 96I-Ford XB	GY	170.947	21.059s	12	194	Running		
16	Parker Johnstone (USA)	49	Brix Comptech Motorola Reynard 96I-Honda	FS	167.253	21.524s	19	193	Running		
17	Robby Gordon (USA)	5	Walker Valvoline/Cummins/Craftsman Reynard 96I-Ford XD	GY	171.510	20.990s	10	191	Running		
18	*Jeff Krosnoff (USA)	25	Arciero-Wells Racing MCI Reynard 96I-Toyota	FS	165.912	21.698s	22	191	Running		
19	Juan Manuel Fangio II (RA)	36	All American Racers Castrol Eagle Mk.V-Toyota	GY	165.483	21.755s	23	187	Running		
20	*Eddie Lawson (USA)	10	Galles Racing Delco Electronics Lola T96/00-Mercedes	GY	165.368	21.770s	25	184	Running		
21	Eliseo Salazar (RCH)	7	Team Scandia Cristal/Copec/Mobil 1 Lola T96/00-Ford XB	GY	164.195	21.925s	26	184	Running		
22	*Mark Blundell (GB)	21	PacWest Racing Group VISA Reynard 96I-Ford XB	GY	172.329	20.890s	9	183	Suspension		
23	*Michel Jourdain Jr. (MEX)	22	Team Scandia Herdez/Perry Ellis/Alta Lola T96/00-Ford XB	GY	165.466	21.757s	24	182	Running		
24	*P.J. Jones (USA)	98	All American Racers Castrol Eagle Mk.V-Toyota	GY	160.696	22.403s	27	181	Running		
25	Roberto Moreno (BR)	34	Payton/Coyne Data Control Lola T96/00-Ford XB	FS	166.409	21.633s	21	179	Running		
26	Raul Boesel (BR)	1	Brahma Sports Team Reynard 96I-Ford XD	GY	172.470	20.873s	8	128	Accident		
27	Stefan Johansson (S)	16	Bettenhausen Alumax Aluminum Reynard 96I-Mercedes	GY	166.840	21.578s	20	78	Handling		
28	Hiro Matsushita (J)	19	Payton/Coyne Panasonic/Duskin Lola T96/00-Ford XB	FS	160.031	22.496s	28	61	Exhaust		

* denotes Rookie driver   ** no point awarded for pole position

Caution flags: Laps 0–4, spin/Johnstone; laps 133–152, accident/Boesel; laps 188–193, accident/Blundell; laps 196–198, spin/Moore; lap 200, accident/Johnstone and Krosnoff. **Total:** five for 35 laps.

Lap leaders: Paul Tracy, 1–38 (38 laps); Michael Andretti, 39–71 (33 laps); Tracy, 72–76 (5 laps); Al Unser Jr., 77–137 (61 laps); Andretti, 138–157 (20 laps); Unser, 158–194 (37 laps); Andretti, 195–200 (6 laps). **Totals:** Unser, 98 laps; Andretti, 59 laps; Tracy, 43 laps.

Fastest race lap: Michael Andretti, 22.093s, 162.949 mph, on lap 196.

Championship positions: 1 Vasser, 97; **2** Unser, 75; **3** Andretti, 51; **4** Pruett, 50; **5** Moore, 46; **6** Tracy, 45; **7** Ribeiro, 43; **8** de Ferran and C. Fittipaldi, 41; **10** Rahal, 32; **11** E. Fittipaldi, 29; **12** Gugelmin, 28; **13** Moreno, 24; **14** Johnstone and Lawson, 18; **16** Zanardi and Fernandez, 15; **18** Gordon, 14; **19** Blundell, 10; **20** Johansson, 8; **21** Boesel and Herta, 6; **23** Matsushita and Hearn, 3; **25** Goodyear and Greco, 1.

Official Information Technology Provider **EDS**

DETROIT

Michael C. Brown

Left: With the Canadian bank of the Detroit River providing a scenic backdrop, Michael Andretti leads Newman/Haas teammate Christian Fittipaldi and the third-placed Pennzoil Reynard of Gil de Ferran in the closing stages of the race.

Stefan Johansson *(bottom)* brought Tony Bettenhausen's Alumax Reynard home in seventh place, having started 22nd.

For Christian Fittipaldi, one slight slip proved the difference between victory and defeat in an action-filled ITT Automotive Detroit Grand Prix. The 25-year-old Brazilian displayed brilliant car control as he led handsomely during the wet early stages in his Kmart/Budweiser Lola-Ford/Cosworth XD. He continued to hold the upper hand once the rain had moved away and the tricky Belle Isle Raceway had dried over. Nevertheless, the similar Kmart/Texaco Havoline car of Fittipaldi's more experienced Newman/Haas teammate, Michael Andretti, remained a constant shadow as the race drew toward its conclusion.

On lap 66, soon after the race had resumed following one of several full-course cautions, Fittipaldi left his braking just a fraction too late for Turn Four. Andretti required no more. As Fittipaldi skidded wide and lost momentum, Andretti, ever the opportunist, filled the gap before speeding away toward the checkered flag.

'I just really feel bad for Christian because he was doing a great job,' praised Andretti. 'He deserved to win this race. I was just trying to have patience and luckily the race came to me.'

Fittipaldi, to his credit, did not dwell on feeling sorry for himself: 'Michael beat me fair and square,' he said. 'We chose to run a full wet setup on the car, because it rained all morning, and when it was dry it was a little bit harder for me. But I'm still happy. It was a great day for the team.'

Also for Ford/Cosworth, Lola and Goodyear. By contrast, it was not a great day for Firestone, its tires totally outclassed in the wet conditions.

Saturday had provided an altogether different scenario, as the Firestones appeared to hold a significant advantage in the dry. But race-day dawned wet and miserable. The Belle Isle Raceway remained shrouded by low clouds.

Fittipaldi set the tone for the afternoon by posting comfortably the fastest time in the half-hour warmup. Bobby Rahal was next, a full second adrift, followed by Gil de Ferran, Mark Blundell and Robby Gordon. The two Castrol Eagle-Toyotas of Juan Fangio II and P.J. Jones were 13th and 16th, marking far and away their most competitive performance to date. All were making full use of their wet-weather Goodyear Eagles. The fastest Firestone runner was Greg Moore, a

QUALIFYING

The opening practice session Friday morning gave no hint of what was to come in qualifying. Gil de Ferran led the way in Jim Hall's Pennzoil Reynard-Honda, followed by Bobby Rahal's Miller Reynard-Mercedes, Christian Fittipaldi's Lola-Ford and the Valvoline Reynard-Ford of Robby Gordon. The fact that four different chassis–engine combinations were represented was not unusual, although it was interesting to note that all four were equipped with Goodyear tires.

Andre Ribeiro, however, having set the pace in the opening minutes, had missed the final half of the session after clipping a wall with Steve Horne's LCI International Lola-Honda. He bounced back magnificently in the afternoon and rewarded Steve Ragan and the crew – and Firestone – with the provisional pole.

Ribeiro again set the pace on Saturday morning, followed by Tasman teammate Adrian Fernandez. In the final session of qualifying, though, neither of the Tasman twins was able to match the effort of Scott Pruett *(above)*, who, in his 82nd Indy Car start, overcame all manner of problems to secure a sensational first-ever pole in Pat Patrick's Firestone Lola-Ford.

'It's a good rush, a real confidence builder,' said a delighted Pruett, who was only 15th on Friday after spinning off the track and then experiencing a brief fire in the pit lane. 'The car's been pretty good. We still need to make it a little bit better on the bumps – just like everybody else.'

Ribeiro felt the warmer weather conditions proved detrimental to his hopes of maintaining the pole: 'We had to adjust the car to the conditions,' he explained, 'and it took us a little too long to adjust the car perfectly. By then the tires were past their best.'

Fernandez maintained his recent improvement to take third on the grid, while Parker Johnstone also made an impressive leap to fourth in Brix Comptech Racing's Motorola Reynard-Honda. Alex Zanardi completed Firestone's sweep of the top five positions, with Christian Fittipaldi the fastest Goodyear runner in sixth.

Andretti's probation is lifted

Michael Andretti had good cause for celebration after winning in Detroit, especially as his third victory of the season elevated him to third place in the PPG Cup point standings, just four markers behind Al Unser Jr. and 27 adrift of series leader Jimmy Vasser.

'I approached this race knowing we needed to score some points for the championship,' said Andretti. 'When I was behind Christian, I was pretty much ready to settle for second place. He basically had me handled all weekend, so I feel bad that he didn't win the race. He deserved to. But we'll take it. Maybe my luck has changed.

'It's been an amazing few weeks,' he continued. 'First of all I won on my home track at Nazareth. Then I won on [team co-owner Carl Haas'] home track in Milwaukee. And now I've won on Kmart's home track. The only problem is we're running out of home-towns!'

Andretti's recent run of success, allied to his unblemished record, led IndyCar Chief Steward Wally Dallenbach to rescind the probation order that had been issued following a succession of incidents with other drivers during the early-season races.

'He's been an honor student since he has been on probation, so he is off the hook,' said Dallenbach, himself a former Indy Car winner.

Andretti, however, joked that he wasn't too concerned one way or the other: 'I've won three out of four races since I've been put on probation,' he said. 'Maybe I should stay on probation.'

Michael C. Brown

lowly 14th and more than four seconds slower than Fittipaldi.

The precipitation eased in time for the 1.15 p.m. start, but IndyCar Chief Steward Wally Dallenbach still made a wise decision by starting the 26-car field in single-file formation on the narrow, slippery, 2.1-mile course which is lined by cement walls.

Scott Pruett made full use of his first-ever pole position to lead Andre Ribeiro through the tricky Turn One. But the leading Goodyear contenders already were pushing forward. Fittipaldi led the way, from sixth on the grid, and by the end of the first lap he had elevated himself into second.

The Kmart/Budweiser car sliced easily past Pruett's similar Firestone Lola-Ford prior to Turn 13 on lap two, then began to establish a clear advantage at the front of the field.

De Ferran soon followed in second ahead of Paul Tracy, who jumped from 11th to third inside just three laps. Robby Gordon also was on the move, having overtaken Parker Johnstone and Michael Andretti in one bold maneuver at Turn 10. After slicing past Pruett into fourth, however, on lap four, Gordon left his braking just a little too late at the end of The Strand and plowed straight on into the tire wall. Exit the Valvoline Reynard-Ford.

Gordon's incident brought out the pace car for the first time. Fittipaldi's lead was immediately erased. But not for long. The Brazilian took off again at the restart, pulling away from de Ferran initially at the rate of a second per lap.

By lap 20, with the track beginning to dry, Fittipaldi's lead had stabilized at around six seconds. De Ferran, meanwhile, was coming under increasing pressure from Tracy and Andretti. The four leaders were more than 25 seconds clear of Al Unser Jr., who moved past Pruett on lap 18 and quickly pulled away.

Soon afterward, the caution flags waved once more after Moore's attempt to pass Ribeiro for ninth place resulted only in a synchronized spin at Turn 13.

The focus switched onto pit lane as all of the teams took the opportunity to change onto dry weather tires and replenish their cars with fuel. Fittipaldi resumed in the lead, while teammate Andretti moved up to second after taking advantage both of a super-fast stop by Tim Bumps' crew and a quick spin for de Ferran at the pit exit.

'When I came out of the pits I forgot to turn off the speed limiter,'

Michael C. Brown

Taking full advantage of his Kmart/Budweiser Lola's full wet setup, Christian Fittipaldi *(left)* drove superbly in the early stages of the race, when track conditions were at their most treacherous.

Adrian Fernandez *(right)* kept out of trouble to take fourth place with the Firestone-shod Tecate/Quaker State Lola. Al Unser Jr. was not so lucky.

Bottom: Mark Blundell, Raul Boesel and Eddie Lawson battle for the minor placings. The English rookie's fifth place equaled his best result to date.

admitted de Ferran sheepishly. 'When I realized what I'd done I pressed the button but I had too much throttle and too much power, so I spun around. It was a silly mistake.'

De Ferran rejoined in fourth ahead of Unser and Rahal. Then came Pruett and Fernandez, who remained best-placed among those on Firestone Firehawks.

Andretti soon recognized that on a Belle Isle track notorious for its lack of overtaking opportunities, he would be hard pressed to find a way past his teammate. So he settled into a comfortable rhythm and was content to circulate a few seconds in arrears. His pace was fast enough such that Tracy receded rapidly in his mirrors.

'My car was set up for the wet,' explained Tracy, 'and once the track dried out my handling deteriorated. It was all I could do to hold on.'

A couple of minor errors on lap 41 allowed both de Ferran and Rahal to slip past Tracy, who instead came under increasing pressure from Unser. But rather than allow his

teammate an easy passage, Tracy fought tooth and nail to retain his position. He even refused to cede any ground after sliding wide in Turn Three on lap 47, which enabled Unser to draw alongside prior to the following complex of corners. It was not a wise move. Unser, on the outside line, which was still damp, locked up his brakes before slithering directly across the nose of Tracy and into the tire wall. He was not amused.

'When the track started to dry out, my Marlboro car really came to life,' related Unser. 'I was turning faster lap times than Paul and I tried to pass him lap after lap. It's a shame to be racing that hard with anyone in the middle of the race, especially when you are teammates.'

Enough said.

Tracy's eventful afternoon continued as he banged wheels with Pruett in Turn Seven and came off worst, nosing into the tire wall and out of the race. The incident also served to tweak the front suspension on Pruett's Lola, causing him to make a mistake while pressuring de Ferran

for third place in the final stages. Pruett was a little more fortunate. He was able to extricate his car from the tire wall and salvage three PPG Cup points after finishing a disappointed 10th.

Rahal, too, found the barriers after straying fractionally off the line under braking for Turn 13.

'I feel bad,' said Rahal, 'because the team gave me a strong car and they deserve better than this. We had a golden opportunity to score some important points.'

The demise of Unser, Tracy and Rahal, allied to Pruett's delay, ensured de Ferran an easy passage to third place.

'I'm happy and not so happy,' said the Brazilian. 'I wasn't quite fast enough to catch the first two but I hope this is the beginning of a comeback in the championship.'

Fernandez also drove well in the difficult conditions to claim fourth in his Tecate/Quaker State Lola-Honda. The Mexican was followed by Blundell, Eddie Lawson and Stefan Johansson, all of whom made spectac-

ular progress from lowly grid positions. Raul Boesel, too, secured a welcome boost for Barry Green's Brahma Sports Team. But perhaps the most impressive effort came from P.J. Jones, who drove the wheels off his previously unheralded Eagle and was rewarded with the first-ever PPG Cup points for Toyota.

Championship leader Jimmy Vasser endured another tough weekend, as did Target/Chip Ganassi teammate Alex Zanardi. Both drivers crashed during practice, while veteran race engineer Morris Nunn had a minor fender-bender of his own on the streets of Detroit. The misery continued as the team's two pit-carts expired. 'Things can only get better,' sighed team manager Tom Anderson.

Newman/Haas, meanwhile, experienced the opposite extreme on the scale of emotion: 'It was a great race for us,' said Andretti after securing his third win from the last four races. 'Winning in Kmart's home town is great for us, and finishing one-two is even better.'

Jones earns points for Eagle

Rain, as the saying goes, is the great equalizer in auto racing. P.J. Jones certainly used the inclement conditions to his advantage during the early part of the race as he hauled Dan Gurney's Castrol Eagle-Toyota into a points-paying position for the very first time.

Like his father, 1963 Indianapolis 500 winner Parnelli Jones, P.J. cut his racing teeth on the dirt. Indeed he still races occasionally in the midget ranks, simply because he loves to experience the thrill of competition.

P.J.'s early years in the sport were fraught with incidents, courtesy of his devil-may-care attitude. More often than not, it seemed, Jones would ruefully survey a mangled race car, usually with a broad smile across his face.

But under the expert guidance of both his father and the equally widely respected Dan Gurney, Parnelli Jr. matured enormously after joining Gurney's All American Racers team in 1991. He readily accepted number two status alongside Juan Manuel Fangio II, nephew of the five-times Formula 1 World Champion, who had three years of seniority on the team, and selflessly helped Fangio, AAR and Toyota win two straight IMSA GTP championships.

Jones waited patiently for his opportunity to drive the Indy car. He made a low-key debut at Milwaukee, but as soon as the rain began to fall in Detroit, he knew that the disadvantage of his underpowered Toyota RV8A engine would be minimized. The 27-year-old could barely disguise his glee. Sure enough, Jones flew past teammate Fangio, Jeff Krosnoff and series leader Jimmy Vasser on the opening lap. He then picked off Eddie Lawson, Mauricio Gugelmin, Raul Boesel, Emerson Fittipaldi and Roberto Moreno inside the first 20 laps.

Of course, once the track dried, Jones and his Eagle-Toyota were no match for the more sophisticated opposition. But by then he had moved up among the points, there to stay for the remainder of the afternoon. And deservedly so.

SNIPPETS

• **Roberto Moreno** (above) produced another sterling performance aboard Dale Coyne and Walter Payton's Data Control Lola-Ford. The underrated Brazilian embarrassed many more well-funded teams by qualifying 13th, and ran as high as ninth before being hobbled by a broken exhaust system.

• The **Firestone** enclave was a hive of activity following the race morning warmup as technicians worked feverishly to provide extra grooves within the tread pattern in a vain bid to improve their wet tires' lamentable performance. Ironically, the tire-grooving tools were borrowed from Michelin, which was supplying rubber to the North American Touring Car Championship teams.

'We do know work is needed in this area,' admitted Bridgestone/Firestone Motorsports Manager Al Speyer, 'and we have been developing a new wet tire which will be introduced in the near future.'

• **Ford/Cosworth**'s third victory of the season was enough to take the lead – by 126 points to Honda's 125 – in the battle for the IndyCar Manufacturers Championship. Mercedes, still winless, trailed on 102. Reynard, incidentally, held a narrow lead over Lola, 132 to 130, in the Constructors Championship.

• The #22 **Herdez Lola-Ford** of Michel Jourdain Jr. was withdrawn by Team Scandia owner Andy Evans shortly before the start of the race.

• **Michael Andretti** spoke for all of the drivers when he made reference to the unforgiving nature of the Belle Isle circuit: 'The circuit is challenging but it's just way too bumpy,' said the race winner. 'It's ridiculous. It's way worse than it was last year. And there's just nowhere to pass. We like coming here, it's a great event, but something really needs to be done.'

• **Parker Johnstone** (right), who lost a lap to the field after being forced to make an extra pit stop in the early stages, was contemplating a busy week after the race in Detroit. After taking part in a test session at Mid-Ohio, he was scheduled to travel to his ranch in Redmond, Oregon, for his spring cattle roundup. 'There will be a group of us on horseback with four-legged canine help,' said Johnstone. 'It is kind of like Indy Car racing in that you all have to work together and trust each other and have confidence in each other when you're dealing with unpredictable 700-pound animals. If you are not careful, "understeer" takes on a whole different meaning.'

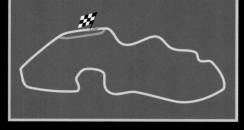

PPG INDY CAR WORLD SERIES • ROUND 8
ITT AUTOMOTIVE DETROIT GRAND PRIX

THE RACEWAY AT BELLE ISLE, DETROIT, MICHIGAN

JUNE 9, 72 laps – 151.200 miles

Place	Driver (Nat.)	No.	Team Sponsors Car-Engine	Tires	Q Speed	Q Time	Q Pos.	Laps	Time/Status	Ave.	Pts.
1	Michael Andretti (USA)	6	Newman/Haas Kmart/Texaco Havoline Lola T96/00-Ford XD	GY	104.057	1m 12.652s	9	72	2h 00m 44.451s	75.136	20
2	Christian Fittipaldi (BR)	11	Newman/Haas Kmart/Budweiser Lola T96/00-Ford XD	GY	104.342	1m 12.454s	6	72	2h 00m 46.860s	75.111	17
3	Gil de Ferran (BR)	8	Hall Racing Pennzoil Special Reynard 96I-Honda	GY	104.333	1m 12.460s	7	72	2h 00m 49.733s	75.081	14
4	Adrian Fernandez (MEX)	32	Tasman Tecate Beer/Quaker State Oil Lola T96/00-Honda	FS	104.913	1m 12.060s	3	72	2h 00m 52.879s	75.049	12
5	*Mark Blundell (GB)	21	PacWest Racing Group VISA Reynard 96I-Ford XB	GY	103.243	1m 13.225s	15	72	2h 00m 54.658s	75.030	10
6	*Eddie Lawson (USA)	10	Galles Racing Delco Electronics Lola T96/00-Mercedes	GY	100.711	1m 15.066s	23	72	2h 00m 55.081s	75.026	8
7	Stefan Johansson (S)	16	Bettenhausen Alumax Aluminum Reynard 96I-Mercedes	GY	100.764	1m 15.027s	22	72	2h 00m 55.318s	75.024	6
8	Raul Boesel (BR)	1	Brahma Sports Team Reynard 96I-Ford XD	GY	103.095	1m 13.330s	18	72	2h 00m 56.621s	75.010	5
9	*P.J. Jones (USA)	98	All American Racers Castrol Eagle Mk.V-Toyota	GY	99.285	1m 16.145s	25	72	2h 01m 01.291s	74.962	4
10	Scott Pruett (USA)	20	Patrick Racing Firestone Lola T96/00-Ford XD	FS	105.290	1m 11.802s	1	72	2h 01m 10.643s	74.865	4
11	*Alex Zanardi (I)	4	Target/Chip Ganassi Racing Reynard 96I-Honda	FS	104.413	1m 12.405s	5	71	Running		2
12	Jimmy Vasser (USA)	12	Target/Chip Ganassi Racing Reynard 96I-Honda	FS	102.981	1m 13.411s	20	71	Running		1
13	Bryan Herta (USA)	28	Team Rahal Shell Reynard 96I-Mercedes	GY	103.187	1m 13.265s	16	71	Running		
14	Parker Johnstone (USA)	49	Brix Comptech Motorola Reynard 96I-Honda	FS	104.449	1m 12.379s	4	71	Running		
15	*Jeff Krosnoff (USA)	25	Arciero-Wells Racing MCI Reynard 96I-Toyota	FS	102.051	1m 14.081s	21	71	Running		
16	Mauricio Gugelmin (BR)	17	PacWest Racing Group Hollywood Reynard 96I-Ford XB	GY	103.059	1m 13.356s	19	71	Running		
17	Paul Tracy (CDN)	3	Marlboro Team Penske Penske PC25-Mercedes	GY	103.660	1m 12.930s	11	71	Running		
18	Juan Manuel Fangio II (RA)	36	All American Racers Castrol Eagle Mk.V-Toyota	GY	100.245	1m 15.415s	24	71	Running		
19	Hiro Matsushita (J)	19	Payton/Coyne Panasonic/Duskin Lola T96/00-Ford XB	FS	98.667	1m 16.622s	26	69	Running		
20	*Greg Moore (CDN)	99	Forsythe Player's Ltd./Indeck Reynard 96I-Mercedes	FS	103.390	1m 13.121s	14	69	Running		
21	Bobby Rahal (USA)	18	Team Rahal Miller Brewing Reynard 96I-Mercedes	GY	104.238	1m 12.527s	8	60	Accident		
22	Al Unser Jr. (USA)	2	Marlboro Team Penske Penske PC25-Mercedes	GY	103.525	1m 13.026s	12	46	Accident		
23	Roberto Moreno (BR)	34	Payton/Coyne Data Control Lola T96/00-Ford XB	FS	103.492	1m 13.049s	13	41	Exhaust		
24	Andre Ribeiro (BR)	31	Tasman Motorsports LCI International Lola T96/00-Honda	FS	104.975	1m 12.017s	2	37	Accident		
25	Emerson Fittipaldi (BR)	9	Hogan Penske Marlboro Latin America Penske PC25-Mercedes	GY	103.107	1m 13.322s	17	36	Accident		
26	Robby Gordon (USA)	5	Walker Valvoline/Cummins/Craftsman Reynard 96I-Ford XD	GY	103.664	1m 12.928s	10	3	Accident		
NS	*Michel Jourdain Jr. (MEX)	22	Team Scandia Herdez/Perry Ellis/Alta Lola T96/00-Ford XB	GY	98.039	1m 17.112s	27	–	Withdrawn		

* denotes Rookie driver

Caution flags: Laps 4–8, accident/Gordon; laps 23–30, accident/Ribeiro and Moore; laps 47–51, accident/Unser; laps 61–64, accident/Rahal; lap 66, accident/Tracy; lap 69, accident/Pruett. **Total:** six for 24 laps.

Lap leaders: Scott Pruett, 1 (1 lap); Christian Fittipaldi, 2–65 (64 laps); Michael Andretti, 66–72 (7 laps). **Totals:** C. Fittipaldi, 64 laps; Andretti, 7 laps; Pruett, 1 lap.

Fastest race lap: Christian Fittipaldi, 1m 14.103s, 102.021 mph, on lap 57.

Championship positions: 1 Vasser, 98; 2 Unser, 75; 3 Andretti, 71; 4 C. Fittipaldi, 58; 5 de Ferran, 55; 6 Pruett, 54; 7 Moore, 46; 8 Tracy, 45; 9 Ribeiro, 43; 10 Rahal, 32; 11 E. Fittipaldi, 29; 12 Gugelmin, 28; 13 Fernandez, 27; 14 Lawson, 26; 15 Moreno, 24; 16 Blundell, 20; 17 Johnstone, 18; 18 Zanardi, 17; 19 Gordon and Johansson, 14; 21 Boesel, 11; 22 Herta, 6; 23 Jones, 4; 24 Matsushita and Hearn, 3; 26 Goodyear and Greco, 1.

PORTLAND

1 – ZANARDI

2 – DE FERRAN

3 – C. FITTIPALDI

Italian rookie Alex Zanardi notched up the first win of his Indy Car career for Target/Chip Ganassi Racing, having driven with the delicacy and restraint of a seasoned veteran when a sharp rain shower soaked the track.

Alex Zanardi, a revelation in his rookie season, scored a long overdue maiden Indy Car victory in the Budweiser/G.I. Joe's 200.

It was a textbook drive by the 29-year-old Italian. He took control of the race from the start, weathered some difficult conditions when a short, sharp shower of rain served to make the track extremely treacherous at the one-third point, then romped home for the Target/Chip Ganassi team's fifth win of the season.

'My car was running like a Stradivarius violin,' declared Zanardi after a flawless performance. 'Everything was perfect. I didn't have any particular problem, except on the last set of tires I had a slight vibration. I was hoping everything would stay together – and, fortunately for me, it did.'

Gil de Ferran, running a similar Reynard-Honda combination for Jim Hall's Pennzoil-backed team, couldn't match the flying Italian and had to settle for second. Christian Fittipaldi once again displayed his wet weather prowess by moving up rapidly when conditions were at their worst. The young Brazilian finished third aboard Newman/Haas Racing's Kmart/Budweiser Lola-Ford/Cosworth.

Zanardi made a clean start to lead the 28-car field into the tight Festival Curves for the first time. Target/Chip Ganassi teammate Jimmy Vasser attempted to follow Zanardi through on the inside of Scott Pruett's Firestone Lola-Ford at the first corner, but wisely decided not to press the issue. Pruett remained in second.

Vasser was pursued by Andre Ribeiro, who made a bold move inside Bryan Herta at the first turn. Paul Tracy took advantage of Herta being forced off line, slipping through into fifth as the pack of cars snaked toward the twisting infield section.

On lap two, Ribeiro tried his luck again under braking for the Festival. But Vasser closed the door firmly. 'Thank you very much,' chuckled Tracy as he nipped past the Brazilian into fourth place.

Tracy wasn't smiling a handful of laps later as he ran wide on the exit of Turn Two, perhaps caught out by a patch of oil. The Canadian, to his credit, sought no excuses: 'Basically I just drove straight off the track,' admitted Tracy, 'and once I got on the grass I couldn't stop and I couldn't turn, so I just went into the tire barrier.'

Tracy's Marlboro Penske-Mercedes was restarted by the IndyCar

QUALIFYING

Alex Zanardi had never before visited the 1.95-mile Portland International Raceway, yet he soon developed an affinity for the European-style road course following a steady diet earlier in the season of ovals and street circuits.

'It's certainly a nice place,' he said on Friday after setting third fastest time behind Vasser and Michael Andretti. 'The track is quite fast. I enjoy it. We are making some improvements on the car, so I'm sure we can go a bit faster tomorrow.'

Zanardi's biggest problem on the first day was a stomach ailment apparently caused by some barbecued chicken he ate for lunch. There were no lingering problems on Saturday, however, and Zanardi rose to the challenge in the final few minutes, eclipsing an early effort from Scott Pruett and securing the pole with a best lap of 59.893 seconds.

'I have to give a lot of credit to the team,' he said. 'We made a lot of changes and it was working extremely well. Of course, I am very 'appy to be on pole. If we can win the race tomorrow, fine, but if not, I'll be happy with some [championship] points.'

Yeah, right!

Pruett's hopes of claiming a second straight pole went up in smoke, quite literally, when his Ford/Cosworth XD engine let go.

Still, second represented a good effort.

Vasser overcame a worrisome case of vertigo, which had bothered him throughout the previous 10 days – a legacy of his crash during practice in Detroit – to qualify a fine third, while Bryan Herta was a delighted fourth on the grid.

'It feels good being the first Mercedes car and the first Goodyear car,' said Herta. 'We've got the car balanced well and I believe we have a good car for the race.'

Andre Ribeiro and Michael Andretti shared row three among a tightly packed field which boasted 15 cars within a second of Zanardi's pole-winning time.

Back in the groove

Emerson Fittipaldi's shift across to the new Hogan Penske team at the end of the 1995 season, effectively making way for Paul Tracy to return to Marlboro Team Penske after a one-year absence, was largely inconsequential. The veteran Brazilian's car was still run from the same shop in Reading, Pa. He worked with the same race engineer, Tom Brown, and crew chief Rick Rinaman. The only major differences – apart from a new paint scheme in deference to the newly formed Marlboro Latin America Team – were a new co-owner, Carl Hogan, who had split with Bobby Rahal at the end of the 1995 season, and a fresh team manager, Tom Wurtz, who joined from the Newman/Haas organization.

Prior to the Budweiser/G.I. Joe's 200, however, Fittipaldi's only tangible success had come at Nazareth and Milwaukee. His wealth of experience and smooth style have traditionally stood him in good stead on the one-mile ovals and, sure enough, Fittipaldi's #9 Penske was a serious contender on both occasions. He deserved better than a couple of fourth-place finishes, ousted in the late running at Nazareth by two bold maneuvers from the more youthful Al Unser Jr. and Greg Moore; and then falling from second to fourth at Milwaukee when his car developed a severe oversteer in the closing stages.

Portland was another track on which Fittipaldi had shone in the past. Nevertheless, after qualifying 16th, there was no real indication he was likely to trouble the leading contenders.

Fittipaldi, however, was among a half-dozen drivers to take on wet tires during his first pit stop, which coincided with a brief shower of rain. He took the opportunity to slice from 11th to fourth before pitting for slicks again just 10 laps later.

Suddenly, it seemed, the old inspiration had returned. He remained in contention until a gearbox oil line burst, which in turn caused the transmission to seize after 78 laps.

'My Hogan Penske team did a beautiful job to prepare the car for the race,' said Fittipaldi, 'and they dealt with the changing weather conditions in giving me three very quick pit stops. It's a shame [the gearbox broke] because we were competitive and had the chance to bring home a good finish and get some points.

'I had fun today,' he added with a smile.

Safety Team, but the car was retired shortly afterward when its rear suspension broke.

Pruett also had a problem in Turn Two on lap 10. He managed to regain control but not before losing several positions. Even before his half-spin, Pruett was not happy with his car, which had been hastily rebuilt following a crash during the final warmup session.

'There was something major wrong with the left rear corner,' he said. 'When I was under braking and turning right, the left rear would break loose.'

Pruett later endured another couple of spins before calling it a day. Herta also posted an early retirement, having been black-flagged due to an oil leak on Team Rahal's Shell Reynard-Mercedes. A cracked block was later discovered. Greg Moore, too, lasted no more than a dozen laps, having moved up to sixth before his similar Player's car succumbed to electrical problems.

Vasser took over in second place

but was unable to match the speed of teammate Zanardi. 'For some reason my fuel consumption was heavier than Alex's,' said Vasser. 'I had to turn back the mixture, and without the power I simply couldn't stay with him.'

Zanardi set a torrid pace at the front of the field. His advantage over Vasser stretched from a little over five seconds on lap 10 to more than 11 seconds by lap 20. Soon afterward, a menacing dark cloud that had been approaching steadily from the southwest began to deposit the first spots of rain. The initial precipitation caused no problems, but gradually the rain drops became larger, then more frequent. By lap 32, most of the circuit was wet. Nevertheless, it was apparent that the shower would soon pass. Brighter weather was on the way.

Coincidentally, it was almost time for the first round of pit stops. The teams and drivers were faced with a quandary: wet tires or slicks?

Ribeiro, who had moved up to

fourth in the LCI International Lola-Honda, was the first of the leaders to make a pit stop – on lap 31. He chose to remain on dry-weather tires. Tasman teammate Adrian Fernandez, running farther back in 12th, elected to switch to rain tires.

The bulk of the field pitted next time around. Again the reactions were mixed. Zanardi, Vasser and de Ferran stayed on slicks, despite the worsening conditions. Al Unser Jr., who had taken advantage of the early attrition to move into a challenging position, decided on wets. So did Robby Gordon, Emerson Fittipaldi, Mark Blundell and Stefan Johansson.

Christian Fittipaldi wisely stayed out on the track as long as possible, stretching his fuel and taking full advantage of the fact his tires were already at their optimum working temperature. Those drivers resuming after pit stops on fresh, cold rubber faced a far more difficult task.

'It was very, very slippery,' confirmed Zanardi, who slowed by as much as 15 seconds per lap when the track was at its wettest. 'The car was sliding all over the place. I just tried to be very, very careful.'

Vasser, Pruett and de Ferran were among those to fall foul of the decidedly tricky conditions. All rejoined, although Vasser, having stalled his engine, lost more than two laps before being retrieved by the IndyCar Safety Team. He eventually finished just out of the PPG Cup points in 13th.

'I'm disappointed, obviously,' said Vasser, 'because I had a good opportunity to pad my points lead and it didn't happen. But that's racing, right? There's nothing I can do about it now.'

Zanardi led by more than 16 seconds when Fittipaldi pulled onto pit lane on lap 35. By then the worst of the rain had passed and the track was beginning to dry. But wet tires still represented the optimal choice. Unser, indeed, carved into Zanardi's advantage, and on lap 39 he showed the effectiveness of his Goodyear rain tires by slicing easily past in Turn Nine.

But the balance of power was shifting. Two laps later, Zanardi regained the point when he flew past Unser under braking for the Festival Curves.

'I couldn't believe how quickly I caught him,' said Zanardi. 'I almost hit him in the rear because he braked so early.'

Unser was the last of those who

Zanardi on target

Alex Zanardi made a favorable impression from virtually the first moment he became involved in the PPG Indy Car World Series. Team owner Chip Ganassi, of course, was delighted with the pace showed by Zanardi during his initial test in Florida, but he was equally taken by the 29-year-old Italian's cheerful approach and dedication to the job at hand.

'Anytime you bring someone new on board to any team situation, you are looking for somebody that is going to mix well with the people you already have,' said Ganassi. 'I think we could have really had our pick of about probably 20 drivers out there, and a large part of that was finding somebody that would fit well with [teammate] Jimmy [Vasser]. Alex was the perfect choice.'

Zanardi, like so many other champions, began his career in karting. Success came quickly, and when he graduated directly into the Italian Formula 3 Championship in 1988, it seemed only a matter of time before he would continue his winning ways. He finished second in the 1990 championship – and claimed pole in the prestigious race in Monaco – then moved up to Formula 3000 for 1991. He placed first or second in six of the 10 races, but four retirements proved crucial in determining the championship, which he lost by a slender margin to Christian Fittipaldi.

Zanardi was invited to contest the final three Grand Prix races of the season for Eddie Jordan's team, but for one reason or another his Formula 1 career failed to take off. It didn't help that he was seriously injured in a crash during practice at Spa-Francorchamps in 1993.

Now his career is back on track. Indeed, in only his second race for the Target/Chip Ganassi team, Zanardi started on the pole and looked to be on course for victory until his crew made a mistake on its pit strategy. Instead he ended up fourth. Later, in the U.S. 500, Zanardi again was in control before being halted by a massive engine failure.

In Portland there was nothing to stand in his way. Even a brief shower of rain, which caught out several rivals, including his own teammate, failed to interrupt his inexorable progress. The victory was both popular and well-deserved.

'It feels like a dream,' said the soft-spoken, impeccably mannered Zanardi. 'Fortunately, it's not.'

Overleaf: Owner-driver Bobby Rahal overcame handling difficulties to take sixth place with the Miller Reynard, having qualified in a lowly 18th place.

Parker Johnstone *(right)* boosted his points tally with fifth place after a typically tenacious drive at the wheel of the Motorola Reynard-Honda.

Below: Christian Fittipaldi leads his Newman/Haas teammate Michael Andretti. The Brazilian once again demonstrated his skill in the wet on his way to his second podium finish in succession.

chose wet tires to make an extra stop for slicks, on lap 43. He rejoined in sixth.

Zanardi assumed a huge lead of over 20 seconds over de Ferran, who was followed closely by C. Fittipaldi. Bobby Rahal had used all of his experience in the wet to move quietly from 11th to fourth in his Miller Reynard-Mercedes – a fine effort – while Ribeiro held a lonely fifth.

Equally impressive was the oldest driver in the field, Emerson Fittipaldi, who posted a string of fast laps as he gradually worked his way closer to Unser, who in turn was closing on Ribeiro, who was also edging near to Rahal.

Things were just beginning to get interesting when Michel Jourdain Jr. beached Team Scandia's Herdez Lola-Ford in the gravel trap at the Festival Curves, bringing out the pace car for the first and only time.

Robby Gordon, who was running directly ahead of the race leader in eighth place, dived immediately into the pits for service. Zanardi, surprisingly, failed to follow suit. All the other leaders took the opportunity to make pit stops.

'At that point I really thought I'd lost the race,' confessed Zanardi, 'because if I got caught behind the pace car, I'd be screwed. But fortunately that didn't happen.'

Indeed, the pace car failed to pick up the #4 Target car, so Zanardi was able to complete an extra lap at full speed before diving into the pits. He duly resumed in the lead. It was a lucky break, but no more than he deserved.

Zanardi took off at the restart and quickly reestablished his superiority over de Ferran as the top positions remained unchanged to the checkered flag.

'I was trying hard in case Alex had a problem or made a mistake, but it became obvious that we were not fast enough to challenge Alex,' said de Ferran. 'I'm actually pretty happy because we had a good result and it puts me in a good position in the championship with seven races to go.'

Ditto Christian Fittipaldi, who chased hard despite intense pressure from Unser. Emerson Fittipaldi's fine run ended early due a broken transmission, but fourth place for Unser was enough to move him to within 11 points of Vasser in the fight for the PPG Cup title.

Parker Johnstone finished fifth after another strong drive for the Brix Comptech team. Rahal experienced some handling problems in the closing stages but persevered for sixth ahead of Ribeiro, who was afflicted by a painful cramp in his right thigh. Blundell, the final unlapped finisher, overcame an appalling two days of practice and qualifying to move up from 21st to eighth in Bruce McCaw's VISA/PacWest Reynard-Ford.

Photos: Michael C. Brown

SNIPPETS

• The last time an **Indy Car podium** was bereft of at least one North American driver was at Milwaukee in 1993, when Britain's Nigel Mansell finished ahead of Brazilians Raul Boesel and Emerson Fittipaldi.

• The **Arciero-Wells Reynard-Toyota** of Jeff Krosnoff featured an attractive new blue-and-orange paint scheme in deference to the team's new major sponsor, MCI.

• **Michael Andretti**'s hopes of winning three in a row were dashed on the pace laps when his Ford/Cosworth engine refused to run cleanly. Andretti ducked into the pits at the end of the first lap but lost almost two laps while the cause was diag-

nosed and over-come. He charged hard all the way to the end of the race and moved up from 12th to 11th, earning an additional PPG Cup point, when Adrian Fernandez ran out of gas on the final lap.

• **Gil de Ferran**'s regular race engineer, Bill Pappas, was taken ill with a serious case of food poisoning on race morning. Hall Racing Team Manager Gerald Davis took over the radio communication duties.

• **Christian Fittipaldi** endured a high-speed crash during a test at Michigan International Speedway the previous Monday. The incident began when his engine blew and deposited oil beneath the car's rear tires. Fittipaldi was fortunate to escape with

nothing more than some bruising to his chest, caused by the seat belts.

• **Scott Pruett**'s Firestone Lola-Ford (right) was among the quickest cars during the final warmup on race morning, in wet-dry conditions, but ended the session parked solidly against a tire barrier after Pruett lost control shortly after switching to dry tires. Tony Van Dongen and the crew cannibalized the rear suspension and undertray from the spare car in order to effect repairs.

• As a further indication of the continually changing face of the PPG Indy Car World Series, **Alex Zanardi** became the sixth driver in the last two years to add his name to the list of first-time winners.

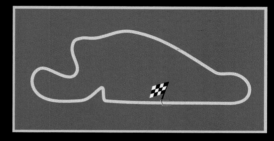

BUDWEISER/G.I. JOE'S 200
PRESENTED BY TEXACO/HAVOLINE

PORTLAND INTERNATIONAL RACEWAY, PORTLAND, OREGON

JUNE 23, 98 laps – 191.100 miles

Place	Driver (Nat.)	No.	Team Sponsors Car-Engine	Tires	Q Speed	Q Time	Q Pos.	Laps	Time/Status	Ave.	Pts.
1	*Alex Zanardi (I)	4	Target/Chip Ganassi Racing Reynard 96I-Honda	FS	117.209	59.893s	1	98	1h 50m 25.401s	103.837	22
2	Gil de Ferran (BR)	8	Hall Racing Pennzoil Special Reynard 96I-Honda	GY	116.137	1m 00.446s	9	98	1h 50m 34.538s	103.694	16
3	Christian Fittipaldi (BR)	11	Newman/Haas Kmart/Budweiser Lola T96/00-Ford XD	GY	115.870	1m 00.585s	11	98	1h 50m 37.073s	103.654	14
4	Al Unser Jr. (USA)	2	Marlboro Team Penske Penske PC25-Mercedes	GY	115.841	1m 00.600s	12	98	1h 50m 40.306s	103.604	12
5	Parker Johnstone (USA)	49	Brix Comptech Motorola Reynard 96I-Honda	FS	115.332	1m 00.868s	15	98	1h 50m 43.658s	103.551	10
6	Bobby Rahal (USA)	18	Team Rahal Miller Brewing Reynard 96I-Mercedes	GY	114.761	1m 01.171s	18	98	1h 50m 59.518s	103.305	8
7	Andre Ribeiro (BR)	31	Tasman Motorsports LCI International Lola T96/00-Honda	FS	116.489	1m 00.263s	5	98	1h 51m 01.220s	103.278	6
8	*Mark Blundell (GB)	21	PacWest Racing Group VISA Reynard 96I-Ford XB	GY	113.909	1m 01.628s	21	98	1h 51m 21.852s	102.959	5
9	Stefan Johansson (S)	16	Bettenhausen Alumax Aluminum Reynard 96I-Mercedes	GY	114.340	1m 01.396s	19	98	Running		4
10	Robby Gordon (USA)	5	Walker Valvoline/Cummins/Craftsman Reynard 96I-Ford XD	GY	115.408	1m 00.828s	14	97	Running		3
11	Michael Andretti (USA)	6	Newman/Haas Kmart/Texaco Havoline Lola T96/00-Ford XD	GY	116.430	1m 00.293s	6	97	Running		2
12	Adrian Fernandez (MEX)	32	Tasman Tecate Beer/Quaker State Oil Lola T96/00-Honda	FS	115.522	1m 00.768s	13	97	Running		1
13	Jimmy Vasser (USA)	12	Target/Chip Ganassi Racing Reynard 96I-Honda	FS	116.989	1m 00.005s	3	96	Running		
14	Juan Manuel Fangio II (RA)	36	All American Racers Castrol Eagle Mk.V-Toyota	GY	113.216	1m 02.005s	24	96	Running		
15	*Eddie Lawson (USA)	10	Galles Racing Delco Electronics Lola T96/00-Mercedes	GY	114.301	1m 01.417s	20	96	Running		
16	Mauricio Gugelmin (BR)	17	PacWest Racing Group Hollywood Reynard 96I-Ford XB	GY	116.074	1m 00.479s	10	96	Running		
17	*Jeff Krosnoff (USA)	25	Arciero-Wells Racing MCI Reynard 96I-Toyota	FS	113.452	1m 01.877s	23	95	Running		
18	Eliseo Salazar (RCH)	7	Scandia Cristal/Copec/Mobil 1 Lola T96/00-Ford XB	GY	109.708	1m 03.988s	28	93	Running		
19	Roberto Moreno (BR)	34	Payton/Coyne Data Control Lola T96/00-Ford XD	FS	113.491	1m 01.855s	22	84	Electrical		
20	Emerson Fittipaldi (BR)	9	Hogan Penske Marlboro Latin America Penske PC25-Mercedes	GY	114.951	1m 01.070s	16	78	Transmission		
21	Hiro Matsushita (J)	19	Payton/Coyne Panasonic/Duskin Lola T96/00-Ford XB	FS	112.596	1m 02.347s	26	64	Engine		
22	*Michel Jourdain Jr. (MEX)	22	Team Scandia Herdez/Perry Ellis/Alta Lola T96/00-Ford XB	GY	112.913	1m 02.172s	25	60	Accident		
23	Scott Pruett (USA)	20	Patrick Racing Firestone Lola T96/00-Ford XD	FS	117.021	59.989s	2	47	Handling		
24	*P.J. Jones (USA)	98	All American Racers Castrol Eagle Mk.V-Toyota	GY	111.664	1m 02.867s	27	42	Accident		
25	*Greg Moore (CDN)	99	Forsythe Player's Ltd./Indeck Reynard 96I-Mercedes	FS	116.147	1m 00.441s	8	12	Electrical		
26	Bryan Herta (USA)	28	Team Rahal Shell Reynard 96I-Mercedes	GY	116.861	1m 00.072s	4	10	Oil leak		
27	Paul Tracy (CDN)	3	Marlboro Team Penske Penske PC25-Mercedes	GY	116.254	1m 00.385s	7	10	Suspension		
28	Raul Boesel (BR)	1	Brahma Sports Team Reynard 96I-Ford XD	GY	114.886	1m 01.104s	17	8	Engine		

* denotes Rookie driver

Caution flags: Laps 62–66, tow/Jourdain. Total: one for five laps.

Lap leaders: Alex Zanardi, 1–33 (33 laps); Christian Fittipaldi, 34 (1 lap); Zanardi, 35–38 (4 laps); Al Unser Jr., 39–40 (2 laps); Zanardi, 41–98 (58 laps). Totals: Zanardi, 95 laps; Unser, 2 laps; C. Fittipaldi, 1 lap.

Fastest race lap: Alex Zanardi, 1m 02.572s, 112.190 mph, on lap 28.

Championship positions: 1 Vasser, 98; **2** Unser, 87; **3** Andretti, 73; **4** C. Fittipaldi, 72; **5** de Ferran, 71; **6** Pruett, 54; **7** Ribeiro, 49; **8** Moore, 46; **9** Tracy, 45; **10** Rahal, 40; **11** Zanardi, 39; **12** E. Fittipaldi, 29; **13** Gugelmin, Johnstone and Fernandez, 28; **16** Lawson, 26; **17** Blundell, 25; **18** Moreno, 24; **19** Johansson, 18; **20** Gordon, 17; **21** Boesel, 11; **22** Herta, 6; **23** Jones, 4; **24** Matsushita and Hearn, 3; **26** Goodyear and Greco, 1.

Official Information Technology Provider EDS

Michael C. Brown

143

CLEVELAND

1 – DE FERRAN

2 – ZANARDI

3 – MOORE

A crocodile of Indy cars headed by race winner Gil de Ferran, Adrian Fernandez and Bobby Rahal winds its way through the vast expanses of the Burke Lakefront Airport.
Photo: Michael C. Brown

Bryan Herta *(right)* confirmed the growing competitiveness of the Shell Reynard with a strong fifth place.

Far right: Like de Ferran, Greg Moore opted for a conservative strategy and was rewarded with another podium finish.

Alex Zanardi *(below right)* maintained his late charge up the point standings with second place for Chip Ganassi.

The Medic Drug Grand Prix of Cleveland provided a classic tale of the tortoise versus the hare . . . if one allows for the fact that the tortoise – in this case Gil de Ferran's Pennzoil Reynard-Honda – emerged to beat the hare – Alex Zanardi's Target Reynard-Honda – at an average speed of no less than 133.736 mph!

De Ferran's Hall Racing pit crew played a major role in ensuring his well-earned victory. The Brazilian, along with most of the front-runners, took the opportunity to make a pit stop during the first (and only) full-course caution on lap 20. But the various teams employed divergent strategies. Zanardi's Target/Chip Ganassi crew opted to stop twice more, running virtually flat-out the whole way. Ditto Michael Andretti's Newman/Haas team and Al Unser Jr.'s Marlboro Team Penske. De Ferran, along with Greg Moore (Player's/Forsythe Racing Reynard-Mercedes) and Andretti's Newman/Haas teammate, Christian Fittipaldi, chose a different approach. Instead they gambled on a slightly more conservative pace with the intention of making only one additional stop.

Zanardi, who had clearly the fastest car during the dramatic closing stages, emerged several seconds in arrears of de Ferran after making his final fuel stop. Zanardi made up the deficit and even nosed briefly ahead on the white flag lap, but the Brazilian kept his cool – and the lead – before crossing the finish line just 1.033 seconds in front. The fuel strategy had worked out perfectly.

'We didn't have much left,' declared team owner Jim Hall. 'I think I could have had it for a cocktail.'

PPG Cup series points leader Jimmy Vasser led the 26-car field away from the start. He held a useful advantage into the tight Turn One hairpin, although a slight bobble on the exit of the corner allowed teammate Zanardi, who started second, to slip past. Paul Tracy, after qualifying eighth, made an opportunist maneuver around the outside line and emerged a startling third in his Marlboro Penske-Mercedes, followed by Bryan Herta's Shell Reynard-Mercedes. Andre Ribeiro ran fifth ahead of de Ferran, who had locked up his brakes and nudged lightly into the back of his countryman's LCI International Lola-Honda.

Zanardi quickly opened up a lead over Vasser. By lap 14 the gap was over six seconds – and growing. Tracy kept pace with the #12 Target car, as did Ribeiro, who snuck ahead of Herta with a nice pass down the inside into Turn One on lap four. De Ferran also later demoted Herta, who was troubled by a handling imbalance after missing virtually all of the final warmup session due to an oil leak.

The pivotal moment of the race occurred on lap 20, when the pace car was sent out following an incident in Turn One between Eddie Lawson and Parker Johnstone which left Lawson's Delco Electronics Lola-Mercedes stranded in the middle of the track.

The caution came a little earlier than the majority of teams had hoped, falling a few laps outside 'the window' which would allow them to complete the race on just two fuel stops. Nevertheless, Zanardi, the leader, peeled off into the pit lane for service. Vasser, running second, did not.

'It was a dumb call,' admitted Target/Chip Ganassi Team Manager Tom Anderson. 'There's nobody to be mad at but myself. We should have done what Alex did.'

Tracy and Ribeiro, third and fourth, also eschewed the opportunity to pit. But they were in a distinct minority. Everyone else followed Zanardi's lead and took on service.

Vasser, Tracy and Ribeiro inherited the lead at the restart and, running on significantly lighter fuel loads, quickly edged away from the pursuing pack. Zanardi led the chase until, crucially, he made a slight slip in Turn Eight on lap 25. The Target car lost valuable momentum, whereupon de Ferran took full advantage by drawing alongside – and then taking over fourth position – on the next straightaway.

The full consequence of that pass did not become apparent until much later in the contest. But it meant that de Ferran was able to control the pace through the middle stages of the race. Zanardi was never quite close enough to redress the balance.

De Ferran took over the lead when Vasser, Ribeiro and Tracy made their first routine stops, right on schedule, at around one-third distance. Andretti, who moved up two positions thanks to a super-fast first pit stop by Tim Bumps and the crew, ran third ahead of Herta, whom he had passed soon after the restart. Unser made several aggressive moves of his own to rise from 16th on the grid to fifth by lap 33.

The top six cars, completed by Adrian Fernandez, were equally spaced, a second or so apart, at the halfway point. The race seemed in danger of developing into little more than a high-speed procession. But then the differing tactics came into play.

Andretti was the first of the leaders to make his second pit stop, on lap 50. The Newman/Haas team hustled its man back into the fray after taking only a partial load of fuel. The Penske crew followed suit, realizing that Unser would have to make another pit stop and hoping the time saved would gain him track position. It did.

De Ferran, meanwhile, stretched his fuel until lap 55 before stopping for service. Moore and Christian Fittipaldi completed yet another lap before making pit stops.

Andretti assumed the lead once everyone had taken on fresh tires and fuel. Zanardi ran second after his slightly longer pit stop, due to taking on more fuel, and lost more time shortly afterward when he was trapped for several laps behind Bobby Rahal, who was already three laps down following a boost control problem earlier in the race.

'I'm quite surprised a guy with his experience would do something like that,' said an irate Zanardi. 'He did the same to me in qualifying. I had to take a hell of a risk to outbrake him.'

De Ferran and Unser ran close together in third and fourth, pursued by Herta, Rahal and Moore, who had steadily made up ground after losing several positions both at the start and following the early caution period.

Andretti turned a sequence of consistently fast laps and held onto the lead until ducking into the pits for a final stop on lap 69. He was on course at least for a top-three finish until suffering a broken differential after 81 laps.

'Considering where we started and the way we battled ourselves back, it's a real shame not to finish this race on the podium,' said Andretti, who also endured two engine failures during practice and qualifying. 'It was a really tough race to come home with nothing.'

Zanardi extended his lead over de Ferran to a full 17 seconds before pitting for a splash of fuel on lap 80. His advantage was such that he was able to continue in second place. At that stage most people still assumed de Ferran, too, would require one more pit stop. Not so.

'We were in full conserve mode,' he explained. 'I was on a fuel economy run but the car was handling great, so I was able to run decent lap times and still save fuel.'

After setting comfortably the fastest time during the first qualifying session late on Friday afternoon, Jimmy Vasser seemed on course toward regaining some of the early-season momentum that had catapulted him into a clear lead in the PPG Cup standings.

'Hopefully this will be the beginning of a new streak,' said Vasser after stopping the clocks at 58.336 seconds in Chip Ganassi's Target Reynard-Honda. His best was more than four-tenths faster than teammate Alex Zanardi and over seven-tenths clear of Gil de Ferran.

Curiously, Vasser was the only driver not to improve his time during the final session on Saturday. Nevertheless, his stunning effort from the previous day remained good enough for the pole – his third of the season and the fifth for the team as Zanardi's best came up a scant 0.014 short.

'I was right on the limit,' declared Zanardi. 'I almost equaled my time but I couldn't beat it.'

Bryan Herta produced another fine performance to secure a fourth top-four grid position in the last five races in Team Rahal's Shell Reynard-Mercedes. He, too, was within one tenth of a second of Vasser's pole-winning time.

'The car's working well and [race engineer] Ray Leto and I are getting on really well together,' noted Herta, who switched to the Goodyear primary tire after running the optionals on Friday. Incidentally, Herta was the only Goodyear runner to break into the top six.

Greg Moore vaulted from 11th to fourth, his progress on the first day having been halted by a blown engine, while fellow Firestone representatives – and Tasman Motorsports teammates – Andre Ribeiro and Adrian Fernandez shared row three of the grid. The Mexican's performance was particularly meritorious as he jumped from 16th on the provisional grid to sixth.

'I knew we could do it,' said the steadily improving Fernandez. 'It was just a matter of finding the right balance on the car.'

Michael Andretti also was content with the balance of his Kmart/Texaco Havoline Lola, although he languished a disappointing 13th on the grid after his engine blew early in the final period of qualifying.

'We were ready to go with our new tires on,' said Andretti. 'The engine just let go with no warning. I think we could have been fifth quickest. It's always better if the engine blows during qualifying rather than in the race, but it's never a good situation.'

Photos: Michael C. Brown

Consistency puts de Ferran in contention

Gil de Ferran has enjoyed mixed fortunes during his two visits to Burke Lakefront Airport. In his rookie Indy Car season, de Ferran dominated the race before tangling with the twice-lapped car of Scott Pruett in the closing stages. Some harsh words were exchanged at the time, but after learning he and Pruett had qualified alongside one another on row two of the provisional grid for his second appearance on the shores of Lake Erie, de Ferran insisted there were no hard feelings.

'That is all in the past,' said de Ferran. 'Scott is an excellent driver and I have a lot of respect for him. What happened then was unfortunate but it's history now.'

De Ferran, hindered by excessive understeer, slipped to seventh on the final grid, while Pruett fell even further, to 12th. The Brazilian, however, soon began to move toward the front once the race was underway. His eventual victory was all the more rewarding for the fact he had guided Jim Hall's Pennzoil Reynard-Honda to third- and second-place finishes in the previous races at Detroit and Portland.

'I hope that's a trend we can continue,' said de Ferran. 'The team has given me a good product to race all season and we have run up front in almost every race. When we had misfortunes from time to time, the guys on the team never got discouraged. The result was that when we finally won, the consistency that we had earlier in the year really paid off and we moved up to a challenging position in the points.'

In fact, de Ferran's victory moved him to within 10 points of series leader Jimmy Vasser in the chase for the PPG Cup title.

'Our goal this year is to win the championship,' he declared. 'If any other problems we had in earlier races could be called "bad luck," we hope that is all behind us.'

Bottom: **After a bright start to his Indy Car career, Robby Gordon appeared to have lost his way. A helpful track marshal suggests that maybe it's time for a change of direction.**

'Obviously I'm just a bit disappointed that we had a great show and we finished behind de Ferran, but that's the way racing goes,' said Zanardi philosophically. 'Today they played a good strategy and it paid off. We had the fastest car – I don't think there is any doubt about that – but they won the race. Still, I'm pretty happy.'

Moore also parlayed a conservative strategy to finish on the podium for the third time in his Player's Reynard-Mercedes.

'It was a long race,' said the Canadian rookie. 'We had a boost problem, so there was no chance of catching those guys. I just did the best I could.'

Unser was equally pleased with fourth, especially since Vasser could manage no better than 10th following a disappointing performance. Vasser, who confessed to losing his rhythm after falling to 20th position when he made his first pit stop under green, also required an extra pit stop after collecting a couple of marker cones during a brief off-course excursion. The slip allowed Unser to close within three points of the PPG Cup lead. De Ferran also moved into serious contention, only 10 markers shy with six races remaining . . .

De Ferran refused to be flustered when Zanardi made inroads into his advantage. The two leaders ran virtually nose to tail for the final four laps, but only once, when they came up behind Stefan Johansson's Alumax Reynard-Mercedes on lap 89, did de Ferran seem likely to lose his grip.

'I thought Stefan was going to let me by going into Turn Three,' related de Ferran, 'so I went inside him – and then he turned [in]! I had to back off, so Alex got a run on me.'

De Ferran adopted a defensive line for the next corner, but Zanardi braked as late as he dared on the outside line and inched ahead of his rival as he attempted to make the turn.

'I almost made it,' smiled Zanardi. 'The trouble is, with the heat [over 90 degrees Fahrenheit], we put down a lot of rubber and there were a lot of "marbles" just off the racing line. It's unbelievable. The car just slides away. I was only about one inch off line but that was enough.'

De Ferran was able to sweep ahead once again on the exit. 'It was a great race,' said de Ferran, who held on for his second Indy Car victory as Zanardi ran out of time to mount another challenge.

Photos: Michael C. Brown

SNIPPETS

- **Mark Blundell** (above) drove another fine race, rising from a dismal 21st on the opening lap, following a poor start, to 11th at the checkered flag. Along the way he survived a flash fire during his second pit stop when he was signalled out fractionally too early. Airjack/vent man Tim Douthat suffered a sprained right ankle during the confusion.

- The **Brahma Sports Team**

endured another tough weekend, with Raul Boesel encountering a broken clutch and two blown engines during practice and qualifying. Boesel made good progress on the handling of his Reynard after regular race engineer Tino Belli had been joined by Reynard's Paul Owens and veteran F1/F3000 engineer Roberto Trevisan, but hopes of a strong finish were dashed by a broken throttle sensor.

- **Casey Mears**, youngest son of former Indy Car driver Roger Mears, posted a promising Indy Lights

- **Gil de Ferran** was much in demand following his overdue first win of the season. The Brazilian's name had been connected to Jackie Stewart's new-for-'97 Formula 1 team, which seemed logical in light of his successful formative years in Formula Vauxhall and Formula 3 with Paul Stewart Racing. De Ferran, however, said he would be more than happy to remain in the PPG Cup series: 'I can see no good reason to move. I'm very happy over here [in North America]. The Indy Car series is extremely competitive, I'm with a very good team, and it's quite good fun, too.'

debut at Cleveland. Filling in for another second-generation driver, Robby Unser, who was busy practicing for the Pikes Peak Hill Climb, Mears showed well in Team Medlin's Lola-Buick, working his way from 18th on the grid to eighth.

- **Emerson Fittipaldi** became a proud grandfather prior to the Cleveland race weekend when daughter Juliana gave birth to a baby boy, Pietro Fittipaldi da Cruz, who tipped the scales at six pounds, eight ounces.

- **Jimmy Vasser** (below) remained upbeat despite seeing a once commanding

lead in the PPG Cup championship standings eroded to just three points over closest challenger Al Unser Jr. 'The last month has not been too good,' admitted Vasser. 'I call it the June Swoon. But that's behind us now. We're still in good shape. I have a great team and a great package, so it's up to me to make the most of it.'

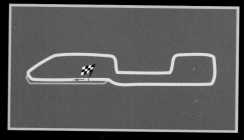

PPG INDY CAR WORLD SERIES • ROUND 10
MEDIC DRUG GRAND PRIX OF CLEVELAND

BURKE LAKEFRONT AIRPORT, CLEVELAND, OHIO

JUNE 30, 90 laps – 213.210 miles

Place	Driver (Nat.)	No.	Team Sponsors Car-Engine	Tires	Q Speed	Q Time	Q Pos.	Laps	Time/Status	Ave.	Pts.
1	Gil de Ferran (BR)	8	Hall Racing Pennzoil Special Reynard 96I-Honda	GY	144.932	58.884s	7	90	1h 35m 39.326s	133.736	21
2	*Alex Zanardi (I)	4	Target/Chip Ganassi Racing Reynard 96I-Honda	FS	146.159	58.350s	2	90	1h 35m 40.359s	133.712	16
3	*Greg Moore (CDN)	99	Forsythe Player's Ltd./Indeck Reynard 96I-Mercedes	FS	145.633	58.561s	4	90	1h 35m 55.729s	133.355	14
4	Al Unser Jr. (USA)	2	Marlboro Team Penske Penske PC25-Mercedes	GY	143.176	59.566s	16	90	1h 36m 07.595s	133.081	12
5	Bryan Herta (USA)	28	Team Rahal Shell Reynard 96I-Mercedes	GY	146.039	58.398s	3	90	1h 36m 14.636s	132.919	10
6	Adrian Fernandez (MEX)	32	Tasman Tecate Beer/Quaker State Oil Lola T96/00-Honda	FS	145.229	58.724s	6	90	1h 36m 25.197s	132.676	8
7	Christian Fittipaldi (BR)	11	Newman/Haas Kmart/Budweiser Lola T96/00-Ford XD	GY	144.672	58.950s	10	90	1h 36m 42.046s	132.291	6
8	Scott Pruett (USA)	20	Patrick Racing Firestone Lola T96/00-Ford XD	FS	144.410	59.057s	12	89	Running		5
9	Paul Tracy (CDN)	3	Marlboro Team Penske Penske PC25-Mercedes	GY	144.881	58.865s	8	89	Running		4
10	Jimmy Vasser (USA)	12	Target/Chip Ganassi Racing Reynard 96I-Honda	FS	146.194	58.336s	1	89	Running		4
11	*Mark Blundell (GB)	21	PacWest Racing Group VISA Reynard 96I-Ford XB	GY	143.387	59.478s	15	89	Running		2
12	Stefan Johansson (S)	16	Bettenhausen Alumax Aluminum Reynard 96I-Mercedes	GY	142.237	59.959s	19	88	Running		1
13	Juan Manuel Fangio II (RA)	36	All American Racers Castrol Eagle Mk.V-Toyota	GY	139.028	1m 01.343s	25	88	Running		
14	Roberto Moreno (BR)	34	Payton/Coyne Data Control Lola T96/00-Ford XB	FS	140.138	1m 00.857s	22	88	Running		
15	Bobby Rahal (USA)	18	Team Rahal Miller Brewing Reynard 96I-Mercedes	GY	144.532	59.007s	11	87	Running		
16	*Jeff Krosnoff (USA)	25	Arciero-Wells Racing MCI Reynard 96I-Toyota	FS	139.039	1m 01.338s	24	85	Electrical		
17	Hiro Matsushita (J)	19	Payton/Coyne Panasonic/Duskin Lola T96/00-Ford XB	FS	139.171	1m 01.280s	23	85	Running		
18	Robby Gordon (USA)	5	Walker Valvoline/Cummins/Craftsman Reynard 96I-Ford XD	GY	144.061	59.200s	14	84	Running		
19	Michael Andretti (USA)	6	Newman/Haas Kmart/Texaco Havoline Lola T96/00-Ford XD	GY	144.344	59.084s	13	81	Transmission		
20	Andre Ribeiro (BR)	31	Tasman Motorsports LCI International Lola T96/00-Honda	FS	145.603	58.573s	5	81	Exhaust header		
21	Mauricio Gugelmin (BR)	17	PacWest Racing Group Hollywood Reynard 96I-Ford XB	GY	144.709	58.935s	9	70	Engine		
22	Emerson Fittipaldi (BR)	9	Hogan Penske Marlboro Latin America Penske PC25-Mercedes	GY	142.067	1m 00.031s	20	27	Engine		
23	*P.J. Jones (USA)	98	All American Racers Castrol Eagle Mk.V-Toyota	GY	137.866	1m 01.860s	26	24	Transmission		
24	*Eddie Lawson (USA)	10	Galles Racing Delco Electronics Lola T96/00-Mercedes	GY	141.423	1m 00.304s	21	18	Accident		
25	Parker Johnstone (USA)	49	Brix Comptech Motorola Reynard 96I-Honda	FS	142.508	59.845s	18	18	Accident		
26	Raul Boesel (BR)	1	Brahma Sports Team Reynard 96I-Ford XD	GY	143.099	59.598s	17	18	Engine		

* denotes Rookie driver

Caution flags: Laps 19–22, accident/Lawson and Johnstone. **Total:** one for four laps.

Lap leaders: Alex Zanardi, 1–19 (19 laps); Jimmy Vasser, 20–30 (11 laps); Paul Tracy, 31 (1 lap); Gil de Ferran, 32–55 (24 laps); Michael Andretti, 56–67 (12 laps); Zanardi, 68–80 (13 laps); de Ferran, 81–90 (10 laps). **Totals:** de Ferran, 34 laps; Zanardi, 32 laps; Andretti, 12 laps; Vasser, 11 laps; Tracy, 1 lap.

Fastest race lap: not given.

Championship positions: 1 Vasser, 102; **2** Unser, 99; **3** de Ferran, 92; **4** C. Fittipaldi, 78; **5** Andretti, 73; **6** Moore, 60; **7** Pruett, 59; **8** Zanardi, 55; **9** Ribeiro and Tracy, 49; **11** Rahal, 40; **12** Fernandez, 36; **13** E. Fittipaldi, 29; **14** Gugelmin and Johnstone, 28; **16** Blundell, 27; **17** Lawson, 26; **18** Moreno, 24; **19** Johansson, 18; **20** Gordon, 17; **21** Herta, 16; **22** Boesel, 11; **23** Jones, 4; **24** Matsushita and Hearn, 3; **26** Goodyear and Greco, 1.

TORONTO

PPG INDY CAR WORLD SERIES • ROUND 11

1 – FERNANDEZ

2 – ZANARDI

3 – RAHAL

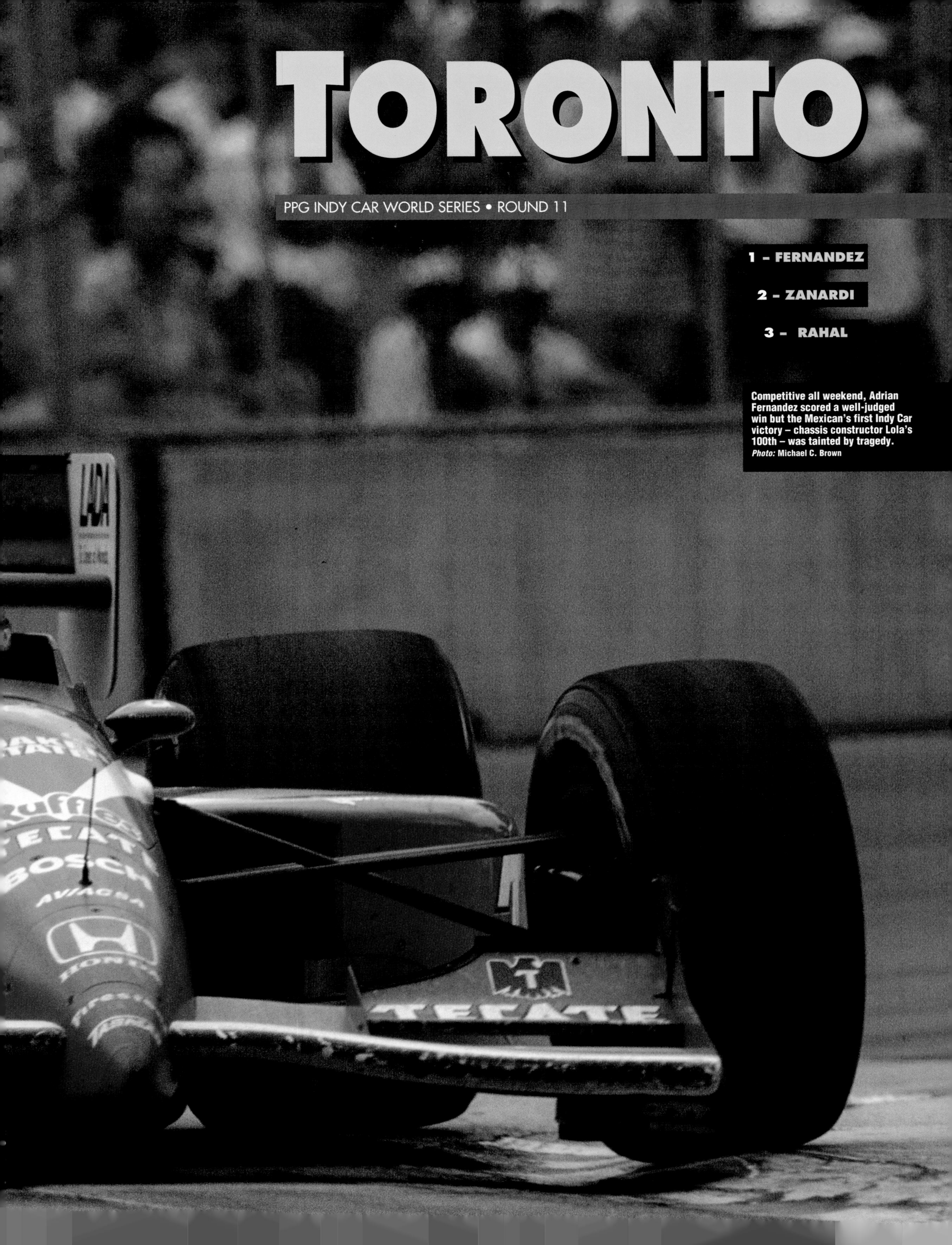

Competitive all weekend, Adrian Fernandez scored a well-judged win but the Mexican's first Indy Car victory – chassis constructor Lola's 100th – was tainted by tragedy.
Photo: **Michael C. Brown**

Michael C. Brown

Right: Paul Tracy holds off an attack from Michael Andretti. The hometown favorite profited from the misfortunes that befell several of the leading runners on the first lap to take fifth place at the finish.

Mexico's newest sporting hero, Adrian Fernandez, scored a magnificent first-ever Indy Car victory in the Molson Indy Toronto. Tragically, his triumph in Steve Horne's Tecate/Quaker State Lola-Honda was overshadowed by the news that Jeff Krosnoff and a course marshal, Gary Avrin, had died as a result of injuries sustained in a crash which caused the race to be halted two laps short of its scheduled distance.

The incident occurred on the fastest part of the track, Lakeshore Boulevard, where the Indy cars reached in excess of 175 mph. It came shortly after a full-course caution while the field was still packed closely together. Krosnoff, whose MCI Reynard-Toyota had been running strongly, was involved in a tight battle with Stefan Johansson's Alumax Reynard-Mercedes when the two cars made contact at the beginning of the braking area. Krosnoff's car was launched over the right-rear wheel of Johansson's Reynard, whereupon it cleared the concrete wall, was partially arrested by a debris fence, and then slammed into a tree. The chassis disintegrated upon contact.

The IndyCar Safety Team reached the scene moments after the remnants of the car had come to rest in the middle of the track, but the popular Californian was already beyond help. He was pronounced dead at Toronto Western Hospital at 4.20 p.m. local time, little more than a half-hour after the accident.

Avrin, too, was killed instantly when he was hit by the car as it careened over the wall. Another course worker, Barbara Johnston, was taken to the hospital. Thankfully, she was released later in the evening after receiving treatment for a minor head laceration.

Official word of the fatalities was not released until all the immediate family members had been informed some two hours after the race had been concluded. The teams and, especially, the drivers, who had to negotiate a path through the debris, knew the accident had been serious, but no one at that stage realized the full extent of the carnage. All anyone knew for certain was that Fernandez had won the race.

'I've been waiting for this for a long time,' said Fernandez. 'I owe it all to the guys. They did a great job. I love the guys from Tasman; without them I wouldn't be here.'

The Tasman team secured a good setup for its pair of Lola-Hondas, such that both Fernandez and Andre

QUALIFYING

Firestone tires once again appeared to be the hot ticket when the Indy cars were turned loose on the 1.784-mile course within Exhibition Place. Indeed, by the time final qualifying had been completed on Saturday afternoon, Firestone-shod cars filled the top six grid positions.

Andre Ribeiro *(above)* led the way on Friday, bouncing back from an incident in morning practice when he damaged the left-side suspension of his LCI International Lola-Honda in Turn One. The Brazilian also glanced off the wall in the afternoon, but not until after he had claimed the provisional pole with an impressive lap at 58.060 seconds.

'You go until you find the limit,' declared Ribeiro. 'The limit, unfortunately, is the wall. I was motivated because I was angry when I found out we had lost the pole position at one point. I'm glad we got it back. The track was improving, the car was improving and I was improving as well.'

Ribeiro reckoned there was more to come on Saturday. But after the morning practice session was held in damp conditions following overnight rain, a dramatic increase in heat and humidity prevented most drivers from improving their times. The pole, his first on a road course, was safe.

Alex Zanardi, who was alone among the Firestone contingent in preferring to remain with the harder prime tires, was not content after failing to beat Ribeiro in the final session. 'I should have gone faster,' he confessed. 'The car was better but the traffic was bad and I couldn't put a good lap together.'

Adrian Fernandez set the fastest time in the final session, good enough to move him from fifth to third, immediately behind his Tasman teammate on the starting grid.

Scott Pruett and Greg Moore also improved their times fractionally, but not by enough to prevent Fernandez from leapfrogging ahead. Parker Johnstone completed the Firestone romp after another fine performance in the Brix Comptech team's Motorola Reynard-Honda.

Al Unser Jr. was the fastest Goodyear representative, seventh in the fastest of Roger Penske's cars. Bobby Rahal, Gil de Ferran, Michael Andretti, Jimmy Vasser, Bryan Herta and Paul Tracy were close behind, all bracketed by less than two tenths of one second!

Ribeiro's sister LCI International entry were among the fastest throughout the weekend. Ribeiro, in fact, secured the pole – his first on a road course – with Fernandez in third place behind the on-form Alex Zanardi's Target Reynard-Honda.

Ribeiro maintained his advantage away from the start, but only as far as Turn Three, where Zanardi took the lead by virtue of a perfectly judged outbraking maneuver on the inside line. The Italian, Brazilian and Mexican trio duly completed the first lap out in front. Behind, though, several major contenders were already in trouble. Al Unser Jr. lost a front wing from his Penske in the first-lap shuffle. Gil de Ferran also required a pit stop for a new nosecone. Scott Pruett picked up a puncture. Parker Johnstone, meanwhile, was an innocent victim of a concertina movement in Turn Six which left his Motorola Reynard-Honda stranded in the middle of the road.

A couple of laps later, with Johnstone still immobile, the first full-course caution of the afternoon was called by chief steward Wally Dallenbach. The timing could not have been worse for Unser, who had rejoined ahead of Zanardi, only to be lapped mere moments before the crossed yellow flags were displayed. Thus, according to the new restart procedure, the unfortunate Unser was

obliged to fall back through the pack and assume his correct order in line – a distant 26th. He was not happy.

The biggest beneficiary of the first-lap shenanigans was Unser's Marlboro Penske-Mercedes teammate Paul Tracy, who somehow blustered his way from 13th on the grid to sixth.

Zanardi asserted his superiority as soon as the race was restarted, inching away slowly but surely from the two Tasman cars. The gap reached as high as four seconds by lap 21, then began to diminish as the leaders encountered slower traffic. The first round of pit stops took place between laps 36 and 39. Zanardi resumed with his handy lead intact. Bobby Rahal emerged in second, thanks to a sensational pit stop by Jim Prescott's boys. Ribeiro, by contrast, missed his marks in the pits. The car had to be shuffled into position before refueling could commence. The Brazilian fell to 11th.

The middle stages of the race were largely uneventful. Zanardi stretched his margin over Rahal to around seven seconds, while Fernandez chased hard in third place. Tracy, Moore and Rahal's teammate, Bryan Herta, were all fairly well spaced apart in the other top six positions, followed by Jimmy Vasser, who came under increasing pressure from Christian Fittipaldi.

Zanardi pulled onto pit road for the second time on lap 66. He needed to take on only 29 gallons of fuel, although a mix-up among the crew led to him sitting motionless for seven seconds longer than was necessary. The delay allowed both Rahal and Fernandez to move in front once they had pitted, respectively, on laps 67 and 68.

Crucially, however, this time Ed Daood's Tasman crew was able to complete service in just 12 seconds, which enabled Fernandez to rejoin j-u-s-t ahead of Rahal. The Mexican's mirrors were filled by Rahal's Miller Reynard-Mercedes at the end of the back straight, as Rahal tried desperately to regain his advantage, but Fernandez rebuffed the challenge admirably.

'I just tried to stay focused,' said Fernandez. 'That's one of the things I've been concentrating on this year. Steve Horne has been a great help to me, kind of a mentor, and I've learned so much from the Tasman team.'

Moore took over in the lead until finally making his own final stop on lap 78. Fernandez moved into the top position and never looked back.

Zanardi, who lost some ground to Rahal on lap 81 when he left his braking a fraction too late in Turn One, quickly made up the deficit and was able to slip past the Ohioan after he, too, had made a slight bobble coming onto the main straightaway a half-dozen laps later.

'I saw Bobby had gone in the marbles,' related Zanardi, 'so I knew that, because the guy is clever, he would go to the inside and protect his line; and brake a little early. He did, so I was able to pass him on the outside.'

Zanardi immediately pulled away from Rahal and set his sights on Fernandez, who responded by turning a string of fast laps as he fought to maintain his hard-won advantage. The gap between the two cars stayed fairly constant for several laps, but Zanardi was given one last chance when the caution flags flew on lap 85, after Michael Andretti's Kmart/Texaco Lola-Ford expired due to an engine failure. Andretti, incidentally, after running in sixth place for much of the race, had fallen from contention on lap 60 after locking up his brakes and spinning in Turn Three.

The restart came with just six laps remaining. Once again, Fernandez was up to the task. Indeed, he pulled out over two seconds over Zanardi on the very first lap of green.

Michael C. Brown

Patience pays off for Fernandez

Adrian Fernandez drove exquisitely en route to victory. He made a good start, maintained the pressure on teammate Andre Ribeiro throughout the first stint, did not get flustered when he was beaten out of the pits by Bobby Rahal, and in the closing stages withstood a determined challenge from the talented Alex Zanardi.

'I cannot imagine the excitement in Mexico,' said an ecstatic Fernandez on the victory podium, having not yet realized the full severity of Krosnoff's race-stopping accident. 'I was just there before coming to Toronto. I have been criticized sometimes in Mexico for not being aggressive enough. They seem to think if you don't crash, you are not aggressive.

'You have to be a complete driver to win races, and today I think I proved that. Sometimes you panic because you want to be the quickest, but you need to be more than quick to be a balanced driver. Bobby Rahal and Al Unser Jr., for me, are the best drivers out there, and they don't have to be quickest in every session.

'We came here with a different strategy this weekend. We were ninth in the warmup but the car was good. We just made a few little changes and in the race the car was perfect.'

The 30-year-old from Mexico City, who last year moved to Bloomfield Hills, Mich., with his fiancee, Tania, worked long and hard before rising to the top of the auto racing ladder. He began racing in his native Mexico, winning a pair of Formula Vee Championships, then travelled to Europe to compete in the rough-and-tumble world of Formula Ford. The experience stood him in good stead. Fernandez returned to Mexico in 1990, won the following year's Formula 3 title and then earned Rookie of the Year honors in Indy Lights after winning four races.

He graduated into the Indy cars in 1993, with Rick Galles' team, and made a steady improvement. His best finish prior to joining Steve Horne's Tasman Motorsports Group was a third at Michigan in '95.

He settled into the team immediately, impressing Horne with his natural speed and ability. But it took a while before he was able to communicate adequately with race engineer Diane Holl.

'Diane was new and I was new and I needed to be patient,' said Fernandez. 'Steve was instrumental in making this happen. I have to give 100 percent credit to my team, because they've always believed in me and helped me.'

Bobby Rahal (bottom) made his first podium appearance since the 1995 Molson Indy Toronto after a strong showing at the wheel of the Miller Reynard-Mercedes.

make it easy, but he wasn't going to be super-super-tough about it.'

Tracy had to be content with fifth in his hometown race. 'Toward the end of the race I started to get a lot of pickup on the tires,' said Tracy. 'The car was sliding around a lot. Greg was able to get by me and we were just trying to hang in there and not have an accident.'

Another vast crowd in Toronto, enjoying near-perfect weather conditions throughout the weekend, had been treated to the usual quota of excitement. And Fernandez's maiden victory was thoroughly well earned. It was so sad, therefore, that the event had to finish under such a dark cloud.

'Throughout all four years of my Indy Car career I have dreamed of my first win,' said Fernandez. 'To have it occur in such circumstances leaves a hollow feeling which I am not sure will ever dislodge itself from my memory.'

'My left-rear tire had lost a bit of pressure,' explained Zanardi. 'I have to say, quite honestly, I was more concerned with trying to finish the race in the position I was in. I saw [Rahal's] car in both mirrors in every corner, but fortunately I was able to keep him behind me. In any case, Adrian was running very fast at the end. He really deserved the win.'

Rahal finished a close third, best among the Goodyear contingent, while teammate Herta backed him up strongly by finishing sixth.

'It was a good day for our team,' said a proud Rahal. 'It was tough in traffic today and the track got slick at the end. It was very physical out there – just trying to keep it going in the right direction wasn't easy. Our team is turning things around and I think we'll be strong in many of the remaining races too.'

Moore emerged as the top Canadian finisher in fourth. He, like Zanardi, Rahal and several others, lost some time when his car slid wide in Turn One on lap 77 (Moore also survived a spin in the same place on lap 56) but the youngster rebounded strongly by outbraking no less an adversary than Tracy in the same corner just a few laps before the race was red-flagged to its untimely conclusion.

'You know how hard Paul is to pass,' related Moore, 'but I had a pretty good run on him, so it was a good opportunity to get alongside. He didn't

Michael C. Brown

Michael C. Brown

Photos: Michael C. Brown

SNIPPETS

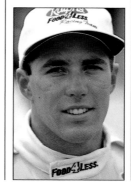

• PPG Cup series leader **Jimmy Vasser** (above) never really got to grips with his Target Reynard-Honda and was outpaced all weekend by his fast-emerging teammate, Alex Zanardi. 'It was a mediocre run at best,' admitted Vasser, who persevered to finish eighth. 'We had problems all day. At one point I was

working on Christian [Fittipaldi] and he drove me into the wall. I decided I didn't want to sacrifice five points to get just one more.'

• **The final two corners** on the 11-turn circuit, plus the pit lane, were dramatically reprofiled due to construction of the 1,000,000 square foot National Trade

Centre. The alterations eliminated what many drivers regarded as one of the most challenging corners on the entire Indy Car schedule.

'I miss the last turn but the changes have opened up a new passing zone [in Turn One], so it should add some extra excitement,' declared Michael Andretti, echoing the thoughts of the vast majority of his colleagues.

• **Bobby Rahal** has amassed an amazing record in the Molson Indy Toronto, scoring no fewer than seven podium finishes in the 11 years the event has been held.

• **Robin Hill**, chief mechanic on Zanardi's Target/Chip Ganassi Racing Reynard-

Honda, was rushed to hospital a couple of days before he was due to leave his home in Indianapolis for the trip to Toronto. Hill was diagnosed as suffering from Lyme Disease. Happily, he made a spectacular recovery and was back in action for the following race at M.I.S.

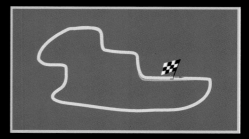

• **Richie Hearn** (left) wasn't feeling up to par after crashing heavily a few days before the race while conducting an IRL test in New Hampshire. 'I was OK for the first 30 laps, then my back got so sore I couldn't hold on,' said the reigning Player's Toyota Atlantic champion, who finally called it quits after 50 laps in John Della Penna's Ralphs/Food 4 Less Reynard.

• **Scott Goodyear** (above), who still considers Toronto his home town, despite the fact he now lives in Carmel, Ind., made a welcome return to Derrick Walker's Valvoline team. Out of action since suffering a serious back injury in Brazil, Goodyear prepared for his Indy Car comeback by finishing third at Le Mans for the factory Porsche team.

PPG INDY CAR WORLD SERIES • ROUND 11
MOLSON INDY TORONTO

EXHIBITION PLACE, TORONTO, ONTARIO, CANADA

JULY 14, 93 laps – 165.912 miles

Place	Driver (Nat.)	No.	Team Sponsors Car-Engine	Tires	Q Speed	Q Time	Q Pos.	Laps	Time/Status	Ave.	Pts.
1	Adrian Fernandez (MEX)	32	Tasman Tecate Beer/Quaker State Oil Lola T96/00-Honda	FS	109.838	58.471s	3	93	1h 41m 59.809s	97.598	20
2	*Alex Zanardi (I)	4	Target/Chip Ganassi Racing Reynard 96I-Honda	FS	110.455	58.145s	2	93	1h 42m 01.760s	97.567	17
3	Bobby Rahal (USA)	18	Team Rahal Miller Brewing Reynard 96I-Mercedes	GY	108.825	59.016s	8	93	1h 42m 03.379s	97.541	14
4	*Greg Moore (CDN)	99	Forsythe Player's Ltd./Indeck Reynard 96I-Mercedes	FS	109.748	58.519s	5	93	1h 42m 04.135s	97.529	12
5	Paul Tracy (CDN)	3	Marlboro Team Penske Penske PC25-Mercedes	GY	108.507	59.189s	13	93	1h 42m 04.880s	97.519	10
6	Bryan Herta (USA)	28	Team Rahal Shell Reynard 96I-Mercedes	GY	108.533	59.175s	12	93	1h 42m 05.498s	97.508	8
7	Christian Fittipaldi (BR)	11	Newman/Haas Kmart/Budweiser Lola T96/00-Ford XD	GY	108.450	59.220s	14	93	1h 42m 07.122s	97.482	6
8	Jimmy Vasser (USA)	12	Target/Chip Ganassi Racing Reynard 96I-Honda	FS	108.634	59.120s	11	93	1h 42m 08.267s	97.464	5
9	Robby Gordon (USA)	5	Walker Valvoline/Cummins/Craftsman Reynard 96I-Ford XD	GY	107.615	59.680s	18	93	1h 42m 18.130s	97.307	4
10	Scott Pruett (USA)	20	Patrick Racing Firestone Lola T96/00-Ford XD	FS	109.803	58.490s	4	93	1h 42m 19.461s	97.286	3
11	*Mark Blundell (GB)	21	PacWest Racing Group VISA Reynard 96I-Ford XB	GY	108.053	59.437s	16	92	Running		2
12	Mauricio Gugelmin (BR)	17	PacWest Racing Group Hollywood Reynard 96I-Ford XB	GY	107.998	59.467s	17	92	Running		1
13	Al Unser Jr. (USA)	2	Marlboro Team Penske Penske PC25-Mercedes	GY	108.852	59.001s	7	92	Running		
14	Emerson Fittipaldi (BR)	9	Hogan Penske Marlboro Latin America Penske PC25-Mercedes	GY	108.283	59.311s	15	90	Accident		
15	*Eddie Lawson (USA)	10	Galles Racing Delco Electronics Lola T96/00-Mercedes	GY	105.316	1m 00.982s	24	90	Running		
16	*Jeff Krosnoff (USA)	25	Arciero-Wells Racing MCI Reynard 96I-Toyota	FS	107.400	59.799s	20	89	Accident		
17	Stefan Johansson (S)	16	Bettenhausen Alumax Aluminum Reynard 96I-Mercedes	GY	106.605	1m 00.245s	21	89	Accident		
18	Gil de Ferran (BR)	8	Hall Racing Pennzoil Special Reynard 96I-Honda	GY	108.727	59.069s	9	89	Running		
19	Scott Goodyear (CDN)	15	Walker Valvoline DuraBlend Reynard 96I-Ford XB	GY	105.943	1m 00.621s	23	89	Running		
20	*P.J. Jones (USA)	98	All American Racers Castrol Eagle Mk.V-Toyota	GY	105.253	1m 01.019s	25	89	Running		
21	Andre Ribeiro (BR)	31	Tasman Motorsports LCI International Lola T96/00-Honda	FS	110.616	58.060s	1	88	Accident		1
22	Michael Andretti (USA)	6	Newman/Haas Kmart/Texaco Havoline Lola T96/00-Ford XD	GY	108.666	59.102s	10	82	Engine		
23	Roberto Moreno (BR)	34	Payton/Coyne Data Control Lola T96/00-Ford XB	FS	106.386	1m 00.369s	22	52	Clutch		
24	Raul Boesel (BR)	1	Brahma Sports Team Reynard 96I-Ford XD	GY	107.534	59.724s	19	50	Electrical		
25	*Richie Hearn (USA)	44	Della Penna Ralphs/Food 4 Less/Fuji Reynard 95I-Ford XB	GY	104.612	1m 01.392s	26	50	Driver fatigue		
26	Parker Johnstone (USA)	49	Brix Comptech Motorola Reynard 96I-Honda	FS	108.947	58.949s	6	38	Suspension		
27	Hiro Matsushita (J)	19	Payton/Coyne Panasonic/Duskin Lola T96/00-Ford XB	FS	102.692	1m 02.541s	28	23	Water pump		
28	Juan Manuel Fangio II (RA)	36	All American Racers Castrol Eagle Mk.V-Toyota	GY	104.312	1m 01.569s	27	10	Clutch		

* denotes Rookie driver

Caution flags: Laps 3–5, tow/Johnstone; laps 84–88, tow/Andretti; laps 92–93, accident/E. Fittipaldi, Johansson, Krosnoff and Ribeiro. **Total:** three for 10 laps.

Lap leaders: Alex Zanardi, 1–36 (36 laps); Greg Moore, 37–38 (2 laps); Zanardi, 39–65 (27 laps); Bobby Rahal, 66 (1 lap); Adrian Fernandez, 67 (1 lap); Moore, 68–77 (10 laps); Fernandez, 78–93 (16 laps). **Totals:** Zanardi, 63 laps; Fernandez, 17 laps; Moore, 12 laps; Rahal, 1 lap.

Fastest race lap: Alex Zanardi, 59.510s, 107.921 mph on lap 84.

Championship positions: 1 Vasser, 107; **2** Unser, 99; **3** de Ferran, 92; **4** C. Fittipaldi, 84; **5** Andretti, 73; **6** Zanardi and Moore, 72; **8** Pruett, 62; **9** Tracy, 59; **10** Fernandez, 56; **11** Rahal, 54; **12** Ribeiro, 50; **13** Gugelmin, E. Fittipaldi and Blundell, 29; **16** Johnstone, 28; **17** Lawson, 26; **18** Moreno and Herta, 24; **20** Gordon, 21; **21** Johansson, 19; **22** Boesel, 11; **23** Jones, 4; **24** Matsushita and Hearn, 3; **26** Goodyear and Greco, 1.

Official Information Technology Provider **EDS**

MICHIGAN

Michael C. Brown

1 - RIBEIRO

2 - HERTA

3 - GUGELMIN

Slick work in the pits by the Tasman team helped Andre Ribeiro to his second win of the season. The Brazilian receives a helping hand as he accelerates back into the race after taking on service.

QUALIFYING

Proof of the steady progress being made by the engine and tire companies was plainly evident during practice and qualifying. In the very first session on Friday, Andre Ribeiro established a new benchmark by turning a lap at 235.714 mph – faster than the best lap seen during the month of May's U.S. 500. On Saturday morning no fewer than six cars bettered 236 mph, with Ribeiro once again emerging on top at an astonishing 238.407 mph.

'It felt good,' said Ribeiro with a broad smile. 'It was a nice experience. It was close to a perfect lap. Obviously, I had a good tow from two or three cars, but to be able to go around the corners at that speed, you have to have a good setup.'

No one expected Ribeiro, or anyone else, to match that speed during single-car qualifying, but it was still a surprise when he managed a 'mere' 231.009, good enough only for a position in the middle of the third row.

'When we practiced, we were concentrating on the race,' he explained. 'So we didn't change the car for qualifying. Of course, it would be nice to be on pole, but this is a 500-mile race. We do have a fantastic car for the race.'

Warmer temperatures also contributed to the lower speeds. Still, it was quite a surprise to see the two Mercedes-powered cars of Greg Moore and Al Unser, plus Scott Pruett's Lola-Ford, atop the timing charts with more than half of the qualifying session completed. The two Target/Chip Ganassi cars, however, had yet to run. Zanardi, who drew 16th, was first to go. He duly posted a pair of scorching laps at 233.553 and 233.643.

Vasser, meanwhile, was waiting patiently in line. When his turn finally came, the Californian shifted into high gear and posted two laps at better than 234 mph.

'It feels great to be on the pole,' said Vasser after clinching his fourth pole of the season and a new track record to boot. 'It's another point for the championship, and good for the team and for Honda and Firestone.'

Andre Ribeiro seems to have developed a special affinity for Michigan International Speedway. The Brazilian drove impressively on his M.I.S. debut in the 1995 Marlboro 500, leading clearly before being hobbled by a minor electrical fire. He was a threat for victory, too, in the PPG Cup series' first of two visits to Roger Penske's high-banked two-mile oval in '96, for the U.S. 500, until a fuel pickup problem dropped him to fourth.

Third time was a charm. Ribeiro qualified only eighth in his LCI International Lola-Honda, but he and race engineer Don Halliday were content after concentrating throughout practice on perfecting their car's setup for the race. The strategy paid off.

The only minor glitch came in the early laps when Ribeiro was sent to the back of the field following a pit stop under yellow. Ribeiro was incensed, having failed to understand the still-evolving new pit lane regulations, but he overcame his emotions and charged back into contention.

As usual for a 500-mile race, attrition took care of several contenders, including Alex Zanardi, Greg Moore, Michael Andretti, Scott Pruett and Ribeiro's own Tasman teammate Adrian Fernandez. Still, at the end he had to push hard to prevent Bryan Herta and Mauricio Gugelmin from stealing his thunder.

The triumph – representing two in a row for Steve Horne's Tasman Motorsports team – was once again tinged by sadness following a violent first-lap accident involving the universally popular and admired Emerson Fittipaldi. Ribeiro was suitably reflective during the traditional post-race festivities.

'We decided not to spray champagne today because of what happened in Toronto and what happened today,' said Ribeiro, who instead merely toasted his success and offered his best wishes for a full recovery to his revered countryman.

Overcast skies and comfortable temperatures greeted the teams on race day. That in itself was good news, since the notorious high heat and humidity of Michigan in July often had served to multiply the stress factor involved in a gruelling 500-mile race.

After one false start, greeted by yellow flags and a shake of the head by starter Jim Swintal, pole-sitter Jimmy Vasser headed Target/Chip Ganassi teammate Alex Zanardi into Turn One. Moore, after recording his best starting position in an Indy Car race, led the chase, but Fittipaldi, who started fifth, was clearly in a racy mood as he rocketed past the rookie's Player's Reynard-Mercedes on the high line between Turns One and Two. Unfortunately, the left-rear tire of Fittipaldi's Marlboro Latin America Penske-Mercedes brushed lightly against Moore's right-front wheel as Fittipaldi completed the pass. It was enough to

High speeds prompt safety concern

Breathtaking action and almost constant wheel-to-wheel racing at speeds reaching over 240 mph ensured the Marlboro 500 was not for the faint of heart. The dangers were amply demonstrated by a series of accidents which resulted in Paul Tracy, Emerson Fittipaldi and Parker Johnstone being admitted to the hospital.

Several drivers, including two of the first three finishers, expressed their concerns about safety issues, and especially about competing on the superspeedways.

'This place is just too fast,' proclaimed Mauricio Gugelmin after claiming his second podium finish at M.I.S. 'We're all friends in this series, so it's tough when you see someone hurt in a crash. Especially when it's a close friend like Emerson. And on this type of race track, it seems like you're always ready to push the eject button, so to speak, to try and get yourself out of the firing line. You're really in the lap of the gods.'

Gugelmin himself was lucky to avoid injury when his car was peppered by debris from Fittipaldi's crash. Indeed he had to make three stops during the extended caution to replace the integral mirror/windscreen cowl which was broken in several places.

Later, when Alex Zanardi hit the wall, an errant wheel bounced off a warning-light gantry extending out from the debris fence in Turn Four and directly into the paths of Jimmy Vasser and Gil de Ferran. Vasser was also in the firing line when Parker Johnstone crashed, as part of a wishbone became embedded in the #12 car's nose.

Last year, too, Bryan Herta had a narrow escape when the onboard camera adjacent to his car's roll-hoop was wiped out by a wheel from Danny Sullivan's car as it disintegrated against the wall.

It is an issue that has not been lost on IndyCar. Bear in mind that the speeds were achieved despite rules which have restricted the cars' cornering ability and reduced the potency of the engines by around 100 horsepower. Expect more safety-minded regulations in the future, including energy-absorbing cockpit collars in 1997 which are aimed directly at preventing the types of injuries sustained by Tracy and Fittipaldi.

'Everyone within IndyCar needs to continue working hard to make this sport safer,' said race winner Andre Ribeiro.

Main photo: *Three abreast. The Hollywood Reynard-Ford of Mauricio Gugelmin is sandwiched by the VISA-backed entry of PacWest teammate Mark Blundell and Bryan Herta's Shell Reynard-Mercedes.*

Emerson Fittipaldi *(inset top right) suffered season-ending injuries in a fiery first-lap crash.*

Inset right: *The Target Reynard of Alex Zanardi comes to rest on the infield after its impact against the wall.*

send Fittipaldi slamming into the outside wall.

After a lengthy delay while Fittipaldi was extricated from his badly damaged car, the race was restarted with 15 laps in the books. Zanardi quickly blew past Vasser into Turn Three, but he wasn't able to get away as Moore and Fernandez joined in a titanic battle for the top positions. Soon, though, Vasser began to drop back.

'The car went big-time loose,' said Vasser, who slipped rapidly down the order. By lap 40 he had fallen to 14th and was in danger of going a lap down to Moore, who had taken over the lead from Zanardi and was obviously suffering no ill effects from the incident with Fittipaldi. A caution for debris saved Vasser's bacon, as did another full-course yellow for similar reasons on lap 64. But it was merely delaying the inevitable.

'It was so bad I could barely do 208 [mph],' noted Vasser as he watched the leaders routinely turning laps at better than 230.

Moore held the upper hand through most of the first quarter of the event, but fell from contention with a familiar problem on the ultra-high speed oval: wheel bearing failure.

Andretti ran comfortably among the leaders until his Ford/Cosworth engine's alternator failed. The Newman/Haas team changed the battery on Andretti's Kmart/Texaco Havoline Lola a couple of times, but to no avail.

'No question about it, we had the best handling car out there,' declared Andretti. 'I thought we might have had a shot at winning.'

Zanardi led a majority of the first 125 laps, although midway through each stint his car would go loose and he would fall back into the clutches of his pursuers. Indeed, just three laps after halfway, while under increasing pressure from the similarly Honda-powered cars of Ribeiro, Gil de Ferran and Fernandez, the Italian slid up into the gray in Turn Four and made heavy side-on contact with the wall.

'I went high to get around traffic and the rear of the car came around,' related Zanardi after climbing uninjured from his damaged Reynard.

One of the Target car's wheels ricocheted off the wall and was collected by both de Ferran and Vasser, who was running two laps behind in 14th. Both continued, but de Ferran slipped off the pace with handling troubles and later lost more time to a broken wheel bearing.

Ribeiro and Fernandez ran up front after Zanardi's demise. The

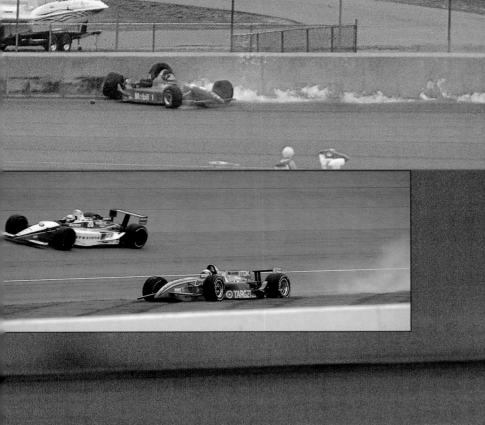

Michael C. Brown

Below: As a thoughtful Andre Ribeiro enjoys his success, team owner Steve Horne and his wife Christine hold aloft the trophy awarded to the victorious entrant.

More power to them

The flat-out nature of Michigan International Speedway always places a premium on horsepower, so it was no surprise to see Honda claim its ninth victory of the season. Nevertheless, there were signs that Mercedes-Benz/Ilmor and Ford/Cosworth had made significant strides toward minimizing the deficit.

The 'Phase II' Mercedes, featuring a revised inlet system, showed its paces during practice when Paul Tracy and Al Unser Jr. headed the time sheets on Friday afternoon. Greg Moore used his new Mercedes to qualify on the front row of the grid, while Bryan Herta finished just over one second behind race winner Andre Ribeiro, albeit after reverting to the tried and tested Phase I engine for the race.

'We've done a lot of work recently and we think it's fair to say we've closed the gap to Honda completely,' said Ilmor's Paul Ray. 'We think there's very little in it now in terms of horsepower.'

Ford/Cosworth also squeezed more power from its XD engine. Consistency, however, remained its Achilles heel.

'The engine let go – again,' said a disappointed Scott Pruett *(above)* after falling by the wayside inside the last 20 miles. 'It's the same old story. We can't get the reliability we need.'

Nevertheless, in contrast to the U.S. 500 in May, all of the XD runners except Pruett and Michael Andretti, who retired with an alternator problem, were around at the finish.

'Honda has earned the right to be considered the leader at this point in the season,' admitted Don Hayward, Ford Indy Car program manager, 'but we've proven ourselves to be their closest competitor with three victories of our own. And we feel whatever gap there is, is quickly being closed.'

Nevertheless, Marlboro 500 winner Andre Ribeiro harbored no doubts about his engine preference: 'The Mercedes has definitely improved, and also the Ford, but the Honda is still going very well,' he said with a knowing smile. 'Scott [Pruett] was running very well when he passed me but there were a few laps to go and I felt I was in control.'

Tasman pair looked extremely strong, and both already had been required to charge through the pack. Ribeiro dropped to 24th when he pitted to replace a flat-spotted tire during the first caution, while Fernandez fell to the rear when he spun the Tecate/Quaker State Lola in pit lane immediately following a routine stop on lap 65.

It was but a minor inconvenience. The Diane Holl-engineered car was hooked up. Fernandez moved swiftly back into contention and set the fastest lap of the race at an amazing 234.020 mph as he chased after Ribeiro.

'The car was perfect,' said Fernandez. 'Steve [Horne] came on the radio and said to take it easy. So I did.'

By this stage nine cars remained on the lead lap. All took on scheduled service when the caution lights flickered on one more time for debris on lap 167. Sadly, Fernandez was unable to leave his pit. A broken clutch was to blame.

'It's a bad feeling on one hand,' said the disappointed Mexican, 'but on the other hand I am happy because today showed how hard we have been working. The car was very good and very fast, and I was waiting for the last 20 laps to battle my teammate, Andre.'

Ribeiro continued in the lead of the race. But he did not have things all his own way. Far from it. Scott Pruett had been biding his time in Patrick Racing's Firestone Lola-Ford/Cosworth. As the race entered its home stretch, Pruett was ready to flex his muscles.

'We played out our strategy just like we planned it,' said Pruett, who was in search of a second straight Marlboro 500 win. 'I was very conservative at the start of the race and we were getting down to the last 50 laps, and especially the last 30, and I became aggressive. The car was good and the tires were great.'

Ribeiro held the lead past the 210-lap mark, but Pruett was little more than a second behind. Gugelmin, too, was within striking distance. Al Unser Jr., Herta and Mark Blundell also remained on the lead lap. Stefan Johansson had just gone a lap down in Tony Bettenhausen's Alumax Reynard-Mercedes.

Everyone made their final scheduled pit stops over the next four laps. The order at the front remained unchanged, save for Blundell falling behind Johansson after a miscue in the PacWest pit. He was obliged to go around one more time.

Pruett rapidly closed a 2.5-second deficit to Ribeiro, and on lap 230 he drafted past on the exit of Turn Two. When Ribeiro returned the favor in the same place on lap 235, it seemed as though the race was building toward a thrilling climax. But at virtually the same moment, Pruett's engine lost its edge. Simultaneously, too, the caution lights came on one final time after a puncture caused Johnstone to crash in Turn Four.

Pruett's engine finally gave up the ghost after a handful of laps under yellow. It was the end of a valiant effort.

'The engine started to go just after

I passed Ribeiro,' said Pruett. 'I called it in right before that last caution. It just wasn't pulling any revs. It was gone.'

Herta overtook Gugelmin for second place right away after the caution. Perhaps he might have something for Ribeiro? But the Brazilian remained cool under pressure. He reeled off the final laps at a relatively relaxed 228/229 mph before crossing the line some 20 yards or so in front of Herta's Shell Reynard-Mercedes.

'He was close all the time but

there were only a few laps to go and I felt in control,' said Ribeiro after scoring the third victory of his short Indy Car career.

Herta was content with second, equaling his career-best finish: 'It feels great. The car was working very well but, to be honest, horsepower is very important on this track. Mercedes did help us out this weekend. It wasn't quite enough for the Big H, but we're definitely getting closer.'

Gugelmin's Ford/Cosworth XB didn't have the grunt to bother either Herta or Ribeiro, yet the underrated Brazilian added a strong third to his magnificent second at the U.S. 500. Teammate Blundell finished sixth, passed by Johansson just three laps from the end after the Englishman's VISA Reynard picked up a puncture.

Ahead of them was the omnipresent Unser, who battled inconsistent handling on his Marlboro Penske-Mercedes and closed to within one point of Vasser in the PPG Cup standings.

'We helped the car in the beginning of the race and at the end we wound up hurting it a little bit because we wound up going loose,' said Unser, who recorded his third top-four finish in four races and his seventh of the campaign. 'It's been a competitive year and we're trying to be as consistent as we can. We moved one step closer to getting that #1 back on the Marlboro car.'

Michael C. Brown

SNIPPETS

Photos: Michael C. Brown

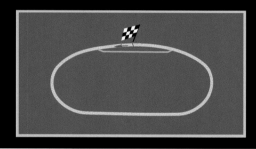

• **Emerson Fittipaldi** (above), a father figure to the growing Brazilian contingent in Indy Car racing and the man largely responsible for the sport's massive growth throughout South America, underwent five hours of surgery a day after his crash to repair a crushed seventh cervical vertebra.

• Marlboro Penske teammate **Paul Tracy** also landed in the hospital after a

hard crash during practice. The telemetry showed Tracy lost control at 212 mph. He hit the wall virtually square-on backward and suffered a 'chip fracture of the Spinous Process (sixth vertebra),' according to IndyCar Director of Medical Affairs Dr. Steve Olvey. Tracy was not able to qualify the car. He also missed the following race at Mid-Ohio.

• **Robby Gordon**, as usual, had a pair of chassis to

choose from. The difference, however, was that in addition to one of his regular Ford/Cosworth XD-powered Valvoline Reynards, Walker Racing also brought one car equipped with the older, proven XB. Gordon qualified the XB car but raced the newer XD.

• Veteran driver/constructor/team owner **Jim Hall** (left) announced immediately after qualifying that he would be retiring from the sport at the end of the season.

• **Jimmy Vasser** endured another tough day at the wheel of Chip Ganassi's #12 Target Reynard-Honda. Aside from his car being loose all day long and twice being hit by debris, Vasser also survived two punctures.

'It was a long day,' he exclaimed after persevering to ninth and emerging with a one-point lead in the PPG Cup standings. 'I thought about parking it a couple of times, but I'm not a quitter.'

• Following an amicable parting of the ways, **Eddie Lawson** was replaced in Rick Galles' Delco Electronics Lola-Mercedes by **Davy Jones** (above).

• **Richard Buck**, crew chief for Al Unser Jr., was trying to tally up the number of days he had spent at Michigan International Speedway during 1996, taking into account both the U.S. 500, back at the end of May, and the Marlboro 500, plus a goodly amount of testing with Marlboro Team Penske: 'I feel like I should've got an apartment up here,' quipped Buck.

PPG INDY CAR WORLD SERIES • ROUND 12

MARLBORO 500

MICHIGAN INTERNATIONAL SPEEDWAY, BROOKLYN, MICHIGAN

JULY 28, 250 laps – 500.000 miles

Place	Driver (Nat.)	No.	Team Sponsors Car-Engine	Tires	Q Speed	Q Time	Q Pos.	Laps	Time/Status	Ave.	Pts.
1	Andre Ribeiro (BR)	31	Tasman Motorsports LCI International Lola T96/00-Honda	FS	231.009	31.168s	8	250	3h 16m 33.425s	152.627	21
2	Bryan Herta (USA)	28	Team Rahal Shell Reynard 96I-Mercedes	GY	229.794	31.332s	11	250	3h 16m 34.803s	152.610	16
3	Mauricio Gugelmin (BR)	17	PacWest Racing Group Hollywood Reynard 96I-Ford XB	GY	228.765	31.473s	13	250	3h 16m 35.717s	152.598	14
4	Al Unser Jr. (USA)	2	Marlboro Team Penske Penske PC25-Mercedes	GY	233.115	30.886s	4	249	Running		12
5	Stefan Johansson (S)	16	Bettenhausen Alumax Aluminum Reynard 96I-Mercedes	GY	228.452	31.516s	14	248	Running		10
6	*Mark Blundell (GB)	21	PacWest Racing Group VISA Reynard 96I-Ford XB	GY	225.872	31.877s	21	248	Running		8
7	Raul Boesel (BR)	1	Brahma Sports Team Reynard 96I-Ford XD	GY	228.405	31.523s	15	247	Running		6
8	Robby Gordon (USA)	5	Walker Valvoline/Cummins/Craftsman Reynard 96I-Ford XD	GY	224.768	32.033s	25	246	Running		5
9	Jimmy Vasser (USA)	12	Target/Chip Ganassi Racing Reynard 96I-Honda	FS	234.665	30.682s	1	245	Running		5
10	Christian Fittipaldi (BR)	11	Newman/Haas Kmart/Budweiser Lola T96/00-Ford XD	GY	226.702	31.760s	19	245	Running		3
11	Eliseo Salazar (RCH)	7	Scandia Cristal/Copec/Mobil 1 Lola T96/00-Ford XB	GY	226.803	31.746s	18	245	Running		2
12	Davy Jones (USA)	10	Galles Racing Delco Electronics Lola T96/00-Mercedes	GY	227.147	31.698s	17	242	Running		1
13	Scott Pruett (USA)	20	Patrick Racing Firestone Lola T96/00-Ford XD	FS	231.783	31.064s	7	241	Engine		
14	Juan Manuel Fangio II (RA)	36	All American Racers Castrol Eagle Mk.V-Toyota	GY	222.609	32.344s	23	240	Running		
15	Hiro Matsushita (J)	19	Payton/Coyne Panasonic/Duskin Lola T96/00-Ford XB	FS	225.994	31.859s	20	240	Running		
16	*P.J. Jones (USA)	98	All American Racers Castrol Eagle Mk.V-Toyota	GY	214.852	33.511s	24	234	Running		
17	*Greg Moore (CDN)	99	Forsythe Player's Ltd./Indeck Reynard 96I-Mercedes	FS	233.501	30.835s	3	227	Running		
18	Parker Johnstone (USA)	49	Brix Comptech Motorola Reynard 96I-Honda	FS	230.411	31.248s	10	220	Accident		
19	Gil de Ferran (BR)	8	Hall Racing Pennzoil Special Reynard 96I-Honda	GY	228.008	31.578s	16	209	Wheel bearing		
20	Adrian Fernandez (MEX)	32	Tasman Tecate Beer/Quaker State Oil Lola T96/00-Honda	FS	232.048	31.028s	6	169	Clutch		
21	*Alex Zanardi (I)	4	Target/Chip Ganassi Racing Reynard 96I-Honda	FS	233.643	30.816s	2	128	Accident		
22	Michael Andretti (USA)	6	Newman/Haas Kmart/Texaco Havoline Lola T96/00-Ford XD	GY	228.808	31.467s	12	99	Alternator		
23	Roberto Moreno (BR)	34	Payton/Coyne Data Control Lola T96/00-Ford XB	FS	225.744	31.895s	22	93	Accident		
24	Bobby Rahal (USA)	18	Team Rahal Miller Brewing Reynard 96I-Mercedes	GY	230.528	31.233s	9	41	Engine		
25	Emerson Fittipaldi (BR)	9	Hogan Penske Marlboro Latin America Penske PC25-Mercedes	GY	232.860	30.920s	5	1	Accident		
NS	Paul Tracy (CDN)	3	Marlboro Team Penske Penske PC25-Mercedes	GY	no speed	no time	–	–	Accident in practice		

* denotes Rookie driver

Caution flags: Laps 0–1, yellow start; laps 2–14, accident/E. Fittipaldi; laps 39–44, debris on track; laps 63–68, debris on track; laps 96–106, accident/Moreno; laps 128–135, accident/Zanardi; laps 167–173, debris on track; laps 235–241, accident/Johnstone. **Total:** eight for 59 laps.

Lap leaders: Jimmy Vasser, 1–15 (15 laps); Alex Zanardi, 16–29 (14 laps); Greg Moore, 30–45 (16 laps); Michael Andretti, 46 (1 lap); Zanardi, 47–48 (2 laps); Moore, 49 (1 lap); Zanardi, 50–51 (2 laps); Moore, 52–65 (14 laps); Andretti, 66–71 (6 laps); Zanardi, 72–127 (56 laps); Andre Ribeiro, 128–210 (83 laps); Scott Pruett, 211 (1 lap); Mauricio Gugelmin, 212–214 (3 laps); Ribeiro, 215–229 (15 laps); Pruett, 230–234 (5 laps); Ribeiro, 235–250 (16 laps). **Totals:** Ribeiro, 114 laps; Zanardi, 74 laps; Moore, 31 laps; Vasser, 15 laps; Andretti, 7 laps; Pruett, 6 laps; Gugelmin, 3 laps.

Fastest race lap: Adrian Fernandez, 30.767s, 234.020 mph on lap 164.

Championship positions: 1 Vasser, 112; **2** Unser, 111; **3** de Ferran, 92; **4** C. Fittipaldi, 87; **5** Andretti, 73; **6** Zanardi and Moore, 72; **8** Ribeiro, 71; **9** Pruett, 62; **10** Tracy, 59; **11** Fernandez, 56; **12** Rahal, 54; **13** Gugelmin, 43; **14** Herta, 40; **15** Blundell, 37; **16** E. Fittipaldi and Johansson, 29; **18** Johnstone, 28; **19** Gordon and Lawson, 26; **21** Moreno, 24; **22** Boesel, 17; **23** P.J. Jones, 4; **24** Matsushita and Hearn, 3; **26** Salazar, 2; **27** Goodyear, Greco and D. Jones, 1.

Official Information Technology Provider **EDS**

161

MID-OHIO

1 - ZANARDI

2 - VASSER

3 - ANDRETTI

Having taken the top two positions on the starting grid, the Target Reynard-Hondas of Alex Zanardi and Jimmy Vasser maintained their stranglehold in the race. Bryan Herta and Michael Andretti follow.

Target/Chip Ganassi Racing had the field covered in the Miller 200. Teammates Alex Zanardi and Jimmy Vasser occupied the top two positions on the starting grid and maintained that form virtually throughout the 83-lap race.

'It's my first 1-2,' said ecstatic team owner Chip Ganassi. 'I've got the best team in the business. The U.S. 500 was a great day for us, and so's this one.'

Ganassi's pair of Target Reynard-Hondas were never seriously challenged as Zanardi rebounded from his accident in the Michigan 500 to break open what was previously a tight battle with Greg Moore for Rookie of the Year honors.

'Everything went perfect,' agreed Zanardi. 'The car was fabulous. I'm very happy Jimmy could finish second and score a lot of points for the championship.'

Vasser echoed those sentiments precisely: 'I drove a little conservatively to save fuel and make sure I got points,' he said after establishing a 128–111 margin over Al Unser Jr. in the PPG Cup standings. 'I've been up before in the points and then it was down to one point, so it's good to be up by a few again.'

Warm, dry weather and hazy sunshine ensured near-perfect conditions for another record crowd on the scenic and challenging Mid-Ohio Sports Car Course. Just about every vantage point was taken around the 2.25-mile parkland venue. It was a spectacular – and colorful – sight.

Zanardi, perhaps, was suitably inspired as he accelerated smartly in anticipation of the starting signal, which, as usual at Mid-Ohio, was given on the long back straightaway rather than on the short chute in front of the pits. Zanardi held a clear advantage as he turned into Turn Four. Behind him Vasser came under strong pressure from the on-form Bryan Herta, who once again had qualified strongly in Team Rahal's Shell Reynard-Mercedes.

Herta pulled alongside Vasser in the braking area but the championship leader was determined not to squander his front row starting position. Vasser braved it out around the outside of the first segment of the Esses, then reclaimed second place as the pair turned left and crested the hill in Turn Five.

Michael Andretti followed in fourth, split from Newman/Haas teammate Christian Fittipaldi by Scott Pruett, who made a strong start from the outside of row three.

Michael C. Brown

Fast learner

With Emerson Fittipaldi hors de combat and Paul Tracy not cleared to drive at Mid-Ohio as a result of neck and back injuries sustained at Michigan, Roger Penske needed to find a replacement driver. His eventual choice, Mercedes Junior Team member Jan Magnussen, represented something of a surprise, since he had never before raced in North America.

The 23-year-old nevertheless had established a fine reputation in Europe. A former world champion kart racer, Magnussen (pronounced 'MAO-noo-ss'n' in his native Denmark) won the prestigious Formula Ford Festival in 1992 and thoroughly dominated the 1994 British Formula 3 Championship, during which he eclipsed Ayrton Senna's record number of wins in a single season. More recently he had been competing for Mercedes in the International Touring Car Championship and carrying out Formula 1 testing duties for Marlboro McLaren International.

Magnussen gathered his first experience of an Indy car during a two-day test at Sebring, Florida: 'My first impression was that the car was very user-friendly,' he said. 'You can drive it hard and go to the limit and still catch it without going off, whereas in a Formula 1 car you never really know where the limit

is until you fall off. I really like it.

'The biggest difference from a Formula 1 car is the brakes. In a Formula 1 car, with carbon discs, it's almost like an on–off switch; but in an Indy car, with steel discs, the brakes are much more progressive. You can feel it's a heavier car than a Formula 1, but there's more power too, so they kind of even each other out. I must say the Indy car is a lot of fun to drive.'

Magnussen admitted that Mid-Ohio represented an altogether tougher challenge: 'It's probably one of the most difficult circuits I've been to. If it had been in a car I've been in all year, I think it would be a different story. I just need to build a little more confidence in the car.'

Magnussen, after qualifying 18th, spent much of the race in close company with Mark Blundell, who, ironically, was his Marlboro McLaren teammate during his Formula 1 debut in the 1995 Pacific Grand Prix at Aida. Finally, on lap 64, the pair tangled in Turn Two as Blundell attempted to make a pass.

'It was strange to get stuck in the gravel and be able to get out and continue the race,' said Magnussen, who finished 14th after gaining assistance from the IndyCar Safety Team. 'All in all, I learned a lot this weekend and really enjoyed myself.'

QUALIFYING

Alex Zanardi and Jimmy Vasser both switched to their backup cars during an eventful first practice session, but it didn't seem to cause any ill effects as the two Target Reynard-Hondas still finished on top of the timing charts. Both men made good progress, although Vasser was slightly concerned after experiencing a broken front suspension wishbone under braking at the end of the main straight.

Lap times continued to tumble on Friday afternoon, with Zanardi once again fastest to claim the provisional pole. This time he was separated from his teammate by an inspired Bobby Rahal: 'You can always be better but generally I'm very pleased,' said Rahal, who had assumed the mantle of Indy Car racing's elder statesman as a result of Emerson Fittipaldi's enforced absence due to injuries suffered at M.I.S. '[Teammate] Bryan [Herta] has been very fast in testing here, so that gave us a good basis to work from. Goodyear has done a great job with the tires, and hopefully there will be more [speed] to come tomorrow. I'd like to think we can get the pole, because it's been a long time since I've had one.' Since Toronto in 1992, to be precise.

Rahal couldn't reproduce his Miller Reynard's balance on Saturday, slipping to a disappointed ninth, but Herta responded with a time good enough for third on the grid – beaten only by the two Ganassi cars.

'I'm really happy,' said Herta. 'The car feels good. We gave it everything we have. Alex and Jimmy did an outstanding job because those are phenomenal lap times.'

Zanardi had absolutely no complaints: 'Today was one of those beautiful days when everything goes right,' he said after securing his third pole and a new track record, eclipsing Jacques Villeneuve's mark from 1995. 'This morning we did a lot of work, not always in the right direction, but we learned what makes the car better. I'm very, very confident for tomorrow because I think we have a very good car.' Prophetic words.

Michael Andretti saw off a spirited challenge from Bryan Herta to take third place in the Kmart/Texaco Havoline Lola, breathing new life into his PPG Cup championship ambitions.

A little farther back, Gil de Ferran completely misjudged his braking point in Jim Hall's Pennzoil Reynard-Honda and rammed hard into the rear of fellow Brazilian Mauricio Gugelmin. De Ferran resumed three laps in arrears after being pulled out of the sand trap and then stopping in the pits for a new nose section. Gugelmin wasn't so lucky. His Hollywood/PacWest Reynard was out due to damaged rear suspension.

The next drama befell rookie Greg Moore, who started strongly but fell to the tail of the field due to an obscure electrical malfunction. Curiously, and again without warning, the engine suddenly began to fire on all cylinders. Moore set about despatching the tail-enders.

Zanardi eked out a significant advantage at the opposite end of the field. Vasser couldn't keep pace with the flying Italian, but he was able to edge clear of a good scrap between Herta, Andretti, Pruett, Fittipaldi, Adrian Fernandez, Bobby Rahal, Andre Ribeiro, Al Unser Jr. and Raul Boesel, who remained tied together as if part of one long express train. Unser contrived to find a way past Ribeiro on lap six, but otherwise there were no changes of position. The drivers seemed content to bide their time until the first round of pit stops.

The order at lap 20 remained the same. Zanardi led Vasser by more than five seconds. Herta was more than nine seconds farther back, having pulled out a little breathing space over Andretti.

Unser was first to peel off into pit lane. Roger Penske, the master strategist, had recognized the fact that Unser was being held up by Rahal and Fernandez. He reasoned that an early stop, fresh tires and, he hoped, a clear track, might give Unser an opportunity to move up a place or two before everyone else took on service. As usual, he was right on the money.

Vasser assumed the lead for a couple of laps after Zanardi had made his pit stop, whereupon the situation remained much as it was before, with Zanardi leading by as much as nine seconds. Herta, though, fell from third to fifth, primarily as a result of being held up for three laps behind backmarkers Eliseo Salazar and Hiro Matsushita, who were more intent upon dicing for 21st place than allowing the leaders easy passage.

'I've got no respect for those guys,' said an angry Herta. 'I don't know what they're doing out there.'

Fittipaldi maintained sixth, but now his mirrors were filled by Unser, who had leapfrogged ahead of both Fernandez and Rahal. Unser's Marlboro Penske-Mercedes was looking strong as the race approached its halfway point. But then, quite abruptly, his tires began to lose grip. The team had switched to a combination of harder primary tires on the front and Goodyear's softer option compound on the rear at the previous stop. Unser soon began to realize he was in trouble.

'We started the race with a push and then the car went loose on me,' related Unser. 'Even though Goodyear came here with good tires this week-

Paul Webb

end, we chose the wrong combination for the race.'

Rahal, meanwhile, was on the move. He passed Fernandez impressively on the outside line into Turn Four on lap 45, and next time around demoted Unser in the same location. Unser also was passed by Fernandez a couple of tours later.

Rahal quickly closed on Fittipaldi's Kmart/Budweiser Lola-Ford, and at that stage the veteran's Miller Reynard-Mercedes was perhaps the fastest car on the track – save for the two Target Reynard-Hondas, of course. Rahal tried on a couple of occasions to find a way past Fittipaldi, once on the inside under braking for Turn Four and once on

the outside; but the Brazilian wasn't conceding any ground at all. Rahal stayed behind.

Boesel's race ended prematurely due to yet another faulty crank trigger after 48 laps, and when he parked Barry Green's Brahma Reynard-Ford on the side of the track there was talk among the IndyCar officials of a full-course yellow. The timing could not have been worse for Unser, whose crew decided to delay his much-needed pit stop for fear of falling a lap down. It turned out to be a moot point. There was no yellow and Unser's car was handling so poorly he lost a lap anyway.

Rahal signaled the beginning of the second round of pit stops on lap

54. By lap 58, everyone else had followed suit. The status quo remained as Zanardi held a handy margin over Vasser. Andretti still ran third, albeit some 25 seconds in arrears of Vasser. Pruett, sadly, lost fourth place when his car lost all drive immediately after taking on scheduled service.

Herta took the position and soon was being pursued by team leader Rahal, whose early stop had enabled him to pass Fittipaldi. The Brazilian also lost places to Fernandez and Moore as his car began slipping and sliding almost uncontrollably.

Then came the first of two late full-course cautions, after Indy Car debutant Jan Magnussen slid into

the gravel trap in Turn Two as he was passed, somewhat lustily, by Mark Blundell for 11th place. The race was suddenly rejuvenated. Except that no one told Zanardi, who took off briskly at the restart and soon reestablished an appreciable cushion over Vasser.

'I was trying as hard as I could,' said the series leader.

'I was hoping I could make some spectacular move and make it onto [ESPN's] SportsCenter, but it was tough. I didn't have anything for Alex. He was just a tick or two faster, and in that situation it doesn't make sense to do anything silly.'

While Vasser was content to settle for second, Herta had no intention of

Like a duck to water

Of the two Europeans making their Indy Car debuts, Jan Magnussen garnered most attention by virtue of driving for the high-profile Marlboro Team Penske. Yet in many ways the performance of Massimiliano 'Max' Papis was more impressive at the wheel of Arciero-Wells Racing's altogether less potent MCI Reynard-Toyota.

Team co-owner Cal Wells III had thought long and hard before settling upon a replacement for Jeff Krosnoff, who had tragically lost his life in Toronto. Marco Apicella, a good friend of Krosnoff from their days together in the All-Japan Formula 3000 Championship, turned down the opportunity for personal reasons. Last year's Player's Toyota Atlantic champion Richie Hearn and 1996 champion-elect Patrick Carpentier were unavailable due to prior contractual obligations. Papis, meanwhile, also had been highly recommended following some spectacular performances, including three wins, aboard Gianpiero Moretti's Momo Ferrari 333SP in the IMSA World Sports Car Championship.

'For me it was important to have someone with a positive approach and a lot of experience,' said Wells. 'Max is a phenomenal talent and I believe he can per-

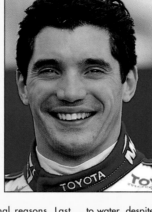

Michael C. Brown

petuate what Jeff started. We fully expect to be winning races a year from now, and therefore the decisions we make now are critical. Max is the type of talent and the kind of athlete that can achieve those aims.'

The 26-year-old from Como, Italy, pursued an almost identical career path to countryman Alex Zanardi, graduating directly from karts into Formula 3 and then progressing through Formula 3000 to Formula 1, in which he drove seven races in 1995 for the Footwork Arrows team. His best result was a seventh at his home Grand Prix in Monza.

Papis took to the Indy car like a duck to water, despite gaining his first experience during a mandatory rookie test just one day prior to the start of practice at Mid-Ohio. Papis was almost immediately quicker than the two Eagle-Toyotas and claimed the team's highest grid position of the season, 19th, just one place and 0.1 second behind Magnussen's Penske-Mercedes.

'I am very pleased with the performance we had because every time I jump in the car we get better and better,' said the thoughtful, upbeat Papis, who also displayed his potential in the race before being forced out by engine woes.

Bobby Rahal *(bottom)* **completed another encouraging weekend for Team Rahal by taking fifth place with the Miller Reynard.**

allowing Andretti an easy passage for the final podium position. Herta drew alongside the Kmart/Texaco Havoline car under braking for Turn Four at the restart, and it took a typically robust move from Andretti to keep him at bay. Herta tried again following one final caution, after a blown engine had ended a good run by Robby Gordon and deposited his Valvoline Reynard-Ford into the gravel in Turn Two. This time Herta and Andretti raced side-by-side through Turns Four and Five, rubbing wheels along the way. Once more, Andretti was able to hold on.

'I knew I could trust Bryan because he is a really good driver, a good, fair driver,' said Andretti. 'I was totally confident that we would come out of that in one piece.'

Andretti secured his third-place

finish, leaving Herta in fourth: 'That kind of racing is really fun. We touched a little bit but there was no real problem,' said Herta.

Rahal also drove a fine race to finish fifth, followed by Fernandez, who maintained a solid pace with a car that was not handling entirely to his liking. Fittipaldi persevered for seventh and Ribeiro limped home eighth with a puncture after Moore attempted an impossible maneuver in Turn Two on the final lap. The miscue also dumped his Player's car into the tire barrier.

Blundell was tops among those a lap down, while a desperate move by Unser to displace Parker Johnstone from 11th place ended with both cars off the road at the end of the back straightaway. It was an ignominious ending to a dismal day for the two-time PPG Cup champion.

Steve Swope Photography

Photos: Michael C. Brown

SNIPPETS

• The bumper crowd had plenty to cheer about as all four drivers representing the two Columbus-based teams qualified among the top 10.

Team Rahal led the way as **Bryan Herta** (right) celebrated the launch of 'Hertamania' – inspired by team co-owner David Letterman –

by securing third on the grid. **Bobby Rahal** was a little farther back in ninth, sandwiched between the Tasman Motorsports Group twins, **Adrian Fernandez** and **Andre Ribeiro** (left).

• **Stefan Johansson** suffered a massive engine failure in final qualifying, such that a gaping hole was punched through his Alumax Reynard's undertray.

• Both **Newman/Haas** drivers spun off the road during first practice. Damage, fortunately, was minimal and both Michael Andretti and Christian Fittipaldi reverted to their primary chassis in time for qualify-

• All of the **Reynards** featured distinctive new wing-extensions on the rear edge of their sidepods, similar to the flaps seen on Formula 1 cars for a couple of years, as well as the 'swoopier' nose-wing design first seen on Rahal's car at Portland.

ing. They atoned for their transgressions by finishing third and seventh.

• The relentless improvement of **Ilmor Engineering**'s Mercedes-Benz IC108C engines was once again exemplified by a series of fastest trap speeds on the back straightaway. Greg Moore's Player's Reynard was swiftest of all, clocked at 188 mph during final qualifying.

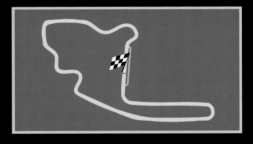

• **Raul Boesel** (above), having had little to cheer about during his first 12 races with Barry Green's Brahma Sports Team, bolstered his confidence by setting fourth best time in the initial practice session. He slipped to 11th on the grid but raced strongly until hobbled by an electrical/engine failure for the fourth time in five races.

PPG INDY CAR WORLD SERIES • ROUND 13
MILLER 200

MID-OHIO SPORTS CAR COURSE, LEXINGTON, OHIO

AUGUST 11, 83 laps – 185.800 miles

Place	Driver (Nat.)	No.	Team Sponsors Car-Engine	Tires	Q Speed	Q Time	Q Pos.	Laps	Time/Status	Ave.	Pts.
1	*Alex Zanardi (I)	4	Target/Chip Ganassi Racing Reynard 96I-Honda	FS	122.100	1m 06.339s	1	83	1h 46m 49.448s	104.358	22
2	Jimmy Vasser (USA)	12	Target/Chip Ganassi Racing Reynard 96I-Honda	FS	121.584	1m 06.621s	2	83	1h 46m 51.362s	104.327	16
3	Michael Andretti (USA)	6	Newman/Haas Kmart/Texaco Havoline Lola T96/00-Ford XD	GY	120.572	1m 07.180s	4	83	1h 46m 52.853s	104.303	14
4	Bryan Herta (USA)	28	Team Rahal Shell Reynard 96I-Mercedes	GY	121.116	1m 06.878s	3	83	1h 46m 53.964s	104.285	12
5	Bobby Rahal (USA)	18	Team Rahal Miller Brewing Reynard 96I-Mercedes	GY	119.981	1m 07.511s	9	83	1h 46m 55.093s	104.267	10
6	Adrian Fernandez (MEX)	32	Tasman Tecate Beer/Quaker State Oil Lola T96/00-Honda	FS	120.130	1m 07.427s	8	83	1h 46m 58.284s	104.215	8
7	Christian Fittipaldi (BR)	11	Newman/Haas Kmart/Budweiser Lola T96/00-Ford XD	GY	120.414	1m 07.268s	5	83	1h 46m 58.770s	104.207	6
8	Andre Ribeiro (BR)	31	Tasman Motorsports LCI International Lola T96/00-Honda	FS	119.912	1m 07.550s	10	83	1h 49m 58.398s	101.370	5
9	*Greg Moore (CDN)	99	Forsythe Player's Ltd./Indeck Reynard 96I-Mercedes	FS	120.140	1m 07.421s	7	82	Accident		4
10	*Mark Blundell (GB)	21	PacWest Racing Group VISA Reynard 96I-Ford XB	GY	119.431	1m 07.822s	13	82	Running		3
11	Stefan Johansson (S)	16	Bettenhausen Alumax Aluminum Reynard 96I-Mercedes	GY	116.912	1m 09.283s	20	82	Running		2
12	Parker Johnstone (USA)	49	Brix Comptech Motorola Reynard 96I-Honda	FS	118.655	1m 08.265s	16	81	Accident		1
13	Al Unser Jr. (USA)	2	Marlboro Team Penske Penske PC25-Mercedes	GY	119.283	1m 07.906s	15	81	Accident		
14	*Jan Magnussen (DK)	3	Marlboro Team Penske Penske PC25-Mercedes	GY	117.813	1m 08.753s	18	81	Running		
15	Eliseo Salazar (RCH)	7	Scandia Cristal/Copec/Mobil 1 Lola T96/00-Ford XB	GY	114.128	1m 10.973s	26	81	Running		
16	Davy Jones (USA)	10	Galles Racing Delco Electronics Lola T96/00-Mercedes	GY	115.408	1m 10.186s	23	81	Running		
17	Gil de Ferran (BR)	8	Hall Racing Pennzoil Special Reynard 96I-Honda	GY	119.297	1m 07.898s	14	79	Running		
18	Robby Gordon (USA)	5	Walker Valvoline/Cummins/Craftsman Reynard 96I-Ford XD	GY	118.448	1m 08.384s	17	75	Engine		
19	Hiro Matsushita (J)	19	Payton/Coyne Panasonic/Duskin Lola T96/00-Ford XB	FS	114.848	1m 10.528s	25	72	Accident		
20	Juan Manuel Fangio II (RA)	36	All American Racers Castrol Eagle Mk.V-Toyota	GY	115.850	1m 09.918s	22	56	Fire		
21	Scott Pruett (USA)	20	Patrick Racing Firestone Lola T96/00-Ford XD	FS	120.201	1m 07.387s	6	55	Transmission		
22	Raul Boesel (BR)	1	Brahma Sports Team Reynard 96I-Ford XD	GY	119.856	1m 07.581s	11	48	Electrical		
23	Roberto Moreno (BR)	34	Payton/Coyne Data Control Lola T96/00-Ford XB	FS	116.580	1m 09.480s	21	40	Transmission		
24	*Max Papis (I)	25	Arciero-Wells Racing MCI Reynard 96I-Toyota	FS	117.596	1m 08.880s	19	40	Engine		
25	*P.J. Jones (USA)	98	All American Racers Castrol Eagle Mk.V-Toyota	GY	115.003	1m 10.433s	24	11	Fire		
26	Mauricio Gugelmin (BR)	17	PacWest Racing Group Hollywood Reynard 96I-Ford XB	GY	119.812	1m 07.606s	12	1	Suspension		

* denotes Rookie driver

Caution flags: Laps 1–2, tow/de Ferran; laps 65–68, accident/Magnussen and Blundell; laps 76–79, accident/Matsushita and tow/Gordon. **Total:** three for 10 laps.

Lap leaders: Alex Zanardi, 1–28 (28 laps); Jimmy Vasser, 29–30 (2 laps); Zanardi, 31–56 (26 laps); Vasser, 57–58 (2 laps); Zanardi, 59–83 (25 laps). **Totals:** Zanardi, 79 laps; Vasser, 4 laps.

Fastest race lap: Alex Zanardi, 1m 08.607s, 118.064 mph on lap 75.

Championship positions: 1 Vasser, 128; **2** Unser, 111; **3** Zanardi, 94; **4** C. Fittipaldi, 93; **5** de Ferran, 92; **6** Andretti, 87; **7** Ribeiro and Moore, 76; **9** Fernandez and Rahal, 64; **11** Pruett, 62; **12** Tracy, 59; **13** Herta, 52; **14** Gugelmin, 43; **15** Blundell, 40; **16** Johansson, 31; **17** Johnstone and E. Fittipaldi, 29; **19** Gordon and Lawson, 26; **21** Moreno, 24; **22** Boesel, 17; **23** P.J. Jones, 4; **24** Matsushita and Hearn, 3; **26** Salazar, 2; **27** Goodyear, Greco and D. Jones, 1.

ROAD AMERICA

QUALIFYING

Alex Zanardi benefited from a productive test session with the Target/Chip Ganassi team a few weeks before the race and returned to set the pace during first practice on Friday. In the afternoon, however, an improvement of only 0.2 seconds left him a distant ninth on the provisional grid, well adrift of Bryan Herta's Shell Reynard-Mercedes. Zanardi and his own Reynard-Honda teammate, Jimmy Vasser, who set the second fastest time, were the only Firestone runners to break into the Goodyear-dominated top 10.

As usual, lap times tumbled on Saturday as the teams and drivers dialed in their cars to the track conditions. The final session began with Gil de Ferran forging his way to the front in the Pennzoil Reynard-Honda. Then Zanardi bounded to the top with the only sub-102-second qualifying lap of the fast, undulating and supremely challenging Road America circuit.

'All the guys, and [engineer] Mo Nunn especially, did a very good job,' praised Zanardi after an engine change and some astute alterations to the setup enabled him to secure his fourth pole. 'We turned the car upside down. Normally we have a good advantage with the Honda engine and Firestone tires, but it doesn't look like that this weekend. It's definitely the best pole position I've had so far – the most satisfying.'

De Ferran actually set a faster time during Saturday morning practice but was unable to match that in the warmer, more humid conditions which prevailed in final qualifying. Nevertheless, the Brazilian reckoned he could have matched Zanardi's best had he been able to find a clear lap on his second set of tires.

Michael Andretti posted his strongest qualifying effort of the season, third, just ahead of Christian Fittipaldi despite differing from his Newman/Haas teammate by choosing the harder Goodyear tire compound. 'I think we were giving up about three-tenths [by running the harder tire],' said Andretti, 'and three-tenths would have been good enough for the pole.'

Mauricio Gugelmin trimmed virtually all the downforce from his Hollywood Reynard to qualify a fine fifth fastest ahead of Herta and Vasser, neither of whom improved upon his Friday time.

IndyCar stewards clamp down on drivers

IndyCar Chief Steward Wally Dallenbach, Chief Steward Designate Dennis Swan (due to take over the role upon former driver Dallenbach's retirement at the end of the season) and Vice President of Competition Kirk Russell issued an array of stringent penalties following the dramatic Texaco/Havoline 200. Citing articles 6.1 and 8.12 in the IndyCar Rule Book, which pertain, respectively, to 'unsportsmanlike conduct' and 'unjustifiable risk,' Andre Ribeiro, Paul Tracy and Alex Zanardi were disciplined for 'rough driving.'

Tracy and Ribeiro, both of whom were involved in more than one incident, were fined $40,000 apiece, of which half was suspended pending no repeat offenses in the final two races of the season. Zanardi, who clashed controversially with Gil de Ferran on the opening lap, was fined $20,000. In addition, de Ferran and Greg Moore were advised they would be under close scrutiny in the year's final two races.

'We have seen some first-class competition in 1996,' said Dallenbach, 'and as the season draws to a close we are determined to maintain correct standards of sportsmanship and driver discipline on the race track. Our drivers are some of the best in the world, but it is inevitable that when it is so competitive, problems on the track will occur. As professionals, I am sure that all our drivers will be concentrating on producing their best possible performance in the year's final races.'

The consensus among all drivers was in favor of some action being taken by the stewards following a series of incidents in recent races. Nevertheless, there was widespread surprise not only at the severity of the fines, which far exceeded anything previously issued by IndyCar – and which made the $5,000 penalties issued at Long Beach in April pale into insignificance – but at the manner in which they were assessed, before the drivers were given an opportunity to explain their side of the story.

Zanardi, for example, was particularly upset about comments made by de Ferran in a television interview soon after their collision when he accused Zanardi of deliberately forcing him off the track and demanded he should be black-flagged and excluded from the race.

'So far as I am concerned, it was a racing accident,' said the Italian. 'The stewards are paid money to decide who is right and who is wrong. The bad thing is that if you scream loud, people take a different perspective and it shouldn't work that way.'

A majesty setting for an extraordinary race. Michael Andretti inherited victory on the last lap after a bizarre sequence of misfortunes had eliminated many of his main rivals.

Even the most imaginative of fiction writers would have been hard pushed to conceive a plot as dramatic or unpredictable as that which unfolded during the Texaco/Havoline 200. Take Al Unser Jr.'s role, for example. The Marlboro Team Penske star arrived at Road America as the nearest challenger to PPG Cup points leader Jimmy Vasser, but having failed to win a race thus far during the 1996 season – and after qualifying a mediocre 12th, almost 1.5 seconds away from Alex Zanardi's pole-winning time – Unser was not expected to be much more than a bit-player.

Then again, as he has shown so often in the past, Unser is no ordinary race car driver. Qualifying has never been his forte, yet his rivals are all too aware he can never be discounted once the race is underway.

This was one such occasion. By lap 22, following a curious variety of circumstances, Unser suddenly found himself in the lead. For Unser, that's akin to showing a red flag to a bull. He retained control of the race through the second round of pit stops and acknowledged the white flag with a slim but apparently secure advantage over Michael Andretti. Just one four-mile lap remained. At last, team owner Roger Penske's longest victory drought in 20 years seemed on the verge of being extinguished.

Unser's Marlboro Penske-Mercedes clearly had the legs on Andretti's Kmart/Texaco Havoline Lola-Ford/Cosworth XD on the long straightaways, and while Andretti might have held a slight advantage through the corners, there appeared no way in which he could alter the balance of power. But then, mere moments before Unser prepared to jump onto the brakes in readiness for Canada Corner, less than a mile from the checkered flag, his previously immaculately behaved Mercedes-Benz engine erupted in a dense cloud of white smoke. The desperately disappointed Unser could only stare in disbelief as Andretti swept past and on to victory.

'This track is just flat unlucky for me,' noted Unser. 'The black cloud started in 1982, when I first raced here in a Can-Am race. I sat on the pole and was leading the race when I broke on the second lap. Then, in 1985, I had a 20-second lead [in the Indy Car race] and ended up [crashing and] breaking my leg. If I ever make it past Canada Corner on the last lap when I'm leading the race, then I'll know I'll be in victory lane.'

The bizarre ending perhaps should have been expected, since the 50-lap race had been punctuated by all manner of dramas. The start itself was orderly enough, with Zanardi clinging to his pole advantage through the first corner despite a robust challenge around the outside line from second fastest qualifier Gil de Ferran. But rather than drop back into line as the leaders swept downhill toward Turn Three, de Ferran clung doggedly to the outside, hoping to coax Zanardi into a mistake. It was de Ferran who came off worst, however, as a clash of wheels sent the Brazilian's Pennzoil Reynard-Honda bounding across the grass and deep into the gravel. Needless to say, the two protagonists offered distinctly different views of the incident.

'My perspective is the reality,' claimed an irate de Ferran, who for the second straight race was making a mere cameo appearance, out of contention almost before the race had begun. 'The reality is, he knew where I was and Alessandro decided not to give me enough room and drove me off the road. All he needed to do was give me another foot of space and I would have braked and tucked in behind him. I don't know what he was thinking.' Zanardi, who rejoined the race in 12th place after a detour through the grass, wasn't buying that story: 'We came up to the first turn and Gil was on the outside. He tried to outbrake me on the outside. We went through side by side and at the following turn I thought I was going to have an easier time. There just isn't room for two. The guy tried to outbrake me on the outside and we hit each other. So far as I'm concerned, we both turned into the corner and I felt him hit me in the back. I was already committed to the corner.'

Andretti, having started on row two of the grid, had a grandstand view of the melee – despite the fact he was rather busy in attempting (vainly) to keep Christian Fittipaldi at bay: 'Basically, if I'd done what Gil did, I'd have gone off in the same place,' declared Andretti, who instead preferred to cede the position to his Newman/Haas teammate.

Fittipaldi and Andretti duly emerged in the lead, followed by Mauricio Gugelmin, who was enjoying by far his most promising outing of the season in his Hollywood Reynard-Ford XB. Paul Tracy, not content with moving from eighth to fourth within the first half-mile, attempted an almost impossible maneuver around the outside of Gugelmin under braking for Turn Five. Not surprisingly, the Canadian found himself on the grass at the exit. He promptly lost two places to Vasser and Bryan Herta. As if that wasn't bad enough, Tracy clipped the rear of Herta's Shell Reynard-Mercedes just a couple of corners later, ripping the left-front wing from his Penske.

For the third time in as many races, the leaders at the end of the first lap were greeted by double yellow flags. The caution enabled Tracy to make a pit stop without losing a lap. Jon Bouslog's crew quickly replaced the damaged nose and Tracy returned in 20th place, only to continue his miserable day by losing control under braking in Turn Three. Cue another caution while the #3 Marlboro Penske was removed from the gravel-trap.

Fittipaldi maintained his lead on the second restart.

Andretti, meanwhile, was outdragged first by Gugelmin, then by Herta. He lost another place to Bobby Rahal's Miller Reynard-Mercedes on lap 13.

'The yellows were killing me,' said Andretti. 'On each restart I was getting eaten alive on the straightaways.'

A couple of laps later, the caution flags waved for a third time after Greg Moore crashed heavily on the back straightaway after making contact with Andre Ribeiro. Moore, who was fortunate to emerge unhurt from a high-speed plunge into the sand pit, placed the blame for the incident firmly at Ribeiro's door. Just a few moments later, Davy Jones lost control in Turn 13, his Delco Electronics Lola-Mercedes coming to rest upside down.

Michael C. Brown

Juan Manuel Fangio II *(above center)* rewarded the faith of team owner Dan Gurney *(top left)* with his first points of the season for AAR.
Above: Al Unser Jr. leads the Newman/Haas Lolas of Christian Fittipaldi and Michael Andretti. A last-lap engine failure cost the Penske driver his first win of the year.
Max Papis *(right)* shone for Arciero-Wells, taking ninth place in the spare MCI Reynard-Toyota.
Far right: Bobby Rahal's Reynard carried a striking new livery commemorating Miller's 25th year in motorsports.

Photos: Michael C. Brown

Rahal on the rebound

Bobby Rahal has enjoyed precious little in the way of success since winning his third PPG Cup championship – in his first season as a team owner – in 1992. But after switching to his fifth different equipment package in as many seasons and forging a new partnership with his talented protege, Bryan Herta, Rahal's season-high second in his Miller Reynard-Mercedes, supported by Herta's fifth in the sister Shell machine, represented the third time in four races both men had finished among the top six.

'We've been up at the front ever since the U.S. 500,' declared Rahal. 'This team's really beginning to come together. He have a good technical package with Reynard, Mercedes and Goodyear, and a great young team of engineers. Plus, I think there's no doubt, having Bryan with us has added a great deal. He's very good in testing.'

Herta, indeed, set the ball rolling when he qualified on the outside of the front row for the U.S. 500. He duly added five more appearances among the top three rows of the grid from the ensuing eight races. Herta, who amassed a meager six points from the opening nine races, due to a combination of bad luck and mechanical problems, had since bolstered his tally to 62, rising from a dismal 22nd in the PPG Cup standings to a challenging 12th. Only Alex Zanardi scored more points in the same period.

'I just feel everything is beginning to come together,' said Herta after taking his fifth straight top-six finish. 'I feel very comfortable in this team. It always takes time to build up new relationships with a crew, and this year has been no different.

'It was my goal to be challenging for wins in the latter part of the season and I think we've achieved that. I'm getting along really well with my race engineer, Ray Leto. We're making progress every time out. You can't ask for much more than that.'

Back from injury, Paul Tracy *(right)* had an eventful race, surviving a number of incidents to pick up a point for 12th place.

Bottom: Stefan Johansson emerged from the mayhem in fourth place, easily his best result of the season with the Alumax Reynard-Mercedes.

Michael C. Brown

The time was ripe for the first round of pit stops. Herta, Rahal and Vasser ducked immediately into pit lane, only to discover that the pits were formally closed. They were forced to trundle through the pits, maintaining the mandatory speed limit, then, along with the rest of the field, stop next time around for service. By then they had fallen to the back of the pack.

Andretti was forced to take violent evasive action in order not to hit Vasser as he exited his pit. Fittipaldi also was delayed slightly. Unser, though, benefited from a super-quick stop by Richard Buck's team, and due to the catalog of disasters suffered by the other front-runners, Unser suddenly found himself elevated from seventh place to second. Only Zanardi lay ahead, and the Italian already was committed to a three-stop strategy after taking fuel and fresh tires during the preceding caution.

Gugelmin, too, had fallen back, due to a slow pit stop, and on lap 20 he was eliminated in another multi-car accident in Turn 12, this time involving teammate Mark Blundell and Ribeiro.

Yet another full-course caution ensued – the fourth inside just 20 laps. Zanardi took the opportunity to make a pit stop.

Incredibly, he, too, was assessed a penalty for stopping while the pits were supposedly closed. The Italian was banished to the back of the pack for the restart in what was turning out to be an extremely scrappy affair.

Unser was left out in front of the field, and he effectively controlled the remainder of the race. Fittipaldi chased hard, only to suffer a blown engine just five laps from the finish. He deserved better.

Andretti chased after Unser in the waning stages, as the race finally came to life, but he was more concerned about the proximity of Rahal than his own chances of victory: 'On the last lap I was mostly driving on my mirrors, making sure I could keep Bobby behind me,' admitted Andretti. 'Then, coming out of the kink, I saw a puff of smoke. I thought, did Al just bottom out? Then I saw more and more smoke and suddenly it went BOOM!'

Rahal redoubled his efforts to get on terms with Andretti but came up 0.541 seconds short at the finish line. Still, second place represented a handsome reward for a magnificent drive, especially since Rahal had lost the use of his clutch after his first pit stop.

'The car was really hooked up,' said Rahal. 'My heart goes out to Al. He had us covered. But we had a car to win today too.'

Zanardi also overcame a series of dramas to finish third ahead of Stefan Johansson, who took advantage of the various shenanigans to claim a deserved fourth, his best result of the year in Tony Bettenhausen's Alumax Reynard-Mercedes. Herta extended his streak of top-six finishes to five after another solid performance, while Vasser profited the most from Unser's cruel misfortune, claiming sixth and reestablishing himself as the firm favorite to win the coveted PPG Cup title.

Andretti, of course, was delighted with his fourth victory of the season, equaling Vasser's tally, yet he sympathized with his good friend Unser's misfortune: 'I felt really sorry for Al, but you know, I've given him a few in the past,' concluded Andretti. 'I stopped in that exact place in 1989, when I ran out of fuel. I feel really bad for him. He earned it. But we'll probably return the favor somewhere down the way.'

Michael C. Brown

SNIPPETS

Photos: Michael C. Brown

• **Stefan Johansson** (above) set the seventh fastest time in each of the two practice sessions but qualified an unrep-

resentative 21st after his Alumax Reynard-Mercedes was plagued by engine problems in qualifying.

• **Gil de Ferran** was obliged to switch to his spare Pennzoil Reynard following a rare Honda engine failure during the race morning warmup. The Brazilian's fourth consecutive failure to score points, following the collision with Alex Zanardi, effectively eliminated him from the championship reckoning.

• **Michael Andretti**'s victory was the 50th since team co-owners Paul Newman and Carl Haas joined forces prior to the 1983 season. Andretti, having joined the team in 1989, contributed exactly half of that tally. The other 25 were compiled by Michael's father, Mario (18), Nigel Mansell (five) and Paul Tracy (two).

• Team Rahal co-owner David Letterman was suitably impressed after flying in on race morning and taking his place alongside Bobby Rahal on the podium: 'This is great,' said the Late Show star. 'You just show up and they give you a trophy.'

• **Robby Gordon**, **Scott Pruett** and **Al Unser Jr.** flew to Michigan International Speedway immediately after qualifying on Saturday for the final IROC race of the season. Gordon was the top finisher, fourth, but the overall series spoils were claimed by race winner Mark Martin. Gordon took the opportunity to confirm he would be joining the NASCAR ranks in 1997, driving for Sabco Racing.

• **Paul Tracy** returned to the Penske fold after a one-race absence due to injury. The Canadian, troubled by discomfort in his lower back, was involved in several scrapes during the race, including one with Parker Johnstone on the final lap.

• **Jan Magnussen** (below),

having switched across to the Hogan Penske team, qualified a strong 10th and set fastest time in the final warmup session. Unfortunately, his race ended at Turn Three when he bounced off Rahal's car and into the pea-gravel while trying to avoid a cloud of dust from the Zanardi/de Ferran incident.

PPG INDY CAR WORLD SERIES • ROUND 14
TEXACO/HAVOLINE 200
ROAD AMERICA, ELKHART LAKE, WISCONSIN
AUGUST 18, 50 laps – 200.000 miles

Place	Driver (Nat.)	No.	Team Sponsors Car-Engine	Tires	Q Speed	Q Time	Q Pos.	Laps	Time/Status	Ave.	Pts.
1	Michael Andretti (USA)	6	Newman/Haas Kmart/Texaco Havoline Lola T96/00-Ford XD	GY	140.771	1m 42.294s	3	50	1h 56m 33.859s	102.947	20
2	Bobby Rahal (USA)	18	Team Rahal Miller Brewing Reynard 96I-Mercedes	GY	139.877	1m 42.947s	9	50	1h 56m 34.400s	102.939	16
3	*Alex Zanardi (I)	4	Target/Chip Ganassi Racing Reynard 96I-Honda	FS	141.179	1m 41.998s	1	50	1h 56m 39.234s	102.868	15
4	Stefan Johansson (S)	16	Bettenhausen Alumax Aluminum Reynard 96I-Mercedes	GY	136.655	1m 45.375s	21	50	1h 56m 40.890s	102.844	12
5	Bryan Herta (USA)	28	Team Rahal Shell Reynard 96I-Mercedes	GY	140.285	1m 42.648s	6	50	1h 56m 42.339s	102.823	10
6	Jimmy Vasser (USA)	12	Target/Chip Ganassi Racing Reynard 96I-Honda	FS	140.100	1m 42.784s	7	50	1h 56m 53.525s	102.659	8
7	Scott Pruett (USA)	20	Patrick Racing Firestone Lola T96/00-Ford XD	FS	138.881	1m 43.686s	16	50	1h 56m 55.834s	102.625	6
8	Juan Manuel Fangio II (RA)	36	All American Racers Castrol Eagle Mk.V-Toyota	GY	134.662	1m 46.934s	24	50	1h 57m 16.864s	102.318	5
9	*Max Papis (I)	25	Arciero-Wells Racing MCI Reynard 96I-Toyota	FS	135.716	1m 46.104s	23	50	1h 58m 14.692s	101.484	4
10	Al Unser Jr. (USA)	2	Marlboro Team Penske Penske PC25-Mercedes	GY	139.221	1m 43.433s	12	49	Engine		4
11	Parker Johnstone (USA)	49	Brix Comptech Motorola Reynard 96I-Honda	FS	136.792	1m 45.269s	20	49	Accident		2
12	Paul Tracy (CDN)	3	Marlboro Team Penske Penske PC25-Mercedes	GY	139.943	1m 42.899s	8	49	Running		1
13	Adrian Fernandez (MEX)	32	Tasman Tecate Beer/Quaker State Oil Lola T96/00-Honda	FS	138.938	1m 43.643s	14	48	Running		
14	Raul Boesel (BR)	1	Brahma Sports Team Reynard 96I-Ford XD	GY	137.582	1m 44.664s	17	46	Electrical		
15	Hiro Matsushita (J)	19	Payton/Coyne Panasonic/Duskin Lola T96/00-Ford XB	FS	132.104	1m 49.005s	26	45	Transmission		
16	Christian Fittipaldi (BR)	11	Newman/Haas Kmart/Budweiser Lola T96/00-Ford XD	GY	140.652	1m 42.380s	4	44	Engine		
17	Robby Gordon (USA)	5	Walker Valvoline/Cummins/Craftsman Reynard 96I-Ford XD	GY	138.921	1m 43.656s	15	41	Electrical		
18	*P.J. Jones (USA)	98	All American Racers Castrol Eagle Mk.V-Toyota	GY	133.846	1m 47.586s	25	27	Transmission		
19	Andre Ribeiro (BR)	31	Tasman Motorsports LCI International Lola T96/00-Honda	FS	137.154	1m 44.992s	18	20	Accident		
20	*Mark Blundell (GB)	21	PacWest Racing Group VISA Reynard 96I-Ford XB	GY	138.984	1m 43.609s	13	19	Accident		
21	Mauricio Gugelmin (BR)	17	PacWest Racing Group Hollywood Reynard 96I-Ford XB	GY	140.519	1m 42.478s	5	19	Accident		
22	Roberto Moreno (BR)	34	Payton/Coyne Data Control Lola T96/00-Ford XB	FS	136.187	1m 45.737s	22	17	Transmission		
23	*Greg Moore (CDN)	99	Forsythe Player's Ltd./Indeck Reynard 96I-Mercedes	FS	139.248	1m 43.413s	11	13	Accident		
24	Davy Jones (USA)	10	Galles Racing Delco Electronics Lola T96/00-Mercedes	GY	136.813	1m 45.253s	19	13	Accident		
25	Gil de Ferran (BR)	8	Hall Racing Pennzoil Special Reynard 96I-Honda	GY	140.818	1m 42.260s	2	0	Accident		
26	*Jan Magnussen (DK)	9	Hogan Penske Marlboro Latin America Penske PC25-Mercedes	GY	139.410	1m 43.292s	10	0	Accident		

* denotes Rookie driver

Caution flags: Laps 1–3, tow/de Ferran and Magnussen; laps 7–9, tow/Tracy; laps 14–16, accidents/Moore and D. Jones; laps 20–23, accident/Ribeiro, Gugelmin and Blundell; laps 37–39, tow/Fernandez. **Total:** five for 16 laps.

Lap leaders: Christian Fittipaldi, 1–15 (15 laps); Alex Zanardi, 16–21 (6 laps); Al Unser Jr., 22–34 (13 laps); Zanardi, 35–37 (3 laps); Unser, 38–49 (12 laps); Michael Andretti, 50 (1 lap). **Totals:** Unser, 25 laps; Fittipaldi, 15 laps; Zanardi, 9 laps; Andretti, 1 lap.

Fastest race lap: Paul Tracy, 1m 43.408s, 139.255 mph on lap 33.

Championship positions: 1 Vasser, 136; 2 Unser, 115; 3 Zanardi, 109; 4 Andretti, 107; 5 C. Fittipaldi, 93; 6 de Ferran, 92; 7 Rahal, 80; 8 Ribeiro and Moore, 76; 10 Pruett, 68; 11 Fernandez, 64; 12 Herta, 62; 13 Tracy, 60; 14 Gugelmin and Johansson, 43; 16 Blundell, 40; 17 Johnstone, 31; 18 E. Fittipaldi, 29; 19 Gordon and Lawson, 26; 21 Moreno, 24; 22 Boesel, 17; 23 Fangio, 5; 24 P.J. Jones and Papis, 4; 26 Matsushita and Hearn, 3; 28 Salazar, 2; 29 Goodyear, Greco and D. Jones, 1.

Official Information Technology Provider **EDS**

VANCOUVER

1 – ANDRETTI

2 – RAHAL

3 – C. FITTIPALDI

Displaying a composure that has not always been evident in the past, Michael Andretti fended off a determined Bobby Rahal to take his second win in succession.

Michael C. Brown

suffered a slightly compressed vertebra and some muscle strain in his neck, 'but the adrenaline carried me through. When you're leading, nothing hurts anyway! Everything seems to hurt more when you lose. When you win, it's the best remedy out there.'

Bobby Rahal also bounced back from an accident – in his case during the damp first practice session on Friday – to claim an excellent second in the Miller Reynard-Mercedes, followed by the Kmart/Budweiser Lola-Ford of Christian Fittipaldi, who fought through impressively from a lowly 14th on the grid.

For only the second time in seven races, neither of Chip Ganassi's Target Reynard-Hondas finished among the top three. Alex Zanardi, however, after starting from his third straight pole, was most definitely the man to beat.

The 29-year-old rookie took off into the lead at the green flag, and for the first eight laps was pursued closely by Andretti and Rahal. Bryan Herta couldn't match their pace in the second Team Rahal Reynard-Mercedes, but he remained in fourth at the head of a long train comprising Jimmy Vasser, Al Unser Jr., Gil de Ferran, Andre Ribeiro, Adrian Fernandez and Scott Pruett.

Zanardi turned up the wick on lap nine as he established what was to stand as the fastest lap of the race. Gradually he began to edge clear of Andretti. By lap 17, when Zanardi came up to lap the Castrol Eagle-Toyota of P.J. Jones, who was embroiled in a battle for 23rd with Scott Goodyear's Valvoline DuraBlend Reynard-Ford, the margin between them had grown to 4.7 seconds.

'He was getting away a little bit

but I know this race,' said Andretti, twice previously a winner on the streets of Vancouver, 'and once you start getting behind traffic, that's when things start to happen. When I saw him come up to lap P.J., I turned up my pace to try to put some pressure on him.'

Zanardi followed the Eagle for more than a lap, during which his advantage over Andretti shrunk by close to two seconds. Then, on the sweeping right-handed turn leading into the final hairpin, the Eagle and Reynard collided – with disastrous consequences for Zanardi, whose car almost flipped over before crashing into the retaining wall.

'He braked right in the middle of the circuit,' said a furious Zanardi. 'How can he do that? I mean, he braked so early even God would not have been able to avoid him. There was no gap either to the left or right of him.'

Andretti, though, apportioned at least some of the blame to Zanardi: 'I think Alex was starting to get frustrated, because it's very difficult to pass on this track. I saw he had been behind P.J. for a couple of laps and I think he just tried to force the issue. I think P.J. should have got out of the way; but he didn't and I think Alex should have been a bit more patient.'

The first full-course caution of the afternoon signaled the first round of pit stops. As usual there were several significant changes in the order. Andretti and Rahal retained the top two positions but a slow stop for Herta relegated him to fifth behind Vasser and Unser. Paul Tracy, who had been running sixth in the second Marlboro Penske-Mercedes, fell all the way to 15th after stalling his

engine, while de Ferran, who earlier had lost 10 places by running into the escape road at Turn Three, dropped another two positions after pulling into the pit lane before the all-clear signal was given. The Brazilian had to go around one more time before taking on fuel and fresh Goodyear tires.

Unser found a way past Vasser immediately after the restart. Pretty soon the top four began to stretch away from Herta and Christian Fittipaldi, who gained three positions during the pit stops and was elevated one more place when Ribeiro was assessed a roll-and-go penalty for running over an air-hose in teammate Fernandez's pit.

Andretti, Rahal, Unser and Vasser remained closely matched through the middle stages of the 100-lap race. It wasn't until the leaders began to encounter some slower traffic that Andretti was able to gain any breathing space.

'Michael got through traffic better than I did, and that really hurt me,' noted Rahal, who was more than four seconds adrift when the caution flags waved again on lap 54 after Ribeiro's attempt to relieve Mark Blundell of 11th position resulted in the Brazilian's LCI International Lola-Honda sitting broadside across the road in Turn Three.

The caution came a little too early for comfort, since most teams realized they would be hard-pressed to reach the finish without stopping one more time for a splash of fuel. Nevertheless, Andretti led the way onto pit road. Everyone else followed suit.

Swift work by Richard Buck's men enabled Unser to resume ahead of Rahal, whereupon team owner (and strategist) Roger Penske pulled what

A cool head and a slice of good fortune were the keys to success in the Molson Indy Vancouver. Michael Andretti possessed both as he sped to an accomplished victory – his fifth of the season – in Newman/Haas Racing's Kmart/Texaco Havoline Lola-Ford/Cosworth.

The bumpy Concord Pacific Place street circuit, centered upon the imposing B.C. Place stadium almost within a stone's throw of downtown Vancouver, is notoriously hard on equipment and drivers. Furthermore, Andretti was not feeling at his best following a hefty crash during an open IndyCar test session at Laguna Seca the previous Tuesday.

'I was a little sore in the middle of the race,' admitted Andretti, who

QUALIFYING

Michael Andretti led the way on the first day of practice and qualifying, although Bryan Herta circulated a mere 0.002 seconds slower after another fine performance in Team Rahal's Shell Reynard-Mercedes. A Goodyear sweep of the top six positions was completed by Al Unser Jr., clearly intent upon putting the agony of Elkhart Lake behind him, plus Bobby Rahal, Gil de Ferran and Paul Tracy. Andre Ribeiro was the fastest Firestone runner in seventh.

The Target/Chip Ganassi pair languished in 12th (Zanardi, who missed most of the session after collecting the wall) and 17th (Vasser). Saturday morning, however, was altogether more productive: 'Much better,' said a relieved Vasser after recording the second fastest time, once more behind Andretti. 'We made a lot of good changes at the get-go and then made the car better during the session. It was a good progression.'

Vasser clipped almost two more tenths from his previous best during afternoon qualifying, vaulting to the top of the charts after the first half-hour. Still, with the fastest 13 from Friday yet to venture onto the track, Vasser was under no illusions.

'I'm not totally pleased with the chassis,' he said. 'We're still making gains with it. I think Michael and Alex and a lot of guys in the other group have the chance to go quick, but this is certainly better than 17th.'

Herta was the first to vault ahead of Vasser, soon to be eclipsed first by his teammate, Rahal, and then by Zanardi, who midway through the session posted a sensational 53.980s. The lap was more than a second faster than Zanardi had managed previously and fully half-a-second clear of Andretti, who jumped to second with less than five minutes remaining.

'I'm obviously very satisfied,' said Zanardi. 'Yesterday the car was running well and I made a mistake and went into the wall. We made a lot of changes to the car this morning and we made the car worse! So Morris Nunn and I sat down for a long time in the trailer and we put a completely different setup on the car for qualifying. It was a shot in the dark really, but we knew it was the right direction and we ended up with a very good car.'

Left: Gil de Ferran locks a wheel during the course of a spirited recovery from an early excursion that eventually netted him fourth place.

Below: Bryan Herta holds station ahead of a frustrated Jimmy Vasser, who was desperate for points to bolster his dwindling lead in the PPG Cup standings.

Bottom: Andre Ribeiro and Michael Andretti have a grandstand view as Jan Magnussen's Penske catches fire.

Al Unser Jr. leads Mark Blundell and Scott Goodyear through the Vancouver streets. A typically bold pit stop strategy by Penske failed to pay dividends after a late-race tangle between Juan Manuel Fangio II and Robby Gordon triggered a full-course yellow.

Michael C. Brown

Never say never

Parker Johnstone had been eagerly awaiting a rare opportunity to test Brix Comptech Racing's Motorola Reynard-Honda during the officially sanctioned, two-day IndyCar open session at Laguna Seca on the Monday and Tuesday prior to the Molson Indy Vancouver. Sadly, the test did not go according to plan.

First of all, on Monday, Johnstone's mileage was restricted by a massive engine failure. Worse, on Tuesday, he crashed on the exit of Turn Four, inflicting heavy damage to the tightly budgeted sophomore team's sole remaining Reynard 96I. (The other chassis had been written off during the Marlboro 500.)

Bowed but not broken, the team packed up and headed back to its base at El Dorado Hills, near Sacramento, Calif., but not before Johnstone had sat down with the entire crew, confessed the accident had been entirely his fault, and apologized profusely. 'He didn't have to do that,' said crew chief Shad Huntley admiringly.

'Parker is really good for morale. He keeps everybody believing. Even though every time we seem to come up tails, sooner or later we're going to come up heads and turn things around.'

The close-knit team earned a moral victory even by presenting itself for duty in Vancouver. The major problem, apart from the cost, was a cracked gearbox casing, yet the impressively equipped Comptech fabrication and machine shops worked virtually around the clock for two days to effect a repair.

Johnstone never really got to grips with the handling of his hastily rebuilt machine during the weekend but he did stay out of trouble. Also, with no sign of a Marlboro car on the final lap, he managed to finish 11th and earn a couple of well-deserved PPG Cup points.

There was more good news the following week at Laguna Seca, as Motorola announced a new three-year commitment of sponsorship to the team.

Experience counts in Vancouver

Is it something in the air? Or the local food? The ambience perhaps? What is it that makes Michael Andretti, Bobby Rahal and Al Unser Jr. perform with such brilliance when they ply their trade in Vancouver?

Seven Indy Car races have been held in the hospitable city at the mouth of the Fraser River – the doorway, so to speak, to the geographical treasures of British Columbia – and still only Unser, with four wins to his name, and Andretti, three times triumphant, have tasted the victor's champagne.

Rahal, meanwhile, has qualified only once out of the top three and has finished second on three occasions. Andretti has added three poles and has yet to qualify lower than fifth. Unser has never failed to finish among the top five.

'It's real unusual, I can't explain it. It just seems to suit the old folks,' said Andretti with a chuckle during the post-race press conference as he cast a glance sideways at second-place finisher Rahal *(above)*.

Curiously, the same trio has enjoyed a similar level of success at the other Canadian venue, Toronto, where Andretti has won five times, Unser twice and Rahal once.

'I'm not sure why I have had such good luck here, but I love racing in Canada,' declared Andretti. 'The courses seem to suit my driving style well. It's been good for Bobby, too.'

Indeed, from the combined total of 19 races run in Toronto and Vancouver, Rahal has qualified among the top five on all bar three occasions – including Toronto in 1996 – and has finished in the top three 10 times.

'Canada has been awfully good to me,' acknowledged Rahal. 'There are some places you just seem to have a liking for, or you just seem to know what the car wants – you have a good basis to work from and you just fine-tune that from year to year. Here and Toronto, we always seem to run well.'

---

appeared to be a master stroke when he called Unser back into the pits for a splash of fuel on lap 59, just before the race was restarted. Robby Gordon and series leader Vasser also pitted, although Vasser was obliged to make an additional stop after an apparently malfunctioning speed-limiter caused him to exceed the 65 mph limit in pit lane.

The restart, on lap 62, saw Andretti and Rahal at the front of the field. Next were Fittipaldi and Fernandez, posting another sensible drive in the Tecate/Quaker State Lola-Honda, and Herta, who once more lost ground in the pits. Unser was ninth behind Juan Manuel Fangio II's well-driven Castrol Eagle-Toyota which was showing by far its best form of the season. Vasser was a distant, and disgruntled, 13th.

Unser took until lap 68 before he was able to find a way past Fangio. Then his worst fears were realized when Gordon misjudged his attempt to pass Fangio under braking for the Turn Five chicane and punted the Argentinean into a spin. Out came the yellows again after the Eagle came to rest, engine dead, at the apex of the corner. Unser's strategy had been shot to pieces. Now the other contenders could cruise behind the pace car for a few laps, saving valuable fuel while Fangio's car was towed to safety.

'Marlboro Team Penske took a gamble today and it didn't pay off,' reflected Unser. 'The yellow flag got us. It's a shame, because the car was working really well. We didn't have to make one change to the car all day.'

The final restart came with 25 laps remaining. Andretti, his fuel

fears allayed, set off at a fast pace and immediately established a cushion of a couple of seconds between himself and Rahal: 'I was just driving flat out and I was able to build up a bit of a buffer,' said Andretti.

Try as he did, Rahal was unable to reduce the deficit.

Second place would have to suffice for the veteran.

'I'm not satisfied with second by any means,' said Rahal, 'but it's not for a lack of trying. We're just going to concentrate on having the best car we can, and when we get that win, I'll be real happy.'

Fittipaldi drove a typically neat and tidy race, rewarded by the final position on the podium. De Ferran also deserved credit for fighting his way through the field to fourth after his early mishap. Unser moved up to fifth when, first, Herta lost a couple of positions due to a moment's indecision while lapping the tardy Hiro Matsushita, and then Fernandez made a mistake at the Turn Three hairpin which dropped the Mexican to eighth.

Herta regained his momentum in time to fend off Vasser, and while Unser pulled away, Vasser became increasingly agitated as he tried in vain to find a way past the Shell Reynard-Mercedes.

'I don't know what Bryan was doing,' said an enraged Vasser. 'If it had been me, I'd have let them go on and fight for the championship. He was slow on the track and I've got to be thinking of the championship and not making any low percentage moves – and he's blocking me! I hope he feels like a hero.'

Herta, though, protested his innocence: 'I was racing for position and he never made an attempt to pass. I know he thinks I should have moved over because he's in the championship race. But I couldn't face [team owner] Bobby [Rahal], my crew and the guys at Reynard, Mercedes and Goodyear if I just moved over for him. I needed the points too.'

So far as race-winner Andretti was concerned, Vasser's outburst merely reflected the pressure he was feeling as the championship battle reached down to the final race at Laguna Seca, with Vasser leading Andretti by 14 points and Unser also holding a mathematical chance just three points further in arrears: 'I don't think Jimmy's going to sleep too well,' declared Andretti with a mischievous grin. 'Next week we know we have to win and that's just the way I like it. The rest is up to Jimmy. The pressure is on him.'

Michael C. Brown

SNIPPETS

• **First practice** on Friday began in wet conditions (left) following a heavy thundershower. The only major incident involved Bobby Rahal, who crashed heavily at Turn Eight. 'I felt kind of stupid because I told Bryan [Herta] to take it easy in the wet,' said Rahal. 'Then I go out and hit the wall! I guess it's "Do as I say, not as I do!" '

• **Jan Magnussen** was obliged to use the Hogan Penske team's backup car after crashing heavily on Friday: 'Frankly, we're not sure what happened,' said the Dane. 'It felt like something broke at the rear of the car in the middle of Turn Two. It's a heavy-down-force, 190 mph turn and when I hit the bumps there it threw the rear end off.'

• **Michael Andretti** was fortunate to emerge without more serious injuries after crashing hard at Laguna Seca during an officially sanctioned test just three days before the start of practice in Vancouver: 'When I hit the wall it was a big THUMP and it hurt,' he recounted. 'At first I thought I was OK, but when I went to get out of the car I couldn't put any weight on my shoulders.' Regular visits during the weekend to Tony Lama's Human Performance Center mobile unit served to alleviate Andretti's discomfort.

• Both PacWest drivers also required treatment – **Mauricio Gugelmin** to his left wrist and **Mark Blundell** to his right wrist as a result of their accident at Road America.

• **Alex Zanardi**'s pair of Target Reynards were assigned nicknames during the season. Chassis 009, designated as the spare car in Vancouver, was known as Bessie, due to her unfailing reliability. The other car, 022, known as 'Ol' Midnight' ('Because we're always up until midnight fixing it,' said crew member Ricky Davis), lived up to her reputation after Zanardi hit the wall during qualifying on Friday!

• Honda clinched its first IndyCar Manufacturers Championship when Gil de Ferran finished in fourth place. **Alex Zanardi** (below) also secured The Friends of Jim Trueman Rookie of the Year Award when rival Greg Moore retired from the contest early due to engine problems.

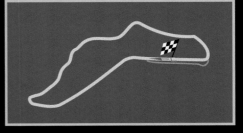

Photos: Michael C. Brown

PPG INDY CAR WORLD SERIES • ROUND 15
MOLSON INDY VANCOUVER

CONCORD PACIFIC PLACE STREET CIRCUIT, VANCOUVER, BRITISH COLUMBIA, CANADA

SEPTEMBER 1, 100 laps – 170.300 miles

Place	Driver (Nat.)	No.	Team Sponsors Car-Engine	Tires	Q Speed	Q Time	Q Pos.	Laps	Time/Status	Ave.	Pts.
1	Michael Andretti (USA)	6	Newman/Haas Kmart/Texaco Havoline Lola T96/00-Ford XD	GY	112.526	54.483s	2	100	1h 48m 16.253s	94.374	21
2	Bobby Rahal (USA)	18	Team Rahal Miller Brewing Reynard 96I-Mercedes	GY	112.477	54.507s	3	100	1h 48m 18.158s	94.347	16
3	Christian Fittipaldi (BR)	11	Newman/Haas Kmart/Budweiser Lola T96/00-Ford XD	GY	111.436	55.016s	14	100	1h 48m 23.341s	94.272	14
4	Gil de Ferran (BR)	8	Hall Racing Pennzoil Special Reynard 96I-Honda	GY	111.929	54.774s	10	100	1h 48m 26.548s	94.225	12
5	Al Unser Jr. (USA)	2	Marlboro Team Penske Penske PC25-Mercedes	GY	112.115	54.683s	7	100	1h 48m 27.773s	94.207	10
6	Bryan Herta (USA)	28	Team Rahal Shell Reynard 96I-Mercedes	GY	112.332	54.578s	4	100	1h 48m 38.347s	94.055	8
7	Jimmy Vasser (USA)	12	Target/Chip Ganassi Racing Reynard 96I-Honda	FS	112.251	54.617s	5	100	1h 48m 38.666s	94.050	6
8	Adrian Fernandez (MEX)	32	Tasman Tecate Beer/Quaker State Oil Lola T96/00-Honda	FS	111.818	54.829s	11	100	1h 48m 51.327s	93.868	5
9	Scott Goodyear (CDN)	15	Walker Valvoline DuraBlend Special Reynard 96I-Ford XB	GY	108.538	56.485s	23	100	1h 49m 06.542s	93.649	4
10	Robby Gordon (USA)	5	Walker Valvoline/Cummins/Craftsman Reynard 96I-Ford XD	GY	111.288	55.089s	15	99	Running		3
11	Parker Johnstone (USA)	49	Brix Comptech Motorola Reynard 96I-Honda	FS	110.776	55.344s	18	98	Running		2
12	*Mark Blundell (GB)	21	PacWest Racing Group VISA Reynard 96I-Ford XB	GY	110.930	55.267s	17	98	Running		1
13	*P.J. Jones (USA)	98	All American Racers Castrol Eagle Mk.V-Toyota	GY	107.317	57.128s	25	97	Running		
14	Davy Jones (USA)	10	Galles Racing Delco Electronics Lola T96/00-Mercedes	GY	108.642	56.431s	22	97	Running		
15	Hiro Matsushita (J)	19	Payton/Coyne Panasonic/Duskin Lola T96/00-Ford XB	FS	102.395	59.874s	27	91	Running		
16	*Michel Jourdain Jr. (MEX)	22	Scandia Herdez/Perry Ellis/Alta Water Lola T96/00-Ford XB	GY	107.336	57.118s	24	81	Accident		
17	Stefan Johansson (S)	16	Bettenhausen Alumax Aluminum Reynard 96I-Mercedes	GY	109.720	55.877s	21	79	Suspension		
18	Paul Tracy (CDN)	3	Marlboro Team Penske Penske PC25-Mercedes	GY	112.244	54.620s	6	74	Accident		
19	Juan Manuel Fangio II (RA)	36	All American Racers Castrol Eagle Mk.V-Toyota	GY	109.857	55.807s	20	67	Accident		
20	Scott Pruett (USA)	20	Patrick Racing Firestone Lola T96/00-Ford XD	FS	111.766	54.854s	12	52	Engine		
21	Andre Ribeiro (BR)	31	Tasman Motorsports LCI International Lola T96/00-Honda	FS	111.978	54.750s	8	52	Accident		
22	*Jan Magnussen (DK)	9	Hogan Penske Marlboro Latin America Penske PC25-Mercedes	GY	110.510	55.477s	19	48	Fire		
23	Raul Boesel (BR)	1	Brahma Sports Team Reynard 96I-Ford XD	GY	111.109	55.178s	16	47	Engine		
24	Mauricio Gugelmin (BR)	17	PacWest Racing Group Hollywood Reynard 96I-Ford XB	GY	111.953	54.762s	9	45	Engine		
25	*Greg Moore (CDN)	99	Forsythe Player's Ltd./Indeck Reynard 96I-Mercedes	FS	111.548	54.961s	13	38	Oil leak		
26	*Alex Zanardi (I)	4	Target/Chip Ganassi Racing Reynard 96I-Honda	FS	113.576	53.980s	1	18	Accident		1
27	Roberto Moreno (BR)	34	Payton/Coyne Data Control Lola T96/00-Ford XB	FS	106.206	57.726s	26	10	Cooling system		

* denotes Rookie driver

Caution flags: Laps 20–23, accident/Zanardi and P.J. Jones; laps 53–60, tow/Ribeiro; laps 68–72, tow/Gordon. **Total:** three for 17 laps.

Lap leaders: Alex Zanardi, 1–18 (18 laps); Michael Andretti, 19–100, (82 laps). **Totals:** Andretti, 82 laps; Zanardi, 18 laps.

Fastest race lap: Alex Zanardi, 55.867s, 109.739 mph on lap 9.

Championship positions: 1 Vasser, 142; 2 Andretti, 128; 3 Unser, 125; 4 Zanardi, 110; 5 C. Fittipaldi, 107; 6 de Ferran, 104; 7 Rahal, 96; 8 Ribeiro and Moore, 76; 10 Herta, 70; 11 Fernandez, 69; 12 Pruett, 68; 13 Tracy, 60; 14 Gugelmin and Johansson, 43; 16 Blundell, 41; 17 Johnstone, 33; 18 Gordon and E. Fittipaldi, 29; 20 Lawson, 26; 21 Moreno, 24; 22 Boesel, 17; 23 Fangio and Goodyear, 5; 25 P.J. Jones and Papis, 4; 27 Matsushita and Hearn, 3; 29 Salazar, 2; 30 Greco and D. Jones, 1.

LAGUNA SECA

Michael C. Brown

Left: A shell-shocked Bryan Herta could only look ahead to 1997 after Alex Zanardi had snatched a sensational victory.

Main picture: Zanardi leads Jimmy Vasser over the brow at the Corkscrew. The Target/Chip Ganassi Racing teammates had different goals on race day; both achieved their aims.
Bottom left: Vasser *(left of picture)* celebrates his PPG Cup title triumph, Zanardi his third race win of the season.

Bryan Herta learned the hard way that nothing comes easily in the increasingly competitive PPG Indy Car World Series. The 26-year-old Californian came within a whisker of claiming his second Indy Car pole, beaten only in the dying moments of the final qualifying session by Alex Zanardi. Even more difficult to bear, by far, was the fact that after passing Zanardi and seemingly taking control as the race entered its final stages, Herta fell victim to a spectacular, even outrageous last-lap pass by Zanardi which denied the American what would have been a well-deserved maiden victory.

'It was obviously risky,' admitted a joyful Zanardi after scoring his third Indy Car win, 'because when you try a move like that you have little percentage of doing it; but when you pull it off you feel very, very good.'

Team owner Chip Ganassi, of course, was mightily impressed by Zanardi's last-gasp victory. And as if that wasn't enough, a conservative drive to fourth place by Target teammate Jimmy Vasser was sufficient to secure the coveted PPG Cup championship.

'I don't think there is any question that this is my best season as a team owner,' said Ganassi. 'To have two race winners in Jimmy and Alex, to win the championship and to win the race the way we did today is just unbelievable.'

The revised Laguna Seca Raceway was in tip-top condition for the PPG Cup finale. Perfect weather conditions and a thrilling battle for the championship also contributed toward attracting a record crowd to the spectacular Californian road course. Happily, the racing lived up to expectations.

Zanardi, however, threatened to turn the Toyota Grand Prix of Monterey, featuring the Bank of America 300, into little more than a high-speed procession as his Target Reynard-Honda edged away from Herta's Shell Reynard-Mercedes in the early stages. But smart strategy by Team Rahal, which entailed running a lean fuel mixture and allowing Herta to complete an extra couple of laps before making his first pit stop, enabled him to close a gap that had extended as high as 6.5 seconds to just a few car lengths once both men had stopped for service. Furthermore, unlike in the early stages, Herta was able to stay with Zanardi once they were back up to speed.

Vasser, who had been content to run steadily in seventh during the

QUALIFYING

The final qualifying session for the Toyota Grand Prix of Monterey truly set the tone for Sunday's thrilling 83-lap race. Curiously, very few drivers improved upon their previous best when the first group of cars took to the track on Saturday afternoon, but soon after the 'fast' group was let loose, Alex Zanardi served notice that Bryan Herta's provisional pole was likely to come under threat as he jumped from fourth to second on his Target Reynard-Honda's first set of Firestone tires.

Mark Blundell, a sensational second fastest on Friday in the PacWest team's VISA Reynard-Ford/Cosworth XB, also posted a slight improvement, albeit not by enough to bump Herta's Shell Reynard-Mercedes from the pole.

The excitement reached a crescendo as the minutes ticked away. First, Blundell's teammate, Mauricio Gugelmin, vaulted to second after a stellar effort in his own Hollywood Reynard. Then Herta stopped the clocks at 1m 08.184s. It wasn't good enough to beat his Friday best, but it was still better than anyone else had managed.

Zanardi, on what would be his last lap but one, slid briefly off-course in Turn Six. Greg Moore also was charging as he attempted to improve upon sixth place with the Player's Reynard-Mercedes. Then, as Jim Swintal prepared to wave the checkered flag, Moore's final effort saw him spin into the wall in Turn Four.

Herta's pole seemed secure. Zanardi, though, remained out on the track. Moments later he flashed across the line and the computer screens up and down pit lane instantly displayed the lap time: 1m 08.004s. Zanardi, by a scant, 0.015s, had snatched away the pole.

'It was a jungle out there in the last few minutes, with a lot of traffic and everyone trying to find a clear lap,' said a relieved Zanardi after securing his fourth consecutive pole, matching the feat last achieved in 1992 by Michael Andretti. Zanardi also equaled the record of eight straight front row starts, previously shared by Bobby Unser (in 1979/80) and Bobby Rahal (1985). 'I'm absolutely delighted. This is definitely my best pole of the year.'

Herta, classy as ever, took the news well: 'I'm disappointed but Alex did a great job and my hat's off to him. We all really wanted this, but you don't win a pole because you want it, you win it because you earned it, and Alex earned this pole.'

Vasser stays calm under pressure

Three drivers – Jimmy Vasser, Michael Andretti and Al Unser Jr. – retained a shot at winning the coveted PPG Indy Car World Series championship at the season finale. Vasser, however, was in the catbird seat, and he knew exactly what he had to do in order to clinch his first PPG Cup title.

'I was basically just out there on a Sunday drive, cruising around the first half of the race, being kind to my engine and tires and conserving fuel. When I saw Michael go into the pits and I realized Al was also having problems, I stepped it up.

'At one point [on lap 48] I went completely off the track. I got lucky I didn't hit the wall. When I got back on the track, that's when I decided to go for it. That's when I decided to stop cruising. The car felt real good. I was able to run a second [per lap] faster than I had been before and it was easy. On the restart I was staying with Bryan [Herta] and Alex [Zanardi] and waiting to see what would happen. I was hoping I could mix it up with those guys at

the end, but then I had a problem with the left-front tire. I got a terrible blister and I barely had any grip in the slow stuff. That's why I fell back toward the end.'

Vasser, indeed, was passed by Scott Pruett on the final lap.

Nevertheless, with Andretti finishing ninth and Unser a disappointing 16th, a fourth-place finish for Vasser was more than enough to clinch the championship and the $1 million bonus.

'It's a wonderful feeling,' said Vasser, smiling broadly as he attended the traditional post-race press conference. 'I have a little bit of relief and I'm going to have a little bit of a party – actually a lot of a party! We had a goal at the beginning of the season and it's great to finally achieve that goal. We go out to do the best we can do. I'm very proud to be champion but you know, I actually have more warmth for my guys than I do pride for myself. I owe a lot to the Target/Chip Ganassi team. They've made this possible for me.'

early stages, also had his first pit stop on lap 30. He, too, took advantage of the additional couple of laps on fully heated tires to move up to third place after taking on fresh tires and fuel.

The only other leading contender to complete 30 laps before stopping was Andre Ribeiro. Unfortunately, after a brilliant stop by Steve Ragan's crew vaulted the Brazilian's LCI International Lola-Honda from seventh to third, Ribeiro squandered

the opportunity by sliding off the road in Turn Four. He then committed exactly the same error on the very next lap, relegating himself to 10th. Team owner Steve Horne was not impressed.

Mauricio Gugelmin, who ran a fine third throughout the first stint, despite a brake problem on his Hollywood Reynard-Ford, continued to hold down fourth place after the pit stops, followed by an intense battle comprising Greg Moore (Player's

Reynard-Mercedes), Scott Pruett (Firestone Lola-Ford), Al Unser Jr. (Marlboro Penske-Mercedes) and Bobby Rahal (Miller Reynard-Mercedes). Pruett slipped past Moore on lap 32, only for the Canadian to return the favor four laps later. Shortly afterward, Moore glimpsed an opportunity to pass Gugelmin under braking for Turn One. He ducked to the inside, braked as late as he dared . . . but couldn't maintain control and gyrated directly in front of Gugelmin's nose. He rejoined a chastened 10th.

A half-dozen laps after the pit stops, it became apparent Zanardi was not able to match his earlier speed. In fact, he was troubled by a blistered left-front tire. 'I honestly don't know why we had the problem,' said Zanardi. 'We had exactly the same compound, exactly the same pressures . . .'

Herta remained close to Zanardi for a while, then saw his opportunity to make a move on the inside for Turn Two. It was a perfectly executed pass. 'It's difficult to get by anyone,' related Herta, 'because when you follow somebody closely, you do lose a lot of downforce. I saw Alex had a little problem getting off Turn 11, so I knew that was my chance. I was able to get a good draft and pull it off.'

Herta soon began to pull clear, despite having to work through heavy traffic. By lap 54 he had extended his lead to more than nine seconds. But then out came the double yellow flags. Stefan Johansson, who had risen from 19th to 12th inside the first 20 laps, had crashed his Alumax Reynard-Mercedes heavily in Turn Two after the rear wing fell loose. It was not the manner in which the likeable Swede had anticipated spending his 40th birthday. He was fortunate to emerge unscathed.

The caution wiped out Herta's advantage, of course, and under the revised regulations introduced midseason, it required all the remaining runners to realign themselves in actual race order. Thus, Zanardi was positioned on Herta's tail for the restart at the end of lap 60. Vasser and Pruett, who moved past Gugelmin right after the green was shown, latched onto the two leaders and soon began to edge away from the Brazilian, who in turn had his mirrors full of the recovered Moore, Rahal and Jan Magnussen, who had moved steadily into contention with Hogan Penske's Marlboro Latin America Penske-Mercedes. Raul Boesel and Ribeiro also remained on

Michael C. Brown

Bryan Herta *(left)* was denied a richly deserved maiden Indy Car victory by Alex Zanardi's opportunism, but the Californian accepted his cruel disappointment with commendable dignity.

Below left: Scott Pruett claimed his third podium finish of the season on the last lap after another strong performance at the wheel of the Firestone Lola-Ford.

Right: Turns 10 and 11 had been reprofiled as part of an extensive program of track improvements.

Michael C. Brown

the lead lap, although neither was to reach the finish.

Pruett couldn't quite match the leaders' pace and dropped away slightly in fourth position. Vasser, meanwhile, stayed in touch until he, like teammate Zanardi earlier, was hindered by a blistered left-front Firestone tire.

So the race boiled down to a simple shoot-out between Herta and Zanardi.

It was an intriguing battle. Herta gradually whittled away his lap times, dropping from mid-1m 11s laps to mid-to-high 1m 10s. Zanardi, though, echoed his every move. And this time, to Herta's chagrin, the Italian's tires showed no signs of duress.

Farther back there were plenty more close battles, too.

Gugelmin, for example, continued to struggle with a long brake pedal yet he managed to keep Moore at bay. Rahal, whose car was not handling to his liking, nevertheless remained close behind in seventh, while Magnussen fell back only in the final few laps. His engine finally expired on the very last lap, but not before the young Dane had garnered his first PPG Cup points.

The minor placings featured some sensational dicing as the race – and the season – drew toward its climax. Christian Fittipaldi, who fell to last place, 29th, after sustaining a puncture on the very first lap, worked his way magnificently from 18th to ninth in the final 22 laps, only to cede the position to his equally hard-working teammate, Andretti, on the final lap. Adrian Fernandez was embroiled in the same fraught battle, as was Roberto Moreno, who drove superbly in Payton/Coyne's underdeveloped Data Control Lola-Ford and was rewarded with the final PPG Cup point for 12th position. Fine effort.

All eyes, however, were on the dice for the lead. Zanardi survived one scare when his car strayed its right-side wheels onto the dirt on the exit of Turn Nine on lap 78, but a deft correction enabled him to gather up the car and set off once again in pursuit of Herta. The pair remained close together throughout the final 20 laps, but Herta appeared to have matters under control. At least, so he believed.

And, to a degree, so did Zanardi: 'I was waiting for Bryan to do a mistake, and for the last 15 laps I was quicker than him but I couldn't get around him. He didn't do anything wrong. And as soon as I came up

close to him I was losing downforce, so I had to drop back.'

Zanardi, however, had one more trick up his sleeve. Climbing toward the top of the hill on the very last lap, Zanardi waited until Herta followed the normal racing line, kinking slightly to the right prior to the infamous Corkscrew, then lunged straight on, leaving his braking almost impossibly late so that he was alongside Herta as the erstwhile leader attempted to turn in to the corner as usual.

'I must admit I didn't expect him

to pass me and I didn't know he was there until I saw a wheel alongside me,' said a shocked Herta, who, to his great credit, instantly straightened his line to prevent Zanardi from slamming into his left flank. The Target car slid straight on past the apex and across the curbs on the opposite side of the road before Zanardi was able to bring it back under control. But by then the advantage was in his favor. Zanardi bounced across the curbs one more time, again forcing Herta to take evasive action, and the race was his.

'It was very risky,' admitted Zanardi, 'but it was definitely worth it. It's incredible. I'm very happy.'

Herta, of course, didn't quite see things in the same light.

But he sought no excuses: 'What can I say? I think that was one of my best drives and Alex made a great pass. It's tough to take. I don't think I've ever been more disappointed or hurt as much as I do inside right now. I wanted to win so badly, not only for me but for all the guys on the team, and for Shell, and it didn't happen. It's very disappointing.'

Andretti takes second on tie-break

Alex Zanardi's dramatic, and successful, last-minute bid for the lead would have had a profound effect on the final PPG Cup standings if not for some remarkably quick thinking on behalf of Newman/Haas Racing.

Michael Andretti's pit crew had been keeping a close watch on positions throughout the contest. Andretti himself, however, never did find a good balance on his Kmart/Texaco Havoline Lola-Ford/Cosworth. He knew he was in no position to challenge Vasser for the championship, and his hopes of finishing second also seemed to have ended when he made a mistake in Turn 11 on his 46th lap.

'I thought I was out of it after I spun out,' admitted Andretti. 'I tried to pass Bobby [Rahal] and locked up my brakes and then, to keep from hitting Al [Unser], I spun and Bobby nailed me. It bent my left steering arm and the car was a real handful after that.'

Andretti fell to 20th place, two laps behind the leaders, but, typically, he refused to give up. Instead he mounted a superb comeback drive. Remarkably, Andretti passed both Unser and Adrian Fernandez on the penultimate lap, moving up to 10th, which would have been enough to secure the runner-up position in the championship assuming Zanardi remained in second place. But when Zanardi overtook Herta on the final lap, Andretti's crew quickly realized he needed to make up one more position. Fortunately, Newman/Haas teammate Christian Fittipaldi was running ninth after also posting a fine recovery following a first-lap delay. So the crew immediately radioed to the Brazilian, requesting him to fall back in line behind Andretti.

'I want to thank Christian for helping me out on that last lap. I'm sure I'll pay him back some day,' said Andretti, who secured the $500,000 second prize from PPG Industries. Zanardi had to be content with the $300,000 award for finishing third.

SNIPPETS

Photos: Michael C. Brown

• Lagu-na Seca Raceway had been completely repaved since the Indy cars last made a visit to the spectacular road course set among the hills overlooking the Monterey Bay. The $1.5 million project also comprised a reconfiguration of Turns 10 and 11 to provide a longer pit lane. The circuit now measures 2.238 miles.

• Just to complete the weekend for Target/Chip Ganassi Racing, series champion **Jimmy Vasser** laid claim to a new Mercedes-Benz E420 Sport under the innovative Marlboro Pole Award program.

• **Raul Boesel**'s miserable season ended on a sour note when yet another bro-

ken crank trigger – the seventh in eight races – sidelined his Brahma Reynard-Ford 14 laps from the finish. 'Raul was doing a great job,' praised team owner Barry Green. 'We didn't give him much of a car to qualify with, so he started in 22nd spot. He worked his backside off to get as high as eighth position. I'm real proud of him.'

• A series of news conferences served to confirm some changes in personnel and equipment for the **1997 season**. Derrick Walker, for example, announced that Gil de Ferran will replace Robby Gordon and maintain his link with Honda by bringing the Japanese/American motors to power a new

Valvoline/Cummins Reynard 97I. Team Rahal confirmed a switch from Mercedes power to Ford/Cosworth for '97, with Bruce McCaw's PacWest Racing Group moving in the opposite direction. PacWest had also changed its allegiance to Firestone tires, but drivers Mauricio Gugelmin (above) and Mark Blundell would be staying on.

• **Brix Comptech Racing** announced long-term con-

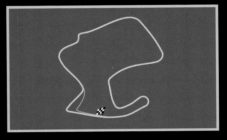

tracts with Parker Johnstone, Honda and Motorola, while **Arciero-Wells Racing** confirmed a commitment through the year 2000 with MCI. **Stefan Johansson** will not return with Tony Bettenhausen's Alumax team for a sixth season, but **Della Penna Motorsports** will conduct a full schedule of PPG Indy Car World Series events in 1997 with driver Richie Hearn and sponsorship from Ralphs and Food 4 Less.

• Erstwhile championship challenger **Al Unser Jr.**, who rose from 13th on the grid to seventh in the early stages, sought no excuses after fading to 16th. 'We just missed on the setup today,' said

Unser (above), who finished fourth in the final PPG Cup standings. 'Jan [Magnussen] did a great job, so obviously the team's car wasn't bad; it was just a miscalculation on my part.'

PPG INDY CAR WORLD SERIES • ROUND 16
TOYOTA GRAND PRIX OF MONTEREY
FEATURING THE BANK OF AMERICA 300

LAGUNA SECA RACEWAY, MONTEREY, CALIFORNIA
SEPTEMBER 8, 83 laps – 185.274 miles

Place	Driver (Nat.)	No.	Team Sponsors Car-Engine	Tires	Q Speed	Q Time	Q Pos.	Laps	Time/Status	Ave.	Pts.
1	*Alex Zanardi (I)	4	Target/Chip Ganassi Racing Reynard 96I-Honda	FS	118.475	1m 08.004s	1	83	1h 48m 32.157s	102.687	22
2	Bryan Herta (USA)	28	Team Rahal Shell Reynard 96I-Mercedes	GY	118.449	1m 08.019s	2	83	1h 48m 33.569s	102.665	16
3	Scott Pruett (USA)	20	Patrick Racing Firestone Lola T96/00-Ford XD	FS	117.054	1m 08.830s	10	83	1h 48m 47.911s	102.439	14
4	Jimmy Vasser (USA)	12	Target/Chip Ganassi Racing Reynard 96I-Honda	FS	117.966	1m 08.298s	5	83	1h 48m 48.247s	102.434	12
5	Mauricio Gugelmin (BR)	17	PacWest Racing Group Hollywood Reynard 96I-Ford XB	GY	118.156	1m 08.188s	3	83	1h 48m 49.937s	102.407	10
6	*Greg Moore (CDN)	99	Forsythe Player's Ltd./Indeck Reynard 96I-Mercedes	FS	117.311	1m 08.679s	6	83	1h 48m 50.307s	102.402	8
7	Bobby Rahal (USA)	18	Team Rahal Miller Brewing Reynard 96I-Mercedes	GY	117.133	1m 08.783s	9	83	1h 48m 51.034s	102.390	6
8	*Jan Magnussen (DK)	9	Hogan Penske Marlboro Latin America Penske PC25-Mercedes	GY	115.971	1m 09.473s	16	83	1h 49m 06.964s	102.141	5
9	Michael Andretti (USA)	6	Newman/Haas Kmart/Texaco Havoline Lola T96/00-Ford XD	GY	116.853	1m 08.948s	11	82	Running		4
10	Christian Fittipaldi (BR)	11	Newman/Haas Kmart/Budweiser Lola T96/00-Ford XD	GY	117.177	1m 08.757s	8	82	Running		3
11	Adrian Fernandez (MEX)	32	Tasman Tecate Beer/Quaker State Oil Lola T96/00-Honda	FS	115.769	1m 09.594s	20	82	Running		2
12	Roberto Moreno (BR)	34	Payton/Coyne Data Control Lola T96/00-Ford XB	FS	114.510	1m 10.359s	23	82	Running		1
13	Parker Johnstone (USA)	49	Brix Comptech Motorola Reynard 96I-Honda	FS	116.843	1m 08.954s	12	82	Running		
14	Davy Jones (USA)	10	Galles Racing Delco Electronics Lola T96/00-Mercedes	GY	115.732	1m 09.616s	21	82	Running		
15	Robby Gordon (USA)	5	Walker Valvoline/Cummins/Craftsman Reynard 96I-Ford XD	GY	116.021	1m 09.442s	15	82	Running		
16	Al Unser Jr. (USA)	2	Marlboro Team Penske Penske PC25-Mercedes	GY	116.706	1m 09.035s	13	82	Running		
17	*Richie Hearn (USA)	44	Della Penna Ralphs/Food 4 Less Reynard 95I-Ford XB	GY	113.838	1m 10.774s	24	80	Running		
18	Scott Goodyear (CDN)	15	Walker Valvoline DuraBlend Special Reynard 96I-Ford XB	GY	113.551	1m 10.953s	27	80	Running		
19	Andre Ribeiro (BR)	31	Tasman Motorsports LCI International Lola T96/00-Honda	FS	117.208	1m 08.739s	7	76	Fire		
20	Raul Boesel (BR)	1	Brahma Sports Team Reynard 96I-Ford XD	GY	115.376	1m 09.831s	22	69	Electrical		
21	Stefan Johansson (S)	16	Bettenhausen Alumax Aluminum Reynard 96I-Mercedes	GY	115.787	1m 09.583s	19	52	Accident		
22	*Max Papis (I)	25	Arciero-Wells Racing MCI Reynard 96I-Toyota	FS	115.902	1m 09.514s	17	39	Engine		
23	Hiro Matsushita (J)	19	Payton/Coyne Panasonic/Duskin Lola T96/00-Ford XB	FS	113.563	1m 10.946s	26	33	Engine		
24	*Mark Blundell (GB)	21	PacWest Racing Group VISA Reynard 96I-Ford XB	GY	118.079	1m 08.232s	4	18	Electrical		
25	Gil de Ferran (BR)	8	Hall Racing Pennzoil Special Reynard 96I-Honda	GY	116.566	1m 09.118s	14	15	Suspension		
26	*Michel Jourdain Jr. (MEX)	22	Scandia Herdez/Perry Ellis/Alta Water Lola T96/00-Ford XB	GY	113.828	1m 10.780s	25	15	Exhaust		
27	*P.J. Jones (USA)	98	All American Racers Castrol Eagle Mk.V-Toyota	GY	112.887	1m 11.371s	29	15	Electrical		
28	Juan Manuel Fangio II (RA)	36	All American Racers Castrol Eagle Mk.V-Toyota	GY	113.237	1m 11.150s	28	5	Engine		
29	Paul Tracy (CDN)	3	Marlboro Team Penske Penske PC25-Mercedes	GY	115.792	1m 09.580s	18	2	Accident		

* denotes Rookie driver

Caution flags: Laps 3–5, accident/Tracy; laps 53–59, accident/Johansson. **Total:** two for 10 laps.

Lap leaders: Alex Zanardi, 1–27 (27 laps); Bryan Herta, 28 (1 lap); Jimmy Vasser, 29 (1 lap); Zanardi, 30–42 (13 laps); Herta, 43–82 (40 laps); Zanardi, 83 (1 lap). **Totals:** Zanardi and Herta, 41 laps; Vasser, 1 lap.

Fastest race lap: Alex Zanardi, 1m 10.148s, 114.854 mph on lap 25.

Final championship positions: 1 Vasser, 154; **2** Andretti, 132; **3** Zanardi, 132; **4** Unser, 125; **5** C. Fittipaldi, 110; **6** de Ferran, 104; **7** Rahal, 102; **8** Herta, 86; **9** Moore, 84; **10** Pruett, 82; **11** Ribeiro, 76; **12** Fernandez, 71; **13** Tracy, 60; **14** Gugelmin, 53; **15** Johansson, 43; **16** Blundell, 41; **17** Johnstone, 33; **18** Gordon and E. Fittipaldi, 29; **20** Lawson, 26; **21** Moreno, 25; **22** Boesel, 17; **23** Fangio, Magnussen and Goodyear, 5; **26** P.J. Jones and Papis, 4; **28** Matsushita and Hearn, 3; **30** Salazar, 2; **31** Greco and D. Jones, 1.

Michael C. Brown

siege WARFARE

Left: Stepping into the seat vacated by Greg Moore, David Empringham seized the initiative at the start of the year and went on to take the title. The highlight was his immaculate victory at Long Beach *(right)*.

Young Brazilian Tony Kanaan *(below right)* secured second place in the standings.

The 1996 PPG-Firestone Indy Lights Championship bore a striking resemblance to the PPG Cup Indy Car title-chase. For starters, it was perhaps the most competitive season since the series was founded (originally as the American Racing Series) in 1986. Secondly, eventual champion David Empringham, like Jimmy Vasser, established a huge advantage in the point standings, then lost his way somewhat and had to be content to pick up points in the later stages to ensure his lead remained intact.

'It was a strange year,' concluded Empringham, 30, from Toronto, Canada, after securing his third championship in four seasons. He also won the Player's Toyota Atlantic crown both in 1993 and 1994. 'It started off just amazing, like I could do nothing wrong, and then a few things happened and it ended up being a bit of a struggle.'

Player's/Forsythe Racing was superbly prepared as the season began in Homestead. Greg Moore, of course, had dominated the series in 1995, so the Fred Crook-managed team had a wealth of knowledge from which to draw. Empringham was fast from the moment he began an extensive test program with race engineer Claude Rouelle, and his confidence benefited even more from a tight relationship with crew chief Tom Howatt and lead mechanic Steve Brody. Empringham duly won from the pole in Florida and added another victory in Long Beach, where he beat pole-sitter Gualter Salles away from the start and then held off a determined challenge from another Brazilian newcomer, Tony Kanaan.

'That win in Long Beach was especially satisfying,' said Empringham, 'because I didn't make any mistakes. I didn't crack under pressure.'

His win from the pole at Michigan, on the series' first visit in seven years to a superspeedway, was equally impressive. Empringham and teammate Claude Bourbonnais struggled to match the ultimate pace in qualifying, so they traveled to Texas World Speedway for a much-needed test session. The results were stunning. A low-drag setup was installed on the cars for the race, whereupon Empringham emerged from a thrilling contest with another victory. After four races, he already boasted a clear lead in the point standings, 80–48 over nearest challenger Mark Hotchkis.

As the season progressed, however, Empringham came under siege from all sides. He struggled to come to terms with the breakup of his marriage; his confidence was upset by the departure of Rouelle, who was at odds with several other team members; and he found himself overdriving the car. In the last half of the season, after winning the pole brilliantly in Detroit, Empringham never qualified better than seventh. But he retained his focus and, apart from being involved in a first-lap crash in Cleveland, always moved up in the race to secure valuable championship points.

Empringham was a deserving champion, as exemplified by his position atop the charts for most wins (three, equal with Gualter Salles), poles (three) and laps led during the season (121 out of 557). He seems likely to remain in the series in 1997 and once again will be a hard man to beat.

Six other drivers enjoyed a taste of victory during a particularly hard-fought season, while at least two more certainly deserved a share of the Chandon champagne.

A trio of Brazilians, two Americans and another Canadian became embroiled in a titanic battle for the runner-up position in the championship, and in the final reckoning it was Kanaan, 21, from Sao Paulo, Brazil, who gained the honors by virtue of a brilliant pole-to-flag victory in the final round at Laguna Seca.

Kanaan, a former champion in the Italian Formula Alfa Boxer series who graduated to Indy Lights via Formula 3, showed his comic facade was no reflection on his ability as he developed quickly into a front-runner with Steve Horne's Tasman Motorsports Group/Marlboro Latin America Team. Kanaan pressured Empringham hard in Long Beach and again at Michigan International Speedway until hobbled by an electrical problem. His first victory came in Detroit and he might have added another at Portland had not Horne made the wrong choice of tires in a wet-dry race. Nevertheless, Kanaan's charge from the back of the field to fifth after a change to slicks represented the single most impressive drive of the season.

Teammate Helio Castro Neves, after learning his trade in Formula 3 both in his native Brazil and in England, also made a good impression. He matured enormously as the year progressed. Castro Neves overcame a series of incidents in the early part of the season and was in a class by himself at Trois Rivieres. The 21-year-old also placed Kanaan under intense pressure at Laguna Seca, marking himself as a young man with a bright future.

Another member of the growing Brazilian contingent, Gualter Salles, displayed the most maturity of the trio. He did not have an extensive budget but he established a good rapport with race engineer Alan Langridge, also a rookie in terms of Indy Lights, and worked wonders in one of Brian Stewart's cars.

Salles, after enduring all manner of misfortunes in the early part of the season, came on strong with a hat-trick of wins at Portland, Cleveland and Toronto. Sadly, accidents during practice at Trois Rivieres and Vancouver effectively put paid to his championship challenge, although Yvan Turcotte and the crew deserved enormous credit for building a fresh car around a bare tub in order for Salles to make the grid in Vancouver.

Claude Bourbonnais, Empringham's teammate, endured a dismal start to his campaign when he crashed during practice at Homestead. But the French-Canadian led strongly at Nazareth and Michigan until forced out by rare engine

by Jeremy Shaw

Brazil's Gualter Salles *(right)* made the most of a tight budget but a couple of practice accidents wrecked his championship chances.

Below: Alex Padilla emerged as a man to watch after a series of impressive late-season performances.

problems. He scored a long-overdue maiden victory in Vancouver and added three more podium finishes as he rose to a strong fourth in the final standings. No one, indeed, scored more points than Bourbonnais in the second half of the season.

Mark Hotchkis, by contrast, began his sophomore Indy Lights season on a hot streak with Genoa Racing. The quiet, amiable Californian netted a fine victory at Milwaukee plus a second and two thirds from the opening five races, but later struggled as some of the immensely talented crop of rookies began to find their feet. Hotchkis, though, qualified on pole at Cleveland, only to be taken out at the first corner. He also drove well to finish third at Vancouver.

Alex Padilla, another gifted young American, came on strong in the latter part of the year with the Superior Performance team, especially after being joined by race engineer Gerald Tyler. Padilla perhaps triggered the opening lap melee in Cleveland, but he made amends by posting a series of excellent drives which netted top-five finishes in each of the last four races to go with his pair of seconds at Detroit and Portland.

David DeSilva was the other race winner, romping to a fine triumph for Genoa Racing at Nazareth in April. It was the perfect way to celebrate his 30th birthday the day before. DeSilva was always a force on the ovals, and toward the end of the season he seemed to gain a better grasp on the road courses as he qualified fifth at Vancouver and seventh at Laguna Seca.

Jose Luis di Palma enjoyed several solid performances in a third Tasman car, although the highlight for the personable Argentinean came

from leading the categories for most laps and miles completed during the season.

Team KOOL Green was expected to be a serious championship contender, especially after Chris Simmons finished a strong second in the season opener. Strangely, however, Simmons and fellow rookie Greg Ray rarely got to grips with their cars. They certainly weren't helped by the fact that no one on the team had any prior experience of Indy Lights. Nevertheless, matters barely improved after they were joined by race engineer Rouelle after his departure from the Forsythe team.

Former motocross star Jeff Ward was a revelation after teaming with Dorricott Racing, although misfortune seemed to dog his every move. He was stricken by a broken gear linkage in Cleveland, a busted halfshaft in Toronto, a faulty coil in Trois Rivieres and a transmission failure in Vancouver, each time while running in the top three. Just one podium finish, a third at M.I.S., represented a travesty.

Teammate Shigeaki Hattori also posted some good drives, while fellow Japanese Hideki Noda enjoyed a third-place finish at Toronto with Sal Incandela's team and could have achieved greater success with a little more good fortune.

From among the additional 27 drivers who entered at least one race, Robby Unser and Nick Firestone claimed a fourth-place finish apiece. Jaki Scheckter displayed his ability during three outings with Peter Faucetta's FRE team, while Casey Mears posted a promising eighth in a one-off drive for Team Medlin at Cleveland. Felipe Giaffone also ran well on occasion, despite having to share Steve Erickson's Autosport Lola-Buick with brother Zeca.

1996 PPG-FIRESTONE INDY LIGHTS CHAMPIONSHIP

Final point standings after 12 races:

Pos.	Driver (Nat.), Sponsor(s)-Team	Pts.
1	David Empringham (CDN), Player's/Indeck-Forsythe Racing	147
2	Tony Kanaan (BR), Marlboro Latin America Team-Tasman Motorsports Group	113
3	Gualter Salles (BR), Kibon/Tang/STP-Brian Stewart Racing	108
4	Claude Bourbonnais (CDN), Player's/Indeck-Forsythe Racing	104
5	Mark Hotchkis (USA), Fountainhead Water-Genoa Racing	101
6	Alex Padilla (USA), SP Aviation/Valvoline-Superior Performance	90
7	Helio Castro Neves (BR), Hudson Oil/Kibon-Tasman Motorsports Group	84
8	David DeSilva (USA), DeSilva-Gates/Men's Fitness-Genoa Racing	61
9	Jose Luis di Palma (RA), Marlboro Latin America Team/Tasman Motorsports Group	56
10	Chris Simmons (USA), Team KOOL Green	54
11	Jeff Ward (USA), Primm Investment/Oakley-Dorricott Racing	53
12	Greg Ray (USA), Team KOOL Green	48
13	Shigeaki Hattori (J), Sesmat/Ibaraki Toyopet-Dorricott Racing	42
14	Hideki Noda (J), Tenoras/GReddy/NCS-Indy Regency Racing	34
15	Robby Unser (USA), ADT Automotive-Team Medlin	25
16	Bertrand Godin (CDN), Player's/Indeck-Forsythe Racing	21
17	Felipe Giaffone (BR), STP/Premier National LeaseAutosport/Leading Edge & Brian Stewart	20
18	Nick Firestone (USA), Firestone Vineyards/STP-Brian Stewart Racing	18
19	Jaki Scheckter (ZA), Kreepy Krauly/Autoquip-FRE Racing	12
20	Dr. Jack Miller (USA), Crest-Brian Stewart Racing	12

Note: All drivers ran identical Lola T93/20-Buick V6 cars

Performance Chart

Driver	Wins	Poles
David Empringham	3	3
Gualter Salles	3	1
Tony Kanaan	2	2
David DeSilva	1	–
Mark Hotchkis	1	2
Helio Castro Neves	1	1
Claude Bourbonnais	1	1
Jeff Ward	–	2

New chassis to be introduced in '97

Indy Lights will have a fresh look in 1997. The new Lola T97/20 chassis was given its first public outing during the season finale at Laguna Seca, as 1995 PPG-Firestone Indy Lights champion Greg Moore took a few leisurely laps in between his Indy Car commitments. The car is the first to be purpose-designed for Indy Lights, rather than being developed from previous use in Formula 3000. In line with the latest Indy Car standards, significant safety improvements have been incorporated into the Lola T97/20, including high structural sidepods, an extra front bulkhead, a longer cockpit and more lateral protection for the driver's head.

star PUPIL

Bespectacled French-Canadian Patrick Carpentier *(right)* **dominated the season at the wheel of Lynx Racing's Ralt RT41** *(far right)*, **recording nine wins from 12 starts.**

Bottom: **Carpentier was in a class apart. Case Montgomery, Lee Bentham, Chuck West, Paul Jasper and the rest of the field give chase at Long Beach.**

Patrick Carpentier entered the 1996 Player's/Toyota Atlantic Championship as one of the clear favorites for honors. The French-Canadian duly lived up to expectations – and more – as he thoroughly dominated the proceedings aboard Lynx Racing's immaculately prepared Ralt RT41. Carpentier virtually rewrote the record books as he sped to an incredible nine victories, including eight in a row to wrap up the championship title. In each of those he also qualified on the pole.

Just as impressive, however, was the way in which the personable 25-year-old from Joliette, Quebec, achieved his success. Through it all, Carpentier retained a firm sense of reality: 'In today's racing you don't win races because you're the best driver,' he said, 'you win races because you know how to make the most out of the car.'

Carpentier took full advantage of two excellent teachers in driver-turned-team manager Steve Cameron and race engineer Jim Griffith. Crew chief Ricky Cameron (brother of Steve), and engine builder Paul Hasselgren also played vital roles as Carpentier enjoyed perfect reliability during the 12-race season.

'Steve taught me a lot about driving,' said Carpentier. 'I spent a lot of time last winter learning about the mechanical side. It helped because I had the best engineer in Jim Griffith, but it's everything put together that gave me a great season.'

While Carpentier took off into a world of his own, three drivers fought a tooth-and-nail battle for runner-up honors. Another Canadian, Lee Bentham, finally took the position after a good sophomore season with Bill Fickling's P1 Racing team. Bentham never won a race but he came close on several occasions, notably in the season opener where he started from the pole and led before indulging in a quick spin while trying to pass slower traffic. Bentham, who recovered to finish second, added another second and five thirds as he edged out top rookie challenger Paul Jasper by 17 points.

The young man from Lake Forest, Ill., amassed an impressive array of sponsors and wisely chose to join Brian Robertson's elite B.D.J.S. team for his first full season of professional racing. Jasper certainly

learned a great deal from the combined experience of Robertson and veteran driver-turned-engineer/crew chief Dave McMillan. He is likely to prove tough to beat if he remains in the category for 1997.

Case Montgomery shone on occasion in Sandy Dells Racing's Microsoft-backed Ralt, but a lack of consistency cost him dear. The highlight for the happy-go-lucky young man from Salinas, Calif., was a fine victory from the pole in Long Beach. He added a trio of seconds at Milwaukee, Toronto and Laguna Seca.

Fifth in the final championship standings was not a true reflection on the ability of Jeret Schroeder. The 1995 SCCA/USAC Formula Ford 2000 National Champion qualified five times on the front row in a second Lynx Racing Ralt, only to suffer a series of accidents – most of them not of his making – and mechanical problems. He deserved credit for keeping his chin up throughout what turned out to be a difficult ordeal.

Photos: Michael C. Brown

Anthony Lazzaro achieved a brilliant victory in Milwaukee, despite running his three-year-old Ralt RT40 on an unbelievably slim budget. In doing so he restored faith in the belief that hard work and sheer talent can bear fruit in this increasingly technical and commercial sport. Unfortunately, the gifted 33-year-old Georgian then blew his opportunity by falling out with his car owner. He returned to the fray with another RT40 but was unable to coax from it the same speed as before.

The similarly impecunious Tony Ave also scored a sensational victory – in the opener at Homestead – with Ove Olsson's RT40. Tragically, Ave sustained devastating leg injuries when he crashed during the non-championship June Sprints at Road America.

Rookie Chuck West raced only five times in his World Speed Motorsports Ralt, yet each time he was impressive. A second at Road America and third at Long Beach hinted at what he might have achieved had he been able to conduct a full campaign.

Former champion Stuart Crow started on the pole and finished second at Nazareth, despite competing only twice in a second B.D.J.S. Ralt. Gentleman racer Charles Nearburg also made the youngsters sit up and take notice when he wheeled out his well-prepared Ralt. Former Canadian Formula Ford hot-shoe Alexandre Tagliani showed some potential in a second P1 Racing Ralt RT41, his best a popular third before a partisan Quebecois crowd in Trois-Rivieres. Eric Lang, Stan Wattles, Robert Sollenskog and Michael David also were consistent campaigners.

The C2 category, for older cars, rarely drew much of an entry. Mike Shank scooped the honors in his self-run Swift DB-4, despite a rash of mechanical problems. Fellow Ohioan Ted Sahley performed well in a '93 Reynard, while veteran Canadian Frank Allers mirrored his achievements by scoring three class wins in a '92 Reynard.

1996 SCCA PLAYER'S/TOYOTA ATLANTIC CHAMPIONSHIP

Final point standings after 12 races:

Pos.	Driver (Nat.), Sponsor(s)-Team Car	Pts.
1	Patrick Carpentier (CDN), Lynx Racing Ralt RT41	239
2	Lee Bentham (CDN), NTN Bearings/TMI Racing-P1 Racing Ralt RT41	149
3	Paul Jasper (USA), Quaker State/Shurtech/Sylvania/Agfa-B.D.J.S. Ralt RT41	132
4	Case Montgomery (USA), Microsoft/Wall Data/Tandem/Compaq-Dells Ralt RT41	129
5	Jeret Schroeder (USA), Ireland Coffee & Tea/Purity Farms-Lynx Racing Ralt RT41	77
6	Anthony Lazzaro (USA), BG Products Ralt RT40	75
7	Alexandre Tagliani (CDN), Agip/Cari-All/Logibec-P1 Racing Ralt RT41	70
8	Eric Lang (USA), LCI International-D&L Racing Ralt RT41	60
9	Michael David (USA), David Engineering & Mfg.-PDR Enterprises Ralt RT41	58
10	Stan Wattles (USA), Metro Racing Systems Ralt RT41	52

Performance Chart

Driver	Wins	Poles
Patrick Carpentier	9	8
Case Montgomery	1	1
Tony Ave	1	–
Anthony Lazzaro	1	–
Lee Bentham	–	1
Stuart Crow	–	1
Paul Jasper	–	1

SCCA PLAYER'S/TOYOTA ATLANTIC CHAMPIONSHIP REVIEW   *by Jeremy Shaw*